A Triumph of Principles

The Story of American Spirituality in Twelve Steps

Benjamin Riggs

The Story of American Spirituality

Copyright © 2020 Benjamin Riggs

All rights reserved.
ISBN: 0692104224
ISBN-13: 978-0692104224

DEDICATION

To my wife, our amazing son, and my
supportive friends and family, without whom
this book would not be possible.

CONTENTS

	Note From The Author	i
1	Bill W. & Dr. Bob: An Introduction	1
2	Religion and Temperance	15
3	The Dr.'s Opinion	38
4	Lack of Power	71
5	Liberty of Conscience	97
6	Tried & True	109
7	"We Agnostics 2.0"	126
8	Will and Life	165
9	The Oxford Group	185
10	Big Chunks of Truth	212
11	The Perfect Objective	260
12	Making Amends	288
13	Spiritual Maintenance	305
14	The God of the Twelve Steps	319
15	Sought Through Prayer and Meditation	333
16	Having Had a Spiritual Awakening	369

NOTE FROM THE AUTHOR

I must begin by acknowledging those who pioneered the ideas and practices treated in this book: Carl Jung, William James, and of course, Bill Wilson, Bob Smith, and their fellow travelers who have not only revolutionized the treatment of addiction, but forged a peerless path of pragmatic spirituality.

This book not only serves as a detailed guide to Twelve Step practice, but it aims to establish the Steps as a distinctly American form of spirituality. It weaves the threads of pragmatism and individual liberty together with the development of the Twelve Steps to submit the Steps as America's most significant contribution to the world of spirituality.

As such, this book demonstrates that the Twelve Steps are accessible and useful to alcoholics and non-alcoholics alike, regardless of their religious or spiritual background. Chapter One tells Alcoholics Anonymous' origin story. Chapter Two explores the complicated relationship between alcohol and religion in American history. Chapter Three unpacks A.A.'s first Step, using alcoholism as an example of "powerlessness," which is broadened in Chapter Four to include vices we all struggle to overcome. The remainder of this book relates the intellectual history and practical instruction for each of the Twelve Steps to a general audience.

1 BILL W. AND DR. BOB: AN INTRODUCTION

"The essence of America, that which really unites us is not ethnicity or nationality or religion. It is an idea, and what an idea it is—that you can come from humble circumstances and do great things."
~ Condoleezza Rice, 2013

Dr. Robert Smith begrudgingly entered the Akron home of Henrietta Seiberling on Sunday, May 12th, 1935. He was there to meet a New Yorker visiting Akron on business, but business was not on their agenda. Bill Wilson long struggled with alcoholism but came to Akron six months sober. Henrietta, a friend of the Smith family, made Wilson's acquaintance the previous day. She thought him a God-send tasked with exorcising Robert's alcoholic demons, so she called to arrange the meeting.

Frustrated with attempts to save both his life and his soul, Dr. Smith begrudgingly agreed to meet with Wilson after his wife guaranteed him the intervention would last no more than fifteen minutes. Robert arrived at Henrietta's house at five o'clock that afternoon. At eleven fifteen that night, the two men emerged with their arms around one another, a foretelling gesture, as Dr. Bob and Bill W. would forever be linked in history.

Today nearly two million people are meeting in over one hundred thousand groups across the globe, all of whom trace their origin back to this initial encounter in Akron, Ohio. The international fellowship that blossomed in the wake of Bill and Bob's meeting is Alcoholics Anonymous.

In the time since, Alcoholics Anonymous has revolutionized the treatment of addiction. The self-titled volume *Alcoholics Anonymous* is one of the best-selling books of all-time (30+ million copies), and is recognized by the Library of Congress as one of the eighty-eight books that shaped America, alongside works like *The Federalist Papers* and *Walden*. Furthermore, this book and its companion text, *Twelve Steps and Twelve Traditions,* articulate a system of spiritual practice that transcends both substance abuse and organized religion, standing as America's most significant contribution to the world of spirituality.

Twelve Step spirituality captures the essence of America. It is a pragmatic spirituality that celebrates individual liberty. The Steps enable aspirants to escape truly humble circumstances and accomplish great things—as evidenced by the story of Bill Wilson, Dr. Bob, and the founding of Alcoholics Anonymous. So how did a tenuous meeting between two unknown, destitute drunks—one a dejected businessman, the other a jittery rectal surgeon—spawn an international movement of such monumental proportions?

The Origins of Alcoholics Anonymous

Bill Wilson was an exceptionally bright and capable fellow with a resume of remarkable accomplishments, but in May of 1935, he was on the mend. His career was sabotaged by both the Crash of 1929 and his fondness for the bottle. The Akron venture was Wilson's first serious foray into the job market in a few years. Just six months earlier, he was puttin' around his Brooklyn home in a robe and slippers drunkenly ranting about Franklin Roosevelt's poor job performance.

On December 11, 1934, Bill purchased four bottles of beer on credit, took the train to Manhattan, and checked himself into Towns Hospital, a well-known drying out spot for New York drunks. When Bill arrived he had but one bottle left, which he frantically waved in the air as he announced to the attending physician, "Doc, I found the cure"—an apparent reference to two philosophy books clasped tightly in his other hand. Of course, he had not found the cure—and the doctor told him as much—but while at Towns, Wilson did discover something extraordinary.

Bill had a spiritual awakening at Towns Hospital. The long-time skeptic suddenly felt as though he stood atop a mountain with a great wind blowing through him. He left the hospital on new footing. Bill committed himself to drying out every drunk in New York, but this proved more challenging than he anticipated. These challenges, coupled with mounting financial woes, broke Bill's resolve. These were the circumstances surrounding his historic trip to Akron.

Wilson came to Ohio with a handful of investors looking to take over National Rubber Machinery, a company that supplied Goodyear and Firestone. He was both financially and emotionally invested in the acquisition. It was a last gasp of sorts. Wilson's adventures as a recovery crusader were primarily financed by his wife's department store salary, which was a source of embarrassment for him. If the acquisition were successful, he would become president of the company, a position that included a handsome salary, thereby relieving Lois of her department store duties and Bill of his embarrassment. This, however, was not to be.

When the deal fell through, Bill was crushed. As he nervously paced the lobby of his temporary residence, the Mayflower Hotel, his despondent mind wandered into the barroom where others shared drinks and camaraderie. Fearing a return to the bottle, Bill took refuge in the only thing that ever insured his sobriety: helping another alcoholic.

Wilson later wrote, "Practical experience shows that nothing will so much insure immunity from drinking as intensive work with other alcoholics." He could say this with confidence because it was his experience. The few months of continuous sobriety Bill secured before arriving in Akron was owed mostly to the feverish pace with which he worked with other alcoholics. After his discharge, Bill regularly walked the halls of Towns Hospital preaching a quasi-religious gospel of sobriety to a captive audience. He saw himself as an alcoholic missionary, but his mission was largely unsuccessful. Not one of the patients Bill tried to rehabilitate achieved lasting sobriety. Disheartened, he confided in his physician, Dr. William Silkworth.

After leaving Towns, Bill joined the Oxford Group, a non-denominational Christian movement that aimed to resuscitate the principles of First Century Christianity. When filtered through the objectives of the Oxford Group, his message of recovery came off as preachy—and if there is one thing alcoholics are unreceptive to, it is proselytizing. Looking at alcoholism through the lens of religion turns it into a moral issue, teeing up a struggle between sin and willpower. Not surprisingly, alcoholics reject this paradigm. Thus, Bill's message repeatedly fell on deaf ears. Still, this ministry safeguarded his sobriety, so in his time of peril, he turned to it again.

Opposite the bar, in the hotel lobby, stood an Akron church directory. Wilson phoned one of the ministers listed, Rev. Walter Tunks. Bill told him he was an alcoholic recovering in the Oxford Groups who desperately needed to work with another drunk. Tunks put him in contact with Henrietta Seiberling, an Oxford Grouper in the Akron chapter. She immediately phoned Anne Smith, Dr. Bob's wife, to arrange a meeting, but Bob was unable to make it that night. It was Mother's Day eve, and he came home with a potted plant for Anne, which he placed on the table. He then proceeded to drink himself under that table, which is where he lied passed out when Henrietta called.

Anne and Henrietta arranged for Bob to meet with Bill the following afternoon. The anticipation got Wilson through the night, but this intervention would surely have gone the way of all his others had he not approached it from a different angle. William Silkworth supplied Bill with a fresh angle.

Bill trusted Dr. Silkworth. He called him "the little doctor who loved drunks." Silkworth was not only the medical director at Towns Hospital, but the person Wilson confided in after his spiritual experience. The doctor verified the transformative effects of his rapturous experience, and further aided his recovery by allowing Bill to work with alcoholic patients following his discharge. Over time, however, Silkworth noticed that Wilson's pitch was becoming increasingly religious. It was informed more by Oxford Group objectives than his personal experience. Just before Bill left for Akron, the New York doctor reminded him that it was not proselytizing that triggered his awakening, but an understanding of the alcoholic problem. Silkworth counseled Bill to lead with his personal experience of alcoholism, rather than God.

Before Bill felt the spirit of God rush through him, he fell into the deepest depression he'd ever known. This was prompted by the foreboding prospects of his alcoholism, not preaching. To better understand his spiritual experience, Bill read *Varieties of Religious Experience* by William James. Silkworth's counsel not only dovetailed with his personal experience, but it also reminded him of a crucial insight proffered by James in that book: All spiritual experiences are born out of a sense of powerlessness.

Bill's understanding of the alcoholic condition was informed by his struggles with the bottle, but Dr. Silkworth's language and ideas helped him articulate his experience. Throughout his career, Silkworth treated tens of thousands of alcoholics. They came from all walks of life, but each exhibited one feature that set them apart from the average person: Once they started drinking, they could not stop. Dr. Silkworth described this reaction as a physical allergy, but this is only half of his alcoholic equation. The destructive cycle triggered by the first drink is not nearly as perplexing as the insanity that compels the alcoholic to pick up that first drink. Dr. Silkworth and Bill described this insanity as an "obsession of the mind."

A despondent Bill felt nostalgia bubbling up as he peered into the Mayflower Hotel's barroom. Suddenly he thought, "I'll go in and have a glass of ginger ale." Then came a moment of clarity: "I don't want a glass of ginger ale. I want to get drunk." Ginger ale was a lower level allurement inviting Bill to relapse. This is an example of alcoholic insanity, the obsession of the mind incessantly plotting the first drink.

Wilson later wrote, "There was always the curious mental phenomenon that parallel with our sound reasoning there inevitably ran some insanely trivial excuse for taking the first drink." This peculiar mental twist not only explains why the alcoholic picks up the first drink, but when coupled with the physical allergy, it confirms what the alcoholic intuits, but lacks the words to express: Once they start drinking they can't stop, and when left to their own devices, they can't stop getting started. This is the foreboding prospect of untreated alcoholism, referred to in the first Step as "powerlessness."

This view of powerlessness bypassed the antiquated model of sin, outlining a new conception of alcoholism. It replaced depravity and weakness with the concept of a disease that affects the whole person, which subsequently justified a spiritual solution. If the mind and spirit are just as sick as the body, then inventory, prayer, and meditation are in order. This new paradigm painted a picture that resonated with the personal experience of alcoholics and made sense of Bill's misplaced spiritual solution.

A hammer without a nail serves no purpose. That's what Bill had before Silkworth intervened. He was shoving a spiritual solution down the throat of drunks who did not understand their problem, and as a result, did not see sense in Wilson's solution. In fact, this was Bill's experience.

Not long before his last drink, Bill was re-acquainted with his childhood friend and drinking buddy Ebby Thatcher. Ebby dropped by Wilson's Brooklyn home. Bill brought him into the kitchen where a bottle of gin and a pitcher of pineapple juice sat on the table, but Ebby wasn't interested in a drink.

"I've got religion," Ebby told Bill before going on about the Oxford Group. "I took ideas peculiar to them and applied them to my drinking," Thatcher said. "Well, if you're in for a penny, you're in for a pound," thought Bill. "So tell me, my friend, what those ideas are?" Ebby proceeded to layout the

Oxford Group's approach: "I had to get honest with myself, talk it out with someone else, make restitution, help others, and ask God to help me do those four things." In response, Bill showed his old friend the door. The final proposition crossed a line Wilson was not yet willing to pass—and there he remained until that fateful night in Towns Hospital.

The morning after his reunion with Ebby, Bill cleaned up and headed to Manhattan for an Oxford Group meeting. He thought, "If it worked for Ebby, then I should at least check it out." On the way he got drunk, but that did not derail his plans. Before the night came to a close, an inebriated Bill was playing the tambourine in front of the congregation at Calvary Mission.

It was after this debacle that Bill checked into Towns for the final time. There Silkworth helped him flesh out an understanding of his alcoholic condition, which brought the nail into sight. Realizing he was powerless made sense of the search for power. The all-too-painful awareness of powerlessness opened Bill's mind to the realm of the spirit. This is the angle Bill took with Bob in their historic first meeting, and it was instrumental in the meeting's success. Had Bill lectured Bob about spirituality without first explaining the problem, their meeting would have lasted fifteen minutes, as originally planned, there would be no Alcoholics Anonymous.

It is important to note that Dr. Bob was no stranger to the Oxford Group. He attended many Oxford Group meetings with Henrietta long before Bill came to Akron. Bob was well aware of their tenets. Moreover, he was an Ivy League-educated physician, well read in theology and philosophy. Bill wasn't going to preach a sermon that Bob hadn't heard; Bob lacked insight into his alcoholism, not religion. "Henrietta, I don't understand it. Nobody understands it," Bob once confessed. Bill understood alcoholism from direct experience, and it was that first-person knowledge that Bob was ripe to receive. Six years after his introduction to Bill Wilson, Bob wrote:

> "The question which might naturally come into your mind would be: 'What did the man do or say that was different from what others had done or said?' It must be remembered that I had read a great deal and talked to everyone who knew, or thought they knew anything about the subject of alcoholism. But this was a man who had experienced many years of frightful drinking, who had had most all the drunkard's experiences known to man, but who had been cured by the very means I had been trying to employ, that is to say, the spiritual approach. He gave me information about the subject of alcoholism which was undoubtedly helpful. Of far more importance was the fact that he was the first living human with whom I had ever talked, who knew what he was talking about in regard to alcoholism from actual experience."

The personal nature of Bill's approach enabled him to develop a rapport with Bob. Then Wilson laid out a new view of alcoholism that appealed to Dr. Bob's medical sensibilities. He explained that the alcoholic is both physically and mentally sick, which not only resonated with Bob but justified the spiritual approach already in his possession.

In Bill, Bob saw a man who personally understood the score of alcoholism, as well as someone released from its grips. Simply put, he saw hope incarnate. The solution Dr. Bob long struggled to employ suddenly became real. Well, not suddenly.

Approximately one month later, Bob left Akron for a medical conference in Atlantic City with 30 days of sobriety under his belt. He attended the American Medical Association Conference every year and had no intention of discontinuing that tradition. Anne had her reservations, but Bob insisted: "I can't stay in Akron forever. I need to see if this really works." Bill, himself a New Yorker in Ohio, agreed and Bob left for Atlantic City. Five days later, he turned up in bad shape.

Bob began drinking not long after the train pulled away from the station. Bill spoke Bob's language and the two enjoyed great camaraderie as a result—but fellowship was only half the battle. Bob did not follow through with the solution. He confused knowledge about spirituality with the application of spiritual principles. Bob failed to conduct a personal inventory, share his story with another person, make restitution, or commit himself to the service of others. In short, he failed to act. Therefore, he remained unchanged. The moment Bob escaped the watchful eye of Anne and the support of Bill, his thoughts turned to the first drink, and having never applied the solution, he was without defense.

At this point, Bill grew frustrated with Bob. He was preparing to return to New York, but Anne convinced him to hang around and help Bob sober back up. The proctologist was to perform an operation a couple of days later and needed it to go smoothly, lest the doctor lose operating privileges at the last hospital in town willing to tolerate him. Bob's deepest secret was his drinking problem. Unbeknownst to him, it was hardly a secret. There was a running joke in Akron: "You literally bet your ass when you go to Dr. Bob Smith because you never know whether he will be drunk or sober." This reputation threatened his career and livelihood. Bill sympathized with Anne and agreed to stay.

Bill bought Bob a beer on the way to the hospital to settle the jittery surgeon's nerves, which Bob appreciated. As he exited the car, Bob told his mentor that he was going to follow through with it. Bill didn't know what "it" was, and didn't bother to ask. He dropped Bob off at the hospital at 10 am. Nineteen hours later, Anne's anxious pacing was interrupted by the sound of a car pulling up to the house. As she peered through the curtains, she said to Bill, "It's him!" Anne greeted Bob with the question, "Where have you been?" to which he replied, "I made amends to everyone I harmed." He followed through with "it," the program of action.

That was June 10th, 1935, celebrated in A.A. as "Founders Day," because it marks the start of the fellowship's unbroken lineage of sobriety. Dr. Bob passed away fifteen years later never having taken another drink.

Alcoholics Anonymous celebrates storytelling and dialogue because the fellowship is born out of a meeting of hearts. Alcoholics Anonymous is an echo chamber where the spirit of that original conversation, that tenuous meeting between two destitute drunks, can be heard reverberating every time one alcoholic shares their "experience, strength, and hope" with another.

Alcoholics Anonymous' success is owed to many people. The Oxford Group, Dr. Silkworth, William James, Carl Jung and countless others placed logs on the fire that keeps A.A.'s fellowship burning bright to the present day. But it was William Griffith Wilson and Dr. Robert Holbrook Smith who, in the late hours of May 12th, 1935, discovered that *the ex-problem drinker properly armed with facts about themselves, can generally win the entire confidence of another alcoholic in a few hours.*

"Because of our kinship in suffering," writes Wilson, "our channels of contact have always been charged with the language of the heart." But for the movement to remain vital—that is, life-giving—it must be joined with a program of action. That is the lesson learned between May 12th and June 10th. In the spirituality of Alcoholics Anonymous, action is the coin in trade.

Every person who walks through the doors of Alcoholics Anonymous hears the familiar refrain that announces the program of action: *"Here are the steps we took...."* Every time those words are spoken in a meeting of Alcoholics Anonymous, Ebby's invitation to Bill resounds. Every time an A.A. member lays the kit of spiritual tools at the feet of a newcomer, Bill's hand can be seen reaching out to Bob. One alcoholic passing on the solution that was freely given to them is the lifeblood of the fellowship, hence the A.A. motto: "I am Responsible. When anyone, anywhere, reaches out for help, I want the hand of A.A. always to be there. And for that: I am responsible."

This book is intended for all spiritual seekers, not just those in recovery. It's not about the fellowship; rather, the Twelve Steps, which stand as America's most significant contribution to the world of spirituality. **As such, alcoholics and non-alcoholics alike can profit from their practice.**

Contrary to popular belief, sobriety is not the primary objective of the Twelve Steps. The Steps aim to affect a spiritual awakening. Sobriety is the focal point of the support groups that utilize the Steps, but only Step One alludes to alcoholism—and even then the emphasis is not on alcohol, but powerlessness, a condition that is pertinent to us all. The remaining Steps focus exclusively on spiritual growth, which applies to all.

In the pages that follow, we will dive deep into the underlying principles and practices that comprise the Twelve Steps, considering their origins, meaning, and application. We will turn to America's storied past to see how her pluralism, religious liberty, and trademark pragmatism shape the Twelve Steps, making them a uniquely American contribution to the spiritual wisdom of mankind. This journey begins with the long and complicated relationship between religion and temperance in the United States.

2 RELIGION AND TEMPERANCE

> "The objection to Puritans is not that they try to make us think as they do, but that they try to make us do as they think." ~ Henry Louis Mencken

The Twelve Steps are a spiritual remedy to alcoholism. As such, they were developed along two historical lines: religion and temperance. From Plymouth to the present day, religion has played a vital role in the American story. America is not only a deeply religious nation, but one with a history of public religion. Religion has always played a prominent role in our political discourse and, for better or worse, has influenced social change. It was especially influential during the Temperance movement.

The social movement to curb alcohol consumption, known as Temperance, took shape in the early days of the Republic. It first gained notoriety in 1784 with the publication of *An Inquiry Into the Effects of Ardent Spirits Upon the Human Body and Mind,* a pamphlet detailing the effects of alcohol abuse by Dr. Benjamin Rush, himself a Founding Father. The Temperance movement peaked with passage of the Eighteenth Amendment in 1919 and fizzled out when the Twenty-first Amendment was ratified in 1933.

In the modern world, addiction falls predominantly within the dominion of medicine and science, but that has not always been the case. Religion and temperance frequently overlap in American history. This is because alcoholism was long thought to be a sin, and therefore within the purview of religion. Enlightenment-era thinkers, like Dr. Rush, conceived of alcoholism as a disease, but during the Second Great Awakening such views fell from favor, and would not regain public support until the publication of *Alcoholics Anonymous* one hundred thirty-nine years later.

Terminating the Age of Reason

The Second Great Awakening was a religious and social reform movement that began at the end of the 18th Century and concluded with the Civil War. It was a populist crusade that was romantic in character and revivalistic in method. It started as a reaction to the Enlightenment, which stressed reason, liberty, skepticism, scientific inquiry, and deism. The Enlightenment climaxed with the American Revolution and is epitomized by some of its central players: Thomas Jefferson, Benjamin Franklin, and Thomas Paine.

The enlightened authors of the new American creed promised "hostility against every form of tyranny over the mind of man." Established religion was second only to monarchy on the founding generations' list of grievances against the Crown. Fixed atop the Bill of Rights are two provisions that democratize the kingdom of heaven. The First Amendment's establishment clause creates a marketplace that forces every sect and denomination to participate without subsidy; whereas the free exercise clause guarantees each individual's right to believe in "twenty gods, or no god" and to practice that belief in the manner best suited to them. Together these clauses constitute "freedom of religion." This freedom is mostly taken for granted today, but was revolutionary at the time of its conception, sparking a populist crusade that turned the established order of religion in America on its head.

For too long, religion trickled down to the masses from the theocratic ivory towers of established religion, but the First Amendment changed that. Religious institutions that benefited only the ruling elites, as well as deterministic belief systems that aggrandized the well-to-do and assigned divine causality to the marginalization of the masses, fell from favor. The denominations that flourished during the Second Awakening were those that catered to populist themes. Just as ideas that failed to serve the multitude were discarded, so too were those wholly unintelligible to the common man.

The average person—disinterested in theological disquisitions, yet yearning no less for salvation—was now free to choose for themselves which faith, if any, to pledge. Those denominations that manned the pulpits and stocked the revival circuit with orators that were both captivating and unassuming in their language thrived during the Second Great Awakening. The Methodists and Baptists saw their memberships explode; whereas established sects, like Congregationalists and Presbyterians, watched as growth stymied; and the Anglican Church, which was loyal to the Crown during the war, saw their membership decline.

The Methodists and Baptists blossomed during this period, in large part, because they ministered to the disenfranchised. These denominations also catered to the pioneers moving West, so their numbers grew as the nation expanded. Moreover, Methodists and Baptists began as religious minorities, and as a result, possessed a view of minority rights that challenged the status quo. They naturally sympathized with the marginalized because they too were marginalized. Preachers, revivalists, and circuit riders focused their ire on everything from slavery and aristocracy to the subjugation of women, inhumane treatment of Native Americans, prison reform, and intemperance—all of which fit neatly under the heading of "sin."

Eden 2.0

The principles of the Enlightenment served the Revolution well, but after dissolving ties with the Crown, America's focus abruptly shifted to social reform. The emergence of America among the "powers of the earth" reissued George Winthrop's invocation to be a "City upon a Hill." When the religious mind is intent on social reform, indispensable is the God who is intimately involved and deeply concerned with the fate of the world. Therefore, stock in the Enlightenment's ambivalent God plummeted in the religious marketplace it established. No longer under the thumb of a distant monarch, the deistic proclivities of the Enlightenment triggered the collective gag reflex of the American populous. And no one was more violently rejected than Thomas Paine.

The fate of Thomas Paine encapsulates the tumultuous transition from the Enlightenment to the Awakening. Paine's enduring claim to fame is the stirring pamphlet, *Common Sense*, without which, John Adams says, "the sword of Washington would have been raised in vain." For this reason, Paine earned the nickname "The Father of the American Revolution." Nearly every rebel who fought for the cause of American liberty read, or heard read aloud, *Common Sense*; that beautiful turn of phrase, "These are the times that try men's souls," still echoes forth from the encampments where General Washington had another of Paine's great works, *The American Crisis*, recited to waning troops. Paine did not live out the rest of his life as a hero, however. His claim to infamy is *The Age of Reason*, which promotes deism and deals a stinging critique of Christianity.

"I begin with your preface. You therein state that you had long had an intention of publishing your thoughts upon religion, but that you had originally reserved it to a latter period in life," Bishop Richard Watson writes in response to Paine's *The Age of Reason*. "I hope there is no want of charity in saying, that it would have been fortunate to the Christian world, had your life been terminated before you had fulfilled your intention." Watson despised Paine because, in his opinion, Paine "unsettled the faith of thousands…rooted from the minds of the unhappy virtuous all their comfortable recompense," and "annihilated in the minds of the flagitious all their fears of future punishment," while giving "the reins of domination" to "every passion."[1] In short, the Awakening judged Paine's irreligious ideas as reckless, claiming they weakened the moral fabric upon which civilization rests. Later, Paine attacked the personage upon which the infant Republic rested, George Washington. Needless to say, the firebrand pamphleteer lacked the social capital to wage a two-front war against the Son of God and the high priest of the Revolution. Quite simply, the world he helped create was intolerant of him and his ideas. Once heralded as a hero, Paine died a wretch with only six people attending his funeral.

The Enlightenment installed reason as the final arbiter of moral concerns, which the Second Awakening saw as a *coup d'etat* that sent the religious conscience into exile, leaving sin unchecked and society in disrepair. Religionists in this era sought to awaken that conscience from its slumber, but not for purely theological reasons.

The Awakening's reformers sympathized with those left behind by the Revolution. The once oppressed that multiplied the now swelling Methodist and Baptist denominations recast their sympathies for the downtrodden as a romantic impulse to restore both the church and creation to their original purity. As though a symbol fated by history—or better yet, ordained by the will of God—the birth of this new nation signaled the

---

[1] Richard Watson, *An Apology for the Bible: In a Series of Letters Addressed to Thomas Paine,* pg 4, 1820

coming of a new Eden, just as the new world had for the Pilgrims a century and a half earlier.

The utopian ideas of the Second Great Awakening were disseminated and dramatized at the great revivals that characterized the era. From the "burned over district" in New York to Cane Ridge in Kentucky, revivals were the evangelistic engine that drove the movement. Contemporaneous reports of these revivals were spectacular, to say the least. They detailed droves of people possessed by a supernatural power, scores floored by an overwhelming conviction in their own sinfulness, and multitudes intoxicated by God's mercy.

"We arrived upon the ground and here a scene presented itself to my mind not only novel and unaccountable, but awful beyond description," the Rev. James Finley recalls in his 1853 autobiography, *Pioneer Life in the West*. This awesome scene, cloistered in the Kentucky Wilderness, was the Cane Ridge Revival. "A vast crowd, supposed by some to have amounted to twenty-five thousand, was collected together. The noise was like the roar of Niagara. The vast sea of human beings seemed to be agitated as if by a storm. I counted seven ministers, all preaching at one time, some on stumps, others on wagons, and one—the Rev. William Burke, now of Cincinnati—was standing on a tree which had, in falling, lodged against another. Some of the people were singing, others praying, some crying for mercy in the most piteous accents, while others were shouting most vociferously. While witnessing the scenes, a peculiarly-strange sensation, such as I had never felt before, came over me. My heart beat tumultuously, my knees trembled, my lip quivered and I felt as though I must fall to the ground."

Revivals were convert factories, but critics questioned the veracity of these mass conversions, and some of the most prominent revivalists agreed. Frequently, the resulting change of heart lasted only as long as the rapturous conditions that evoked it. This led to the "second conversion" or born *again* experience, which became all the rage.

When you are suffering and feel as though you have no recourse against your sinfulness, no terrestrial measures by which to elevate your station, and suddenly the kingdom of God is democratized and all—not just the elite—are welcomed into its promise, that is a seductive, if not intoxicating, prospect. Rebirth is particularly inviting for those on the fringes of society. Uneducated frontiersmen, vagabonds, second-class citizens, and in some cases, slaves attended these revivals, and for the first time, felt a part of God's kingdom dawning in the new republic. They found their suffering suspended, if only temporarily, which offered renewed hope. They also left knowing that salvation, at least in some measure, was attainable on earth, which served as a catalyst for social reform. Religion was no longer a mechanism of control brandished only by elites, but now a revolutionary instrument employed by society at large.

The taste of heaven offered at revivals was just that, a taste. The full measure of salvation's promise was reserved for the coming of God's Kingdom, which the newly empowered felt responsible for ushering in. Thus, the theology of this period emphasized the imminent return of

Christ, and charged believers with the task of preparing America for the Second Coming.

America's Original Sin

The young nation was a blank canvas upon which people of all walks projected their hopes and aspirations. While politicians haggled over finance and industry, religious reformers set themselves to the task of weeding the American garden of sin. There was plenty of sins to choose from, but intemperance and slavery were front and center. In fact, some thought slavery and drunkenness inextricably linked.

Frederick Douglass was a prodigious intellectual and a brilliant orator whose words were emboldened by his experience as a former slave. In recounting the stupefying effects of alcohol on the enslaved, he said, "On each Saturday night it is quite common in the State of Maryland (the slave state from which I escaped) for masters to give their slaves a considerable quantity of whiskey to keep them during the Sabbath in a state of stupidity. At the time when they would be apt to think—at a time when they would be apt to devise means for their freedom—their masters give them of the stupefying draught which paralyzes their intellect, and in this way prevents their seeking emancipation."[2] Thus, said Douglass, "I believe that if we could but make the world sober, we would have no slavery."[3]

---

[2] Frederick Douglass, "Intemperance Viewed in Connection With Slavery: An Address Delivered in Glasgow, Scotland, February 18, 1846." The Frederick Douglass Papers, Yale University Press, 1979. Vol. I, pg. 165

[3] Frederick Douglass, "Intemperance and Slavery: An Address Delivered in Cork, Ireland, October 20, 1845," Truth Seeker. The Frederick

For Douglass, the abolition of slavery and intoxicating spirits went hand in hand. On the question of drunkenness, he had much support but slavery was far more divisive. Slavery proved to be an impasse that would not only rip the nation apart, but destroy families, friendships, churches, and, for our purposes, one of the most successful temperance groups in history.

When tracing the origins of Alcoholics Anonymous through American history, few dates are more significant than April 2, 1840. On that day, six drunks made a pact with one another to never drink again. This mutual-aid group, which precedes Alcoholics Anonymous by nearly one hundred years, is—with the exception of the Oxford Group—A.A.'s most notable forerunner. The Washingtonians, as they came to be known, shared their personal experiences with one another, creating a fellowship based on shared suffering and group support with total abstinence from alcohol as the stated goal.

The Washingtonians took their name from George Washington, a name that in American shorthand is synonymous with honesty and integrity, both of which were core components of their movement. The Washingtonians' two pillars were a personal pledge and peer support, the combined power of which is attested to in this exchange between a member and his wife:

Douglass Papers, New Haven: Yale University Press, 1979. Vol. I, pg. 55

"From this hour I am a changed man—from this hour I will be to you what I was in years long past: the remembrance of which are still dear to me. Last night I threw myself within the sphere of the great moral reformation that is now progressing—the temperance reformation—and I feel, I know, that there is in that sphere a sustaining power that will keep me true to my pledge. For the past, I dare not ask you to forgive me. If you can, let its deeds sink as much as possible into oblivion. But for the future, take hope. In the strength of him whose divine power is present in every good resolution, I will be true to my wife, my children, and myself."[4]

The Washingtonians offered hope to men and families reeling in the despair of drunkenness. Meetings quickly sprang up around the country.

In 1842, a state representative, whose name would one day rival Washington's in American lore, addressed the Springfield Washingtonian Society on the first President's 110th birthday.[5] He was quick to celebrate the hope offered by the movement: "By the Washingtonians this system of consigning the habitual drunkard to hopeless ruin is repudiated," said a thirty-three-year-old Abraham Lincoln. He continued, "They adopt a more enlarged philanthropy. They go for present as well as future good. They labor for all now

---

[4] Six Nights with the Washingtonians: A Series of Temperance Tales, Timothy Shay Arthur, pgs 127-28, 1843

[5] Abraham Lincoln, Temperance Address Springfield, Illinois, February 22, 1842

living, as well as all hereafter to live. They teach hope to all—despair to none."

The Washingtonians were not without controversy. Noticeably absent from their movement was any stress on God or religion. They emphasized a fellowship of support, rather than religious conversion. During the Second Awakening, this did not go without notice or scandal. The Washingtonians' pledge read: "We agree to abstain from all intoxicating liquors except for medical purposes and religious ordinances." Over half-a-million people signed that pledge by the mid-1850s, but its glaring omission of God drew harsh criticism from religious leaders. They thought the Washingtonian pledge placed man's faculties ahead of God and denounced them as "humanists," which was code for "atheist," a damning charge at the time.

Charges of atheism were not the Washingtonian's undoing, however. Their movement was doomed to failure before it began. Their fate was sealed by history. The gravitational pull of slavery was too great. Indeed, Lincoln's address to the Springfield chapter nineteen years before he led the nation through its most perilous time, controversially resurrected the God of reason and waded deep into the waters of slavery. "Happy day, when, all appetites controlled, all poisons subdued, all matter subjected, mind, all conquering mind, shall live and move the monarch of the world." In conclusion, Lincoln proclaimed, "Glorious consummation! Hail fall of Fury! Reign of Reason, all hail! And when the victory shall be complete—when there shall be neither a slave nor a drunkard on the earth—how proud the title of that Land, which may truly claim to be the birthplace and the cradle of both those revolutions, that shall have ended in that victory."

Slavery was a thorn in the proverbial side of the American experiment since Jefferson, himself a slave owner, first put quill to paper in 1776. Now, it loomed so large that it blotted out all others. Many northerners opposed slavery on moral grounds but remained politically apathetic so long as it stayed in the South, out of sight-out of mind. They saw their comfortable indifference disturbed in 1850 with passage of the Fugitive Slave Act. Suddenly, they were party to the institution of slavery. "I have lived all my life without suffering any known inconvenience from American Slavery," said Ralph Waldo Emerson. "I never saw it; I never heard the whip; I never felt the check on my free speech and action, until, the other day, when Mr. Webster, by his personal influence, brought the Fugitive Slave Law on the country."

The tension over slavery continued to build until it reached a crescendo in 1860 with the election of Lincoln. South Carolina submitted the first letter of secession a month later, citing both refusal on behalf of several Northern states to enforce the Fugitive Slave Act and the increasing hostility toward slavery engendered by the election of Lincoln.

Slavery and the war monopolized the nation's attention. Moreover, alcohol played a pivotal role in the war effort. The taxation of alcohol was a significant source of funding, accounting for as much as a third of the Federal budget. The table was set and the temperance movement was placed on the backburner. The drink problem would have to wait until the issue of slavery was resolved on the battlefield.

The Renewal of Temperance

America's obsession with the sin of intemperance lingered in the background throughout the Civil War. Following Reconstruction, it retook center stage. Slavery dispelled, the religious conscience of America was fixed once more upon drunkenness. The drinking problem, however, was no longer a concern limited to holy-rollers hoping to establish America as a shining city on the hill. Intemperance hit home.

According to their biographers, George Washington[6] frequently enjoyed several glasses of wine with dinner, and John Adams[7] drank a gill of hard cider every morning before breakfast. Neither were considered intemperate. In fact, this was moderate drinking at the time. At the turn of the 19th century, Americans annually consumed, on average, six gallons of pure alcohol, which amounts to thirty-four gallons of beer and cider, five gallons of distilled liquor, and just under a gallon of wine.[8] Taverns were a staple in every town, and people literally drank all day.

In the 1830s the average American man consumed roughly seven gallons of distilled spirits annually, nearly three times the present levels.[9] And, as one might imagine, alcoholism was only inflamed by the horrors of war,

---

[6] Ron Chernow, *George Washington: A Life,* pg 135, 2010

[7] David McCullough, *John Adams*, pg 36, 2001

[8] *Drinking in America: A History,* Mark Edward Lender and James Kirby Martin, pg 14, 1987

[9] Ibid, pg 46

particularly a Civil War that claimed over six-hundred thousand lives.

The effects of rampant alcoholism were devastating for both the family and society at large. "Who can calculate the extensive influence of a drunken husband or wife upon the property and morals of their families?" asked Benjamin Rush. "And of the waste of the former, and corruption of the latter, upon the order and happiness of society?"[10] At the time, men were the sole breadwinners. Alcohol not only diminished their earning capacity but squandered what money they managed to earn. This left anxious mothers scrounging to feed their children. Furthermore, drunkenness turns many loving husbands into monsters, and back then, divorce was not an acceptable mode of recourse. The unchecked alcoholism that plagued America's first one hundred fifty years would, by today's standards, be considered a national epidemic.

Alcoholism's impact on the family enlisted throngs of women in the Temperance movement. The demonstrations of civil disobedience organized by Eliza Thompson and the dramatic, if not riotous, acts carried out by the hatchet-wielding Carrie Nation, channeled the frustrations of women everywhere, albeit in wildly different ways. In addition to Thompson and Nation, Susan B. Anthony, Elizabeth Stanton, and Frances Willard, all of whom were indispensable in the passage of the 19th Amendment as well, played pivotal roles in the Temperance movement. These women organized political protests and staged sit-ins that dramatized their

---

[10] Benjamin Rush, *Medical Inquiries and Observations upon Diseases of the Mind,* pg 265, 1812

plight. Their efforts successfully appealed to husbands, fathers, businessmen, and lawmakers, but ultimately failed to effect lasting change.

Alcoholism continued to frustrate both progressive reformers and religious leaders, but this frustration did not deter them. If anything, it radicalized them. The temperance movement continued to pick up steam—so much steam, in fact, that it morphed into the push for prohibition. The prohibitionists' stated goals were eventually met, but their objectives were not. Prohibition became the law of the land, but neither alcohol nor alcoholism vanished from American life.

In retrospect, it is easy to see why the Temperance movement failed. They did not understand the problem of alcoholism, but to be fair, no one did. The nature of the problem had not yet been discovered. So those religiously inclined minds continued to look at "drunkenness" and "intemperance" through the lens of religion, which turned it into a sin, the persistence of which left them with but one option: Prohibition.

In a now famous sermon, remembered simply as the "Booze Sermon," Billy Sunday, perhaps the most influential evangelist of the early 20th century and a staunch prohibitionist, tells the story of his old friend George. Sunday became reacquainted with George while working the "saloon route" as the YMCA Secretary in Chicago. The preacher claimed to count 1,004 men entering a particular saloon in just sixty-two minutes, at which point he entered, and found George throwing back a mint julep. George was enjoying a play at a nearby theater "and came over for a drink between acts." A drink between acts may seem harmless to the average onlooker, but Sunday was an alarmist, not your average onlooker. "George, do you see that old drunken bum, down and out? There was a time when he was just like you. No drunkard ever intended to be a drunkard. Every drunkard intended to be a moderate drinker," Sunday warned. George brushed him off, but the story does not end there. It builds up to Sunday's "I told you so" moment.

"I was standing on another corner less than eight months afterward," the sermon continues, "and I saw a bum coming along with his head down, his eyes bloodshot, his face bloated, and he panhandled me for a flapjack before I recognized him." Of course, "it was George. He had lost his job and was on the toboggan slide hitting it for hell."

Prohibitionists, like Sunday, thought the bottle a conduit of sin that turned good men into drunkards. It never occurred to them that George may suffer from a peculiar sensitivity to alcohol that required treatment, not legislation.

The Eighteenth Amendment

At the onset of the 20th Century, alcoholism was still seen through the lens of Christian fundamentalism. However, the promise of a sinless utopia continued to evade them. The idea that their evangelism was inadequate—or altogether misplaced—never entered their minds. Their religiosity wouldn't permit such thoughts. Instead, they reasoned the crusade against drunkenness failed to produce lasting results because drunks are lily-livered heathens. In effect, "drunkenness" is a manifestation of moral weakness. If drunks are too weak-willed to abstain, abstinence would have to be forced upon them.

The crusade for prohibition was born of a perfect storm. If it is God's plan to establish America as the shining city on the hill—as the religious reasoned—and this light shines forth from her moral superiority—and it does, they added—but obscuring this light is the sin of drunkenness, which the intemperate are constitutionally incapable of overcoming—as was now evident—the only remaining course of action was to bypass temptation by prohibiting the sale of alcohol. If certain people are too feeble minded to resist sin, then sin must be outlawed. In this sense, prohibition is the inevitable conclusion of fundamentalist logic.

The Anti-Saloon League was founded in 1893 by the Reverend Howard Russell. The League was based in Ohio and particularly popular among Methodists and Baptists. Throughout the 19th century both denominations grew in numbers, and as the century drew to a close, they represented a powerful coalition. Generations removed from their humble beginnings, the Baptists and Methodists now wielded considerable influence and were prepared to exert that influence in the political sphere. The Anti-Saloon League was the mechanism that effectively leveraged their influence against lawmakers.

In 1903, an attorney by the name of Wayne Wheeler became the Executive Director of the Anti-Saloon League. Under his leadership, they became a commanding force in

American politics. He not only used the power of religion as a call to action but organized the vast network of churches that supported Temperance and Prohibition into a political *tour de force*. This consolidated Wheeler's base into a formidable bloc, which he weaponized.

The Anti-Saloon League did not care about foreign policy. They had no opinion on trade or civil rights. The League was a single-issue special interest group whose sole focus was Prohibition, and they played for keeps. If you supported their cause, they supported you. If you did not back their agenda, they turned their machine against you with devastating effects. Myron Herrick, a popular Republican Governor in Ohio, saw his bid for re-election wrecked in 1905 because he came down on the wrong side of the Anti-Saloon League. John Pattison soundly defeated Herrick, and politicians around the country repeated the mantra, "Remember what happened to Herrick."

So-called "wet" politicians were not the only obstacle the Anti-Saloon League faced. The federal budget was heavily subsidized by the excise tax on alcohol. The Anti-Saloon League's singleness of purpose demanded they back the 16th Amendment, which gave Congress the power "to lay and collect taxes on incomes." This relaxed the Government's dependency on the excise tax, and with the passage of the 16th Amendment in 1913, the Anti-Saloon League was poised to push for their own amendment, which prohibited "the manufacture, sale, or transportation of intoxicating liquors."

After a protracted battle, the 18th Amendment was ratified on January 16th, 1918. Prohibition was the law of the land. The American statemen, famed Christian fundamentalist, and celebrated orator, William Jennings Bryan, joined a crowd at the First Congregational Church of D.C. where he heralded in the age of prohibition with a rousing speech punctuated by a repurposed verse from the Gospel of Matthew that viciously characterized prohibition's critics: "They are dead that sought the young child's life!" Billy Sunday forecasted the dawn of that long-awaited utopia: "The slums will soon be only a memory. We will turn our prisons into factories and our jails into storehouses and corncribs." Eden was on the horizon, or so prohibitionists thought.

The Twenty-First Amendment

"Understand now, I'm purely a fiction writer and do not profess to be an earnest student of political science," said the novelist F. Scott Fitzgerald, "but I believe strongly that such a law as one prohibiting liquor is foolish, and all the writers, keenly interested in human welfare whom I know, laugh at the prohibition law." This sentiment was shared by more than just the community of writers. In time, the majority of Americans joined this chorus. The idea that you could successfully ban the sale of alcohol not only proved preposterous but it brought forth unintended consequences that were so severe that even Prohibition's most ardent supporters began to second guess themselves.

It is widely believed that drinking continued unabated or even skyrocketed during Prohibition. Will Rogers once quipped, "Instead of giving money to found colleges to promote learning, why don't they pass a constitutional amendment prohibiting anybody from learning anything? If it works as good as the Prohibition one did, why, in five years we would have the smartest race of people on earth." Studies are kinder to the prohibitive effects of the Eighteenth Amendment. The exact figures are unknown, but most estimates show a decrease of alcoholic consumption nearing 20% to 30%. Still, by no means did intoxicating spirits fade from the scene. In rural America, people took to fermenting fruits and vegetables, and in urban centers, saloons were replaced by an explosion of speakeasies. In fact, A.A.'s future co-founder, Bill Wilson, was known to crush grapes and frequent these wet closets.

The degree to which Prohibition curbed drunkenness is debatable, but the collateral damage of the law is not. The aftermath of Prohibition was anything but utopian. "When Prohibition was introduced, I hoped that it would be widely supported by public opinion and the day would soon come when the evil effects of alcohol would be recognized," wrote John D. Rockefeller. "I have slowly and reluctantly come to believe that this has not been the result. Instead, drinking has generally increased; the speakeasy has replaced the saloon; a vast army of lawbreakers has appeared; many of our best citizens have openly ignored Prohibition; respect for the law has been greatly lessened; and crime has increased to a level never seen before."[11]

Rockefeller abandoned Prohibition after witnessing its many shortcomings, but he never gave up the search for an

---

[11] Daniel Okrent, Great Fortune: The Epic of Rockefeller Center, pgs. 246-247, 2003.

antidote to alcoholism. Eight years after penning the above letter, the oil tycoon hosted a swanky dinner in honor of Alcoholics Anonymous. Bill W. and Dr. Bob keynoted the event, which was presided over by Rockefeller's son, Nelson, the 41st Vice President of the United States. In Alcoholics Anonymous, Rockefeller saw a movement that both avoided the excesses of prohibition and provided a more effective remedy to alcoholism. A.A. forced sobriety on no one, whereas Prohibition tried to impose it on everyone. This created a black market and a criminal underworld, the likes of which had never before been seen in America.

Prohibition turned small-time criminals into big-time gangsters, none more infamous than Al Capone. Following the stock market crash of 1929, the nation was gripped by a Great Depression. At the same time, Capone was banking roughly $60 million a year in illegal liquor sales. Criminals like Capone were selling a product that previously employed average Americans, all the while, pocketing tax-free money once used to fund social progress. Furthermore, the government was spending millions to enforce these unenforceable laws. The Eighteenth Amendment obviously created more problems than it solved, so public opinion quickly shifted.

Days after taking office, Franklin Roosevelt signed the *Permit and Tax Beer Act* into law, which legalized the sale of beer, and Congress quickly moved to repeal the 18th amendment. Roosevelt assumed office on March 4, 1933, and by December 5, 1933, the 18th amendment was a relic of the past.

Two years later, just down the road from Anti-Saloon League headquarters in Ohio, Henrietta Seiberling introduced Bill Wilson to Bob Smith. What did Bill W. and Dr. Bob know about alcoholism that the priests, politicians, and reformers did not? Moreover, why did their ideas spark an international movement that accomplished what Temperance and Prohibition couldn't? These questions are complicated and demand complex answers. The pluralistic and pragmatic approach of the Twelve Steps, as well as the peer support offered by the fellowship are key ingredients in A.A.'s success. However, none of this gets off the ground without a revolutionary new take on alcoholism. Therefore, the first step in our journey is to examine "the little doctor who loved drunks" and his "great idea," which informs A.A.'s first Step.
.

3 THE DOCTOR'S OPINION

> "Alcoholism is a devastating, potentially fatal disease. The primary symptom of having it is telling everyone—including yourself—that you are not an alcoholic." ~ Herbert Gravitz

Towns Hospital was founded in 1901 by Charles Towns, a Georgia-born insurance salesman who became an addiction specialist after he acquired a cure for alcoholism from a mysterious country physician, or so the story goes. Charles Towns lacked medical credentials, so he partnered with Dr. Alexander Lambert, personal physician to President Theodore Roosevelt. Together they peddled their alcoholic panacea, creatively dubbed the Towns-Lambert cure, though it is more widely known as the "Belladonna Treatment."

The Belladonna treatment, *according to Towns*, boasted a 90% success rate. This statistic is undoubtedly padded by Towns' convenient rationale, which scored any patient he never saw again as a successful case, omitting the fact that he told every patient, "I do not wish to hear from you after you leave my care."[1]

The Towns-Lambert cure was a racket, but Towns Hospital was a successful enterprise. It was a favorite drying-out spot for well-to-do New York drunks. On Tuesday, December 11, 1934, Bill Wilson made the seven and a half mile trip from 182 Clinton Street in Brooklyn to the Upper West Side of Manhattan, where he, for the fourth and final time, checked into Towns Hospital. At this point, Wilson was anything but well-to-do. His brother-in-law, an Osteopath, named Dr. Leonard Strong, supplied the $125 needed for the five-day detox program. Little did he know, that $125 would secure not only Wilson's sobriety but the sobriety of millions for generations to come.

"So far as people were concerned, the main channels of inspiration for our Steps were three in number," Wilson wrote in the July 1953 edition of A.A.'s magazine, *The Grapevine*. Those three channels were the Oxford Group, William James, and Dr. Silkworth. The latter, according to Wilson, contributed "a very great idea without which A.A. could never had succeeded." The primary objective of this chapter is to better understand that "great idea," and why it was so integral to A.A.'s success. Once we have a working knowledge of this idea, we will unpack Step One and the concept of "powerlessness"—which will be applied to non-alcoholics

---

[1] "I have found that alcoholics taking treatment at my hospital must understand that I do not wish to hear from them after they have left my care." Charles Town, *Habits That Handicap*, pgs. 236-37, 1915

The Allergy

Over the course of his career, Silkworth treated tens of thousands of alcoholics and drug addicts. He observed that neither alcohol nor the desire to consume alcohol were problematic. In a 1937 paper entitled *Alcoholism as a Manifestation of Allergy*, Dr. Silkworth argues, "The majority of people who drink alcohol apparently do so with impunity. Prohibition revealed, among other things, how much people desire to use alcohol on all sorts of occasions, and that this desire, and intention, are not limited to chronic alcoholics."

The religious mind saw sin in every bottle and a future drunk in every drink, which propped up the now debunked Prohibition laws. Silkworth dispelled this theory. The doctor saw an illness, not sin, and it was located in the body, not the bottle. Therefore, it afflicted a particular class of drinker, rather than society writ large.

The 19th century's obsession with eradicating sin confused the desire to partake of intoxicating spirits with drunkenness and drunkenness with alcoholism, but for Silkworth, these were three distinct conditions. "Drunkenness and alcoholism are not synonymous. Intoxication with alcohol, as commonly observed, is a purely superficial manifestation of no diagnostic importance whatever in itself; nor is the desire to take a drink, which is common to many." According to Silkworth, neither the desire to drink nor episodic drunkenness are indicative of a disorder. Moreover, this appetite is not limited to moral degenerates or social outcasts. It transcends class and status: "The judge, the senator, the preacher, all want their alcohol on occasion," and presumably find themselves intoxicated every once in a while. All this led Silkworth to the conclusion that alcoholism is an illness of the mind and body that must be distinguished from casual drinking. The only way to draw such a distinction is to look beyond socio-economic status, race, gender, and religion to the effect alcohol has upon the individual in question.

"We believe," Silkworth writes in his published letter to Alcoholics Anonymous, "and so suggested a few years ago," referencing his 1937 paper, "that the action of alcohol on these chronic alcoholics is a manifestation of an allergy; that the phenomenon of craving is limited to this class and never occurs in the average temperate drinker." According to the doctor, it is a physical allergy to alcohol that distinguishes the alcoholic from the typical drinker.

It is important to note that modern science does not validate Silkworth's theory; nevertheless, it's aged well. One reason for the theory's success is that, while technically incorrect, it does play well with the facts. Alcoholism may not be an actual allergy, but alcoholics do demonstrate an adverse and abnormal reaction to the consumption of alcohol. In short, alcoholism functions *like* an allergy, so for all intents and purposes, Silkworth's theory maps onto reality. Moreover, his imprecision can be seen as an asset. The practical objectives of the Twelve Steps are better served by the simpler allergy model. This model metaphorically conveys the same point, while avoiding an elaborate discussion of enzymes, neurotransmitters, metabolism, and genetics, which only complicate matters for A.A.'s target audience, the layman. It's not altogether clear whether this was Silkworth's intention. On the one hand, he penned a scientific paper espousing the allergy idea; on the other, Bill Wilson claims he "knew this was a misnomer; he used it to express his intuition that something was physically wrong with most of us."[2] At any rate, Dr. Silkworth provided an idea that revolutionized the way we think about and treat alcoholism and drug addiction, situating the malady firmly in the domain of medicine.

It is ironic that Silkworth promoted such ideas, given that twenty years earlier his employer, Charles Towns, wrote in *Habits That Handicap*, "We hear much sympathetic talk of the 'disease of alcoholism'… The sanatorium promoters and proprietors of fake cures continually harp on alcoholism as a disease; and even a few scientists, who should know better, have been misled into acceptance of this theory."[3] Also ironic is the fact that Towns did not count himself among the "proprietors of fake cures." However, the reason Silkworth's ideas were so successful is far more interesting and relevant to our purposes than Towns' lack of self-awareness.[4]

The above quote from Towns suggests that the disease model of alcoholism was in circulation, and to some extent, in vogue, before Silkworth stepped onto the scene. The "Father

---

[2] A.A. World Services, *Pass It On,* pg 388

[3] Charles Barnes Towns, *Habits That Handicap*, pgs 230-31, 1915

[4] Bill Wilson tried to steer clear of this controversy. He did not want to come down on the wrong side of scientific consensus, not then or in the future. Rather than the word "disease," he chose instead to use broad words like malady and illness.

of American Psychiatry," Dr. Benjamin Rush, listed intemperate drinking among the "diseases of the will" in his book *Medical Inquiries and Observations upon Diseases of the Mind*, the first text published in America (1812) that systematically detailed mental illness. Therein, he prescribes a blend of "religious, moral, and physical remedies," including "sober houses," which aim "to rescue persons affected" from the "arm of the law," and "render them subjects of the kind and lenient hand of medicine."[5] Inching closer toward a fixed diagnostic term, the German physician, Christoph Hufeland, coined "dipsomania" in the 1850's. At the turn of the 20th century, the disease theory was still viewed with suspicion, but the teetotaling approach of religionists and moral reformers reached a climax with Prohibition, and to no avail. People were now primed to hear the doctor's opinion.

The stage was set when, in March 1941, Jack Alexander's article in *The Saturday Evening Post* entitled "Alcoholics Anonymous" exposed Silkworth's intriguing ideas to three million readers. "One may be born, they say, with a hereditary predisposition to alcoholism, just as one may be born with a vulnerability to tuberculosis," the exposé reads. "The rest seems to depend upon environment and experience, *although one theory has it that some people are allergic to alcohol, as hay fever sufferers are to pollens.*"

Alexander's article mentioned Silkworth's ideas only in passing. Choosing to focus on the budding fellowship instead.

---

[5] Benjamin Rush, *Medical Inquiries and Observations upon Diseases of the Mind,* pg 262-266, 1812

The article did, however, increase sales in the fledgling book *Alcoholics Anonymous*, which included a detailed account of Silkworth's theories in the foreword entitled, "The Doctor's Opinion." Jack Alexander's piece triggered Alcoholics Anonymous' ascendancy and Silkworth's model of alcoholism enjoyed proportionate success.

Silkworth's impact on the treatment of alcoholism is far-reaching, but outside recovery circles, he seldom gets the credit he deserves. Twelve Step programs and support groups, like Alcoholics Anonymous, are utilized by nearly 75% of substance abuse treatment centers in the United States.[6] "A.A. could never had succeeded," according to Wilson, without Silkworth's allergy idea. Since the impact of Twelve Step programs on the treatment of addiction is of a historic magnitude, and their success is partly owed to the utility of Silkworth's ideas, it stands to reason that Silkworth is deserving of far more credit than he is awarded. But this is a two-way street.

It Just Makes Sense

Silkworth's ideas were, as Bill points out, integral to the success of A.A., but it is also true that the book *Alcoholics Anonymous* played a crucial role in disseminating the doctor's theory. Silkworth's ideas enjoyed wide circulation because they resonated with alcoholics, not because they were adopted by the larger scientific community. In both the fellowship and

---

[6] Substance Abuse and Mental Health Services Administration (SAMSHA), National Survey of Substance Abuse Treatment Services, 2013

the text, Silkworth's ideas find a most effective vehicle. It is a mutually-beneficial relationship between doctor and patient.

This symbiotic relationship is on full display in the opening pages of *Alcoholics Anonymous*. The book begins with "The Doctor's Opinion" because a medical view of alcoholism and the endorsement of a prominent physician lends credibility to the program that follows. However, the doctor's opinion is assuredly legitimized by the ringing endorsement his views receive from the authors of the text, themselves recovered alcoholics. "The doctor's theory that we have an allergy to alcohol interests us," writes Wilson in his prelude to Silkworth's published letter. "As laymen, our opinion as to its soundness may, of course, mean little. But as ex-problem drinkers, we can say that his explanation makes good sense." Bill is essentially saying, Silkworth's theory may or may not stand up to scientific rigor, but it is useful, as evidenced by our personal testimony. Surely this caught the eye of suffering alcoholics, as well as those specializing in the treatment of alcoholism.

The allergy meme quickly replicated itself because it was useful. Silkworth's idea went viral with recovering alcoholics and treatment providers because it corresponds with the experience of alcoholics. It is a pragmatic diagnosis that makes sense of their otherwise perplexing condition—and it does not label them weak or depraved.

The pragmatism of Alcoholics Anonymous is born of necessity. The alcoholic and the drug addict—threatened by "jails, institutions, and death"—can't afford to get bogged down in scientific debates or spin their wheels on subtle points of philosophy and theology. When faced with the pain and despair imposed by addiction on themselves and their families, such intellectual concerns are of little consequence. This is where pragmatism intervenes, suggesting that any manner of living preferable to the current should be dutifully pursued, and the value of a given idea or belief is measured by its ability to bring about that way of life. This rationale settles all academic controversies for the suffering alcoholic.

There is a subtle anti-intellectualism baked into Twelve Step thought that is consistent with the tradition of anti-intellectualism in American philosophy. It isn't an irrational or belligerent turn of mind, but a prevailing common sense that is persuaded by practical results, not abstract reasoning. No one in their right mind would argue that drunkenness is preferable to sobriety. Likewise, most people would resist pressuring an alcoholic or a group of recovering alcoholics to discard an idea that enables them to achieve lasting sobriety simply because it fails to toe the scientific or religious line.

The Admission of Powerlessness

Alcoholics Anonymous generally avoids technical jargon, electing instead for an experiential language more accessible to the lay reader. This conversational tone is also better suited for the mode of personal storytelling practiced in A.A. meetings, which has proven vital to the fellowship's success. In Step One, this is the language of "powerlessness."

Step one reads, "We admitted we were powerless over alcohol—that our lives had become unmanageable." It does not say, "admitted we were alcoholics." This distinction is important, for our purposes, because powerlessness is a condition with which we can all relate, and it can be associated with any number of substances or behaviors. This acknowledgment makes the first Step accessible to those who do not identify as alcoholics or drug addicts, as we shall see in the following chapter. In A.A.'s first Step, powerlessness refers to "alcohol," whereas in Sexaholics Anonymous, powerlessness is qualified by "lust" and in Overeaters Anonymous "food" is the object of powerlessness. Alcohol, and drugs are symptoms; they are not the root cause, which is why anyone can relate to Step One.

"Alcoholism" is technically a diagnostic term subject to clinical standards. Powerlessness, on the other hand, is a subjective term. "The concept fundamental to Alcoholics Anonymous continued to be the pragmatic one of the *alcoholic*, rather than any speculative reaching at some direct comprehension of *alcoholism*," writes historian Ernest Kurtz.[7] Powerlessness describes *how the alcoholic feels*. It also enables prospective members to diagnose themselves. The act of self-diagnosis is called admission in Step One, and it is a crucial part of the recovery process. As the old saying goes, "The first step is to admit that you have a problem." In point of fact, that saying isn't that old. It's a proverbial twist on A.A.'s first Step.

It is important to note that in Step One "admit" does not mean "to mouth" or "say out loud." When we admit something, we "accept it as true" or "let it in," just as an

---

[7] Ernest Kurtz, *Not-God: A History of Alcoholics Anonymous,* pg 59, 1991

admissions office determines who can enroll in the university. In Step One, we are accepting the truth of our powerlessness. This chapter addresses Step One in relation to alcohol. In the next chapter we will explore what that means for the majority of us: powerlessness over food, sex, and other impulsive behaviors. I have decided to lump drug addiction in with alcoholism, since the two are analogous, and because doing so hurries the inclusion of a larger audience.

In the fourth chapter of *Alcoholics Anonymous*, Wilson outlines a handy formula for diagnosing oneself alcoholic: "If, when you honestly want to, you find you cannot quit entirely, or if when drinking, you have little control over the amount you take, you are probably alcoholic." This practical little syllogism triangulates the experience of powerlessness.

Concerning alcohol, there are two possible modes of being: drinking and not drinking. If when you can't control the amount you drink or quit drinking entirely, it is safe to say that you have no control *or power* over alcohol. Hence, you are "powerless." This is a simple diagnostic criteria, but sufficient for its purposes. The standards employed by mental health professionals are far more meticulous, as they should be. Clinicians are diagnosing other people, whereas the Steps are asking the individual to diagnose themselves.

The experience of powerlessness is comprised of two parts, which Bill Wilson calls the "twin ogres." They are a physical allergy coupled with a mental obsession. The physical allergy explains why the alcoholic has little control over the amount they take; the mental obsession explains why they keep taking it; these interlocking ideas form a functional model of addiction.

This model enables the addicted to wrap their mind around the experience of powerlessness, and understanding helps facilitate admission. There is no search for power or spirituality without the admission of powerlessness, so the kit of spiritual tools offered in the remaining Steps are obsolete without this formula. Silkworth's idea is half the equation, so without it, or some variation thereof, A.A.'s Twelve Steps never get rolling. The doctor helps bring the problem into focus (powerlessness), thereby justifying the spiritual solution offered in the remaining Steps (search for power). It exposes the nail, making sense of the hammer.

The Physical Ogre

A newcomer to Alcoholics Anonymous does not need to be converted to powerlessness or convinced of it. Powerlessness is their life experience. They're looking for words that give voice to that experience, which is precisely what they find in Step One.

Alcoholism may not be the literal manifestation of an allergy, but the alcoholic does have an abnormal and adverse reaction to the consumption of alcohol. In other words, alcoholism functions *like* an allergy, and therefore, serves as a helpful metaphor for the addicted struggling to grasp the nature of their condition.

An allergy is a hypersensitivity to a particular substance, usually a food or some airborne particle. Someone with an allergy to peanuts, for example, might experience skin irritation, a runny nose, or in severe cases, constriction of their airways and a drop in blood pressure. These are symptoms or manifestations of an allergy to peanuts. In Silkworth's model of alcoholism, the phenomenon of craving is the manifestation of an allergy to alcohol. The alcoholic's nose doesn't begin to run and their airways do not constrict; instead, they experience an intense craving for more alcohol. This adverse reaction to the first drink is the characteristic that sets the alcoholic apart from other drinkers, according to Silkworth.

Under the sprawling umbrella of alcoholism and addiction you will find daily users, binge drinkers, men, women, black, white, rich, poor, functional, and dysfunctional, but "all these, and many others, have one symptom in common," Silkworth contends: "They cannot start drinking without developing the phenomenon of craving." The "phenomenon of craving" is not a garden variety thirst. Silkworth lifts the phrase from the clinical term, "dipsomania," which is derived from the Greek words for "thirst" and "manic compulsion." He then recasts this insatiable thirst as the manifestation of an allergy.

The phenomenon of craving describes an uncontrollable urge, not a lack of impulse control. In an effort to express the strength of this craving, William James cites, in *The Principles of Psychology*, a first-person account from an apparent alcoholic circa the American Revolution: "Were a keg of rum in one corner of a room, and were a cannon constantly discharging balls between me and it, I could not refrain from passing before that cannon, in order to get at the rum."[8]

Willpower is of no diagnostic interest to Silkworth because the predominance of the craving is priced into the concept. The class of people he labels "alcoholic" are those who demonstrate a craving for alcohol beyond their mental control. This is the only way of accounting for those he says are "entirely normal in every respect except in the effect alcohol has upon them."[9] Those who do not struggle with substance abuse often judge the merits of this idea against their personal experience. This is a mistake.

"The craving for drink in real dipsomaniacs, or for opium or chloral in those subjugated," writes James, "is of a strength of which normal persons can form no conception." When non-addicted persons use their experience to analyze alcoholism or drug addition, skepticism invariably follows because, by definition, they are not sensitive to alcohol or drugs. Their sensitivities lie elsewhere. This mistake was made by the Temperance movement, leading them to the excesses of Prohibition.

Many determined and successful people suffer from alcoholism and drug addiction. Ulysses S. Grant, for example, did not obtain the rank of Commanding General of the U.S. Army or President of the United States because he was a weak-willed person; nevertheless, he struggled to control his

---

[8] William James, *Principles of Psychology*, pg 543, 1918 (can also be found in the aforementioned text by Benjamin Rush)

[9] Bill Wilson, "The Doctor's Opinion," *Alcoholics Anonymous*, 1939

drinking. In fact, Bill Wilson and Dr. Bob provide similar examples; both were successful in their own right before alcoholism brought them to their knees.

Silkworth identifies an entire class of alcoholics who are "able, intelligent, friendly people." He says, "I have had many men who had, for example, worked a period of months on some problem or business deal which was to be settled on a certain date, favorably to them. They took a drink a day or so prior to the date, and then the phenomenon of craving at once became paramount to all other interests so that the important appointment was not met. These men were not drinking to escape; they were drinking to overcome a craving beyond their mental control." Dr. Silkworth is not describing weak-willed people, but a craving so intense that it annuls the strongest of wills, taking precedence over even the most pressing concerns.

The notion that they were "drinking to overcome a craving" distinguishes the doctor's theory from others, and makes it compelling problem drinkers. More often than not, the alcoholic's spree begins with seemingly innocent motives. Perhaps they stop off for a drink after a long day, take a glass of champagne to celebrate the New Year, or reach for a can of beer to close out an otherwise uneventful week. They plan to have just one or two drinks, nothing more—but unbeknownst to them, the first drink triggers an "allergic" reaction, giving rise to the phenomenon of craving. This craving *demands* a second drink, but because the craving is a reaction to the first, it is only made stronger by the second, thereby requiring a third. And so it is with the fourth and fifth, *ad infinitum*.

The desire to drink is hardly peculiar or mysterious. "Men and women drink essentially because they like the effect produced by alcohol," Dr. Silkworth plainly acknowledges. This is true of most everyone, including alcoholics and addicts, but once "allergic types" get started, they find themselves in the grip of a vicious cycle, drinking or using to escape a craving produced by drinking and using. At this point, they pass through the stages of a spree. They binge for a period determined, not by their own faculties, but by events beyond their control. They drink or use until they run out of money, end up in jail, pass out, or meet some other circumstance that renders them incapable of continuing.

This is the physical aspect of powerlessness. When the average person thinks of addiction, their mind focuses exclusively on this feature. They see what happens to the alcoholic or the addict once they get started, but that alone doesn't equal powerlessness. The doctor's theory does not account for the first drink. The alcoholic, like most everyone else, wants to enjoy a drink from time to time, but after a while, they anticipate the resulting bender and its disastrous aftermath. They know the first drink or drug is a bad idea, but that knowledge is of no consequence. Here, the allergy metaphor runs its course.

The Mental Ogre

"These observations would be academic and pointless," Wilson says of the Dr.'s opinion, "if our friend never took the first drink, thereby setting the terrible cycle in motion. Therefore, the main problem of the alcoholic centers in his mind, rather than in his body." The physical component of addiction is of little consequence unless it is triggered, which is why there are no treatment centers for people with sensitivities to shellfish or Twelve Step programs for those who suffer from peanut allergies. When people learn of such aversions, they go out of their way to avoid peanuts and shellfish, but not so with alcoholics or addicts.

Focusing exclusively on the physical ogre reduces addiction to a mere sensitivity, an allergy. If addiction is nothing more than an allergic state, then a period of detoxification followed by a course of complete abstinence is the solution. This simplistic proposition is rebutted by the addicted person's persistent struggles to maintain sobriety, struggles that must be considered native to any conception of addiction. Thus, any serious exploration of addiction must move beyond *what happens once the addict or alcoholic gets started,* and into the far more perplexing matter of *why they get started.*

What happens to the alcoholic once they get started and why they get started in the first place—body and mind, respectively—are the two pillars of powerlessness, the twin ogres. By themselves they are insignificant, but together they are fatal.

"Parallel with our sound reasoning," Wilson explains, "there inevitably ran some insanely trivial excuse for taking the first drink." As I said before, the alcoholic knows the first drink is a bad idea, but running alongside that sane train of thought is the bizarre notion that this time will be different.

"The idea that somehow, someday he will control and enjoy his drinking is the great obsession of every abnormal drinker. The persistence of this illusion is astonishing. Many pursue it into the gates of insanity or death."[10] It is an illusion born of obsession. The addicted mind relentlessly generates rationalizations until one eventually wins out. Here, A.A.'s pragmatic streak reemerges to declare, "Whatever the precise definition of the word may be, we call this plain insanity."[11]

The word insanity is nondescript. It spans a broad spectrum upon which an assortment of abnormal patterns of thought and behavior can be plotted. Wilson defines it as "a lack of proportion, of the ability to think straight," which is essentially a point of view disconnected from reality. It's the conquest of an idea wholly deaf to the counsel of past experience. This idea is beholden not to the body it actually inhabits, the "allergic body," but to a fanciful body that is capable of drinking responsibly. For the addicted, this is an illusory body with potentially fatal consequences for their actual body.

Insanity is the active ingredient in powerlessness. If the alcoholic never takes the first drink, the allergy isn't triggered, and the cycle is never set in motion. This is why Wilson pegs insanity as "the crux of the problem." Moreover, it is the feature of addiction upon which the program of recovery is focused.

---

[10] Bill Wilson, *Alcoholics Anonymous,* pg 30, 1939

[11] Bill Wilson, *Alcoholics Anonymous,* pg 37, 1939

The Twelve Steps aim to restore sanity because insanity is conditioned, and therefore, pliable. It arises from causes and conditions. Consequently, it can be undone; whereas the physical condition appears to be self-existing with no known remedy. This is also why the Twelve Steps are pertinent to us all, not just addicts and alcoholics. The Steps do not target substance abuse. They focus on insanity, which is present and operable in everyone.

The physical and mental aspects of addiction converge on a single point, the experience of powerlessness. Only one of these two forces is malleable. "It is noteworthy," Dr. Silkworth writes in his 1937 paper, "that such patients may be deprived of liquor altogether for a long period, a year or longer for example, and become apparently normal. They are still allergic, however, and a single drink will develop the full symptomatology again." Driving the point home, he writes of the allergy in his published letter to Alcoholics Anonymous: "It has never been, by any treatment with which we are familiar, permanently eradicated." Hence, the prospects for recovery lie not in treating the allergy, but in the restoration of sanity. We must, therefore, dive deeper into this insanity.

Why Insanely Trivial Ideas Win Out

The perplexing question surrounding addiction is not why the addicted lose control once they get started but why, knowing the inevitability of that outcome, they return once more to the bottle, pill, needle, or pipe. "To them their alcoholic life seems the only normal one," writes Silkworth, which, for all intents and purposes, means "the only one." They return to that life because it is the only life they know.

They may concede, in a moment of clarity, that their addicted life is not normal, but on a practical level, it's the only life available to them, as evidenced by the fact that they cannot bring forth any other. "They are restless, irritable and discontented unless they can again experience the sense of ease and comfort which comes at once by taking a few drinks," the doctor says. "Drinks, they see others taking with impunity." But the problem drinkers in question are not "others." They are not their cousin, coworker, neighbor, or some statistical average. Alcoholics cannot take those drinks with impunity, and in the back of their minds, they know that. It is the job of insanity to convince them otherwise, and insanity is good at its job. At the end of the day, the insanely trivial excuse wins out because it represents the only *real* option in the addicted mind.

"The fact is that most alcoholics, for reasons yet obscure, have lost the power of choice in drink," writes Wilson. The "power of choice" refers to the freedom of choice. Addiction is bondage.

Alcoholics and addicts are not weak-willed people. Addiction has nothing to do with fortitude or willpower. "Our so-called willpower becomes practically nonexistent. We are without defense against the first drink," declares Wilson.[12] Addiction is the absence of a defense or viable alternative.

---

[12] Bill Wilson, *Alcoholics Anonymous,* pg 24, 1939

"Insanity" does not imply "unadulterated madness, hysteria, or dementia" in the informal language of the Twelve Steps. Alcoholic insanity attempts to justify the unjustifiable. It tries to rationalize the inherently irrational, namely the alcoholic taking a drink. It does this because it has no other choice. Where there is only one option, there is no power of choice, and without choice, there is no freedom.

Freedom is a necessary condition of choice. When freedom is lacking, willpower is obsolete. The privation of freedom leaves the mind chained to a bad solution, which it tries in vain to rationalize or spin. This "spin" is insanity.

This is a crucial point—key to understanding both powerlessness and the dissemination of Alcoholics Anonymous' theory of addiction. The distinction between a weak-willed person and the faculty of will being neutralized is subtle but critical. It sharply disassociates addiction and cowardice, a link that stigmatized alcoholism for centuries. Wilson is not saying that alcoholics lack the moral courage needed to make a different choice. He is saying, on a *practical* level, there is no other option, and therefore, no opportunity for alcoholics to choose otherwise.

You can have an iron will, but it matters not if there is no alternative to will. *Choicelessness is powerlessness.* Addiction is the negation of free-will by the elimination of alternatives, not a deficit of moral intelligence or willpower, which is why addicts and alcoholics may be reasonable and resolute in all other matters.

Suppose you're starving, but find yourself in the middle of nowhere. Within driving distance there is one diner, so you walk in and take a seat. Strictly speaking, did you choose this diner? You pick up a menu to weigh your options and discover they serve only hamburgers. When the waiter arrives and asks what you would like for lunch, can it be said that you chose a burger? Can a choice be made when there are no options? *Practically speaking,* this is the nature of addiction.

When there is cause to celebrate, the addicted mind reaches for a drink or a drug. At the end of a long day, it is a beer that occupies the alcoholic's thoughts. The addict turns to drugs for a spark at the onset of boredom. When the alcoholic cannot afford the electric bill, their first thought is not to pinch pennies but to buy a case of beer, further exacerbating their financial woes. In good times and bad, a drink or a drug is the only available option in the addicted mind. It is the lone diner, the single item on the menu. This stranglehold gives rise to what Wilson calls "the obsession of the mind."

When triggered, this obsession guarantees relapse because there is no other card to play. The obsession uncontrollably spins around the first drink until the alcoholic relents, which triggers the phenomenon of craving, setting in motion, yet again, the vicious cycle.

Throughout this discussion of choicelessness, I have emphasized words like "practically" and "real." This is an effort to distinguish between actual and hypothetical options. Most dogs are, theoretically, capable of fetching a newspaper, but this is a real prospect only for those trained to do so.

Similarly, if an untrained person steps into the ring with a world class boxer, it is *possible* that they will duck and dodge at exactly the right moments, roll, then land a solid counterpunch that ends the fight—but it's not probable. It's not a real possibility because it is not part of the layman's training. That fantastical outcome depends upon techniques not in his skill set.

Extending this analogy to our discussion of addiction, the sincere but undisciplined aspiration to recover gets in the ring with a well-trained addiction, and we know the rest. The "insanely trivial idea" lands a knockout punch. The addicted mind is undefeated for a reason—and so it will remain unless the aspiration to recover is joined with practice. After all, that's how the addiction became so proficient.

The question now before us is, 'How did the addicted mind lose the power of choice?' This is one of those subtler points that Twelve Step literature does not bother with. Their intentions are entirely practical, so "why" is of no concern. Wilson says the addicted mind lost the power of choice "for reasons yet obscure," and leaves it at that. A.A.'s bases are covered, so long as the alcoholic understands that once they get started, they can't stop, but they can't stop getting started because they have lost the power of choice. Thus, we can only speculate as to the causes, and as a bystander, my powers of speculation are limited. There is, however, a story that comes to mind. It is of interest because it not only shines a light on the phenomenon of choicelessness but neatly connects the loss of choice with insanity.

A few years ago someone in recovery shared with me a story about his first encounter with alcohol. He was thirteen years old, and as all teenage boys do, he wanted to impress a girl. Unfortunately, he was too afraid to approach her. They were hanging out with a handful of other kids at a friend's house. There were no parents around. Nothing stood between him and her, except his anxiety. He sat there quiet and frustrated. Then, someone offered him a swig of alcohol looted from the parent's liquor cabinet. He took the drink. No phenomenon of craving, no drunkenness, but all of his fear melted away. He was suddenly the best looking, funniest person in the room. It was as if he found a magical elixir, a cure for any and all ailments. Thirty years later, he stood before me and said, "After two divorces, estrangement from my children, multiple stints in jail, my mind always remembers that first drink. 'Good looking, funny, fearless,' that's what my mind remembered about alcohol, not the suffering. It always recalled the immediate relief. Despite all the pain, my mind still presents alcohol to me as a cure-all."

I am confident that if, in the midst of his alcoholism, we intervened and asked, "Do you really think a drink is going to help?" he would've responded, "No. I know it will only make things worse." It's not that he intellectually believed, after all the hardship, that alcohol was a cure-all. But *practically* speaking, it was *all* he had for a *cure*. It might have been a bad solution—one he developed an adverse reaction to—but it was his only available solution. This is a critical point often overlooked in addiction. In the addicted mind, alcohol and drugs are not a problem. They are a solution—nay, *the* solution!

Coping skills are acquired through practice. We attempt to actualize what we have observed and learned from others as we struggle against tasks, endure social anxiety, and stumble through relationships. Like learning to ride a bike, if we stick with it, we strike a balance that enables us to ethically and effectively navigate the space where our inner and outer worlds meet. Intoxicating substances bypass this process. They play a cheat code that provokes supernormal bursts of pleasure, which temporarily veil strife, instead of learning how to effectively subdue stress, fear, or anger. In short, alcohol and drugs pursue the illusion of relief instead of coping mechanisms that provide lasting relief and contentment.

When paralyzing fear is instantaneously transformed into charisma, the mind takes note. The next time that mind encounters angst, it is likely to reenlist liquid courage's services. If this second venture proves as profitable as the first, the likelihood of a third increases. As this trend continues, alcohol becomes the mind's preferred weapon in the battle against anger, sadness, boredom, and stress. If it is practiced to the exclusion of everything else, it will monopolize the individual's skill set, becoming the only coping mechanism available.

This trend is also self-reinforcing because the relief it provides is fleeting. As a result, the underlying affliction is bound to return, still with no effective coping mechanism waiting to greet it, which tempts alcohol and drugs, yet again. To be clear, the "underlying affliction" is not fear, anger, sadness, or stress. Those are perfectly normal feelings, inevitabilities of life. The affliction is the inability to process and embody those feelings. True, alcohol released the petrified boy from his fear-induced paralysis, enabling him to wax lyrical, but it did not teach him how to work through fear. Therefore, he is sure to be outmatched every time he encounters fear, forcing him to reach for the bottle with increasing predictability. This is not an effective way to negotiate life.

Substance abuse counselors often say, "Alcoholics and drug addicts stop maturing at the age they start drinking or using." This is because they stop cultivating coping mechanisms when they start drinking or using, which stunts their emotional maturity.

Free will is a controversial subject. No faculty is held in higher esteem than our personal sense of freedom, but it is impossible to conceive of addiction without challenging the freedom of choice. If recovery were merely a matter of choice, the addicted would have chosen differently long ago. At its core, addiction must be conceived of as the absence of choice.

Unmanageability

We are what we practice. We may be intellectually aware of other strategies, but unless we practice those ideas, they are not available to us when we need them most. This is attested to by one of Ben Franklin's more famous aphorisms: "Tell me and I forget. Teach me and I remember. Involve me and I learn." I might intellectually understand the theory of carpentry and even how to use a tape measure, hammer, and saw, but that doesn't mean I can build a stable house; that takes training and repetition. For instance, competency as a typist is not the capacity to recall where on the keyboard certain letters are located, but the ability to reach for them gracefully and with efficiency, a skill acquired through practice, not studying a map of the keyboard.

The brain is a problem-solving machine. In a sense, that's what intelligence is: the ability to solve problems. When questioned, the intellect searches for an answer, but it doesn't search the ether; it searches its database. The human mind is not omniscient. There is a difference between theoretical solutions and actual solutions. Those options that are readily available are those that have been acquired through practice. Star pitchers deliver the baseball with unparalleled precision because they practice the required technique and motion, repeatedly. Only those solutions installed through repetition are available to us in the run of life.

The brain is impatient with chaos, confusion, and discomfort. Faced with a problem, it will push a solution, even if the only available solution is, itself, problematic. The alcoholic mind will search the bottle for ease and comfort when confronted with restlessness, irritability, and discontentment, even if the precipitating dis-ease is directly related to drinking. The situation reaches critical mass when the addiction itself becomes the predominant life problem, and the only remedy on hand is a drink or a drug. This is the impasse of addiction, unmanageability.

When the only fix is destructive, life is unmanageable. The addicted mind will rationalize, romanticize, minimize, and justify the first drink or drug to normalize the behavior. It will say: "One won't hurt," "Beer is better than whiskey," "Marijuana is all-natural," and "It's been a long week; I deserve this!" All in the service of normalizing that first drink, though fears of the impending binge can be heard in the background. The alcoholic knows deep down that none of these rationalizations are true—at least not for them—which is why they are trying to convince themselves otherwise.

Pep talks are for the conflicted. You don't need to be told, "One is okay," unless you know from experience that "One is too many." This relentless gaslighting takes its toll, and, as Silkworth says, the alcoholic "cannot after a time differentiate the true from the false." The addiction is talking them out of what they know, which is to say, talking them into insanity.

Alcoholism, Drug Addiction, and Spirituality

Before we bring this chapter to a close, there is one final point that must be addressed: The relationship between addiction and spirituality. Remember the formula above for self-diagnosing outlined by Wilson: "If, when you honestly want to, you find you cannot quit entirely, or if when drinking, you have little control over the amount you take, you are probably alcoholic." This criterion opens the second chapter of *Alcoholics Anonymous,* "We Agnostics," which introduces the reader to Twelve Step spirituality. Wilson concludes his diagnostic tool with the following prognosis: "If that be the case, you may be suffering from an illness which only a spiritual experience will conquer."

The first two-thirds of Wilson's criteria paint a boilerplate picture of alcoholism. If you cannot control the amount you take once you get started, but, unfortunately, cannot stop getting started, then, perhaps, you are an alcoholic. Simple enough, but the claim that alcoholism is an illness only a spiritual experience can conquer is bizarre. The reasoning isn't at all self-evident.

Initially, the association between addiction and spirituality is tenuous at best. The link comes into sight only after the insanity of addiction is acknowledged and spirituality is realized to be a process by which sanity is restored. It is natural to try and figure out a solution when presented with a problem, but in the case of addiction, the thinking mind is unavailing. When the dilemma is centered in the thinking mind, as A.A.'s theory of alcoholism suggests, the intellect is compromised.

Asking the mind to resolve an issue it is actively creating puts the criminal in charge of the crime scene. When dysfunctional patterns of thought are left to police themselves, madness patrols the alleyways of our mind, which makes for a dangerous neighborhood. The dynamics that engender insanity are then used to measure the truth or sanity of a given idea. This is the epitome of conflicting interests. From this vantage point, one can appreciate the relationship between spirituality and addiction hypothesized by the Twelve Steps. This does not mean that alcoholism is a condition so mysterious that it requires supernatural intervention; rather, as Dr. Kurtz explains, the "tentative understanding of alcoholism as 'an illness which only a spiritual experience will conquer' obviously described the alcoholic rather than analyzed the malady." In other words, it does not describe a biological condition; rather it seeks to *practically* or spiritually navigate the intersection between addiction and human nature.

When you lift the hood, the line of reasoning that leads to the conclusion that alcoholism requires a spiritual solution is surprisingly straightforward. It goes as follows: Since the allergy is immutable, recovery focuses on the insanity of addiction. A purely psychological, self-help styled approach will not suffice because an insane mind cannot think itself sane for the same reason a knife cannot cut itself. Therefore, the solution must tap into a power that transcends thought, which is an objective rightly deemed spiritual in nature. This is where God enters the equation.

The term "Higher Power" is often seen as a stand-in for God, which is fair, but it also zeros in on God. "Higher" is a relative word—in this case, relative to that which it seeks to overcome, the thinking mind. It's not higher in elevation but in order. In the context of the Steps, "God" refers to any idea, belief, or practice that transcends the present circumference of thought, awakening a higher order of consciousness. Much more will be said on this subject in chapters six and seven; for now, it is important to establish the link between addiction and spirituality, and that this connection is established in Step One, not tacked on later in the process. The admission of powerlessness gives rise to the search for power, establishing the connection between addiction and spirituality. The recognition of choicelessness and insanity couples with Step Two's stated goal of restoring sanity, which is realized in Steps Four through Nine where new alternatives are installed by practicing spiritual principles.

Twelve Step spirituality does not begin with Step Two, as is often thought. It starts with the admission of powerlessness in Step One, which is an act of recusal, so to speak. Before there can be an active search for power, there must be an abdication of power. It is tempting for those of us not suffering from drug addiction or alcoholism to skip Step One. The risk here is that the remaining Steps will become an ego trip. The admission of powerlessness is a spiritual practice because it calls the ego to question. We too must enter the path through the gate of powerlessness, and to that end, the next chapter addresses its more common manifestations.

Conclusion

Silkworth seldom gets the credit he is owed for his contribution to the treatment of addiction. For better or worse, the impact of his theory on the treatment of alcoholism and drug addiction is unmatched by any other medical model. This is due primarily to the unrivaled success of the Twelve Steps into which Silkworth's allergy idea is built. "Alcoholism as an allergy" is one half of the first Step that, when paired with the mental obsession resulting from choicelessness, spells out powerlessness and prompts the search for power.

Alcoholism as an allergy is not a scientific view of the disease. Silkworth's idea plays a more practical role than scientific. The doctor's theory is intended to push the suffering alcoholic into the solution. "To modern man science is omnipotent; it is a god," Wilson said in a 1949 address to the American Psychiatric Association. "Hence if science would pass a death sentence on the drunk, and we placed that verdict on our alcoholic transmission belt, it might shatter him completely. Perhaps he would then turn to the God of the theologian, there being no place else to go. Whatever the truth in this device, it certainly had practical merit."[13] No series of words ever uttered better encapsulate Twelve Step thinking than: "Whatever the truth in this device, it certainly had practical merit." Neither science nor religion shapes Twelve Step thinking. American Pragmatism supplies Twelve Step spirituality with its underlying view.

The question is not whether the allergy idea checks out in the laboratory, but whether it provides the suffering prospect with an account of their condition that certifies defeat, thereby reconciling them to the spiritual path ahead. "Almost none of us liked the self-searching, the leveling of our pride, the confession of shortcomings which the process requires for its successful consummation," Wilson sympathetically admits of the remaining Steps. Silkworth's ideas bring in tow a line of reasoning that links addiction to the practices that proved effective not only for Bill W., Dr. Bob, and their collaborators but millions since.

The allergy idea works with the obsession of the mind to bring about the realization of powerlessness. This realization forces the addict to choose between unrelenting suffering and the search for power. "We were in a position where life was becoming impossible, and if we had passed into the region from which there is no return through human aid, we had but two alternatives," Wilson suggests: "One was to go on to the

---

[13] Bill Wilson, *American Journal of Psychiatry*, Vol. 106, 1949

bitter end, blotting out the consciousness of our intolerable situation as best we could; and the other, to accept spiritual help."

"The Doctor's Opinion" is tailored to alcoholics, and though it easily transitions into the realm of drug addiction, the allergy metaphor loses steam without the symbol of intoxicating substances. This book is not a treatise on substance abuse. One of its central purposes is to demonstrate the sophistication and universality of Twelve Step spirituality, which requires a view of the Twelve Steps that applies to all, not just alcoholics and drug addicts. That said, powerlessness is an integral part of the Twelve Steps, so how are those of us who do not identify as alcoholics and drug addicts to relate to the experience of powerlessness? That is the focus of the next chapter.

4 LACK OF POWER

"So convenient a thing to be a reasonable creature, since it enables one to find or make a reason for every thing one has a mind to do." ~ Benjamin Franklin

Non-alcoholics tend to think "powerlessness" overstates their struggles because they do not cross the line of social taboo or bring about debilitating consequences. This reasoning is superficial. Just as alcoholics can live in the suburbs, sit in boardrooms, and perform in operating theaters, powerlessness can afflict those not addicted to illicit substances.

Powerlessness is not defined by social norms. The term does not describe vice. It describes our relationship to it. When we swear off a behavior because it detracts from our happiness, only to find that the behavior persists no matter how hard we try to abstain, then we have identified an area where we are powerless. These areas may be organized around alcohol and drugs, as discussed in the previous chapter; they may also be organized around food, sex, or anger. The Twelve Steps work for almost everyone because they are designed to remedy powerlessness, not alcoholism or drug addiction.

People who do not struggle with substance abuse tend to skip Step One and move onto the "spiritual stuff." Their reasons are obvious: They're not problem drinkers and Step One explicitly mentions alcohol. Unfortunately, this shortcut—which attempts to drop in on the path at an advanced stage—is ineffective because it bypasses the only viable entry point.

Step One is not an appendage that can be discarded. There can be no honest search for a Higher Power without an admission of powerlessness. Consequently, there is no "spiritual part" of the Twelve Steps. The whole kit and caboodle is spiritual, including Step One.

"Lack of power, that was our dilemma," writes Bill Wilson. Alcohol, drugs, food, work, and lust are all negotiable, but powerlessness is not. The previous chapter used Silkworth's allergy theory to paint a picture of powerlessness, but that is the alcoholic formula. It explains why the problem drinker can't stop once they get started. This book does not focus on alcoholism or drug addiction. It demonstrates the universality of the Twelve Steps, including Step One. So we must set the allergy theory aside and paint a new picture of powerlessness.

Powerlessness and Spirituality

Powerlessness is the inability to correct course when you know suffering lies ahead. If we have sincerely tried to amend thoughts and behaviors that predictably beget suffering, yet those patterns persist, then practically speaking, we are "powerlessness." It describes the problem and facilitates surrender, which is indispensable to a spiritual solution.

Spirituality and powerlessness go hand in hand. The experience of powerlessness is close to the truth of selflessness, which is the essence of spirituality. One could say that selflessness and God-consciousness are opposite sides of the same coin. In this sense, "self" refers to the image that our thoughts and feelings are organized around, the ego.

There is a link between truth and power. The ego is powerless because it is false. It is not empowered by truth. When we gloss over Step One, we fail to challenge ego's imagined control. This sabotages the search for a Higher Power.

Spirituality is a transformative way of life, but transformation takes root only in the mind that has debunked the illusion of control. If the ego believes it is in control, it will continue to call the shots, which will reproduce the insufferable conditions that prompted the search for a solution in the first place. Simply put, if we keep doing the same thing, we will get the same results.

The admission of powerlessness is proof against ego's claim of control. It is the act of recusal that forces the mind supplied only with inadequate responses to step aside. For this reason, Step One is essential for alcoholic and non-alcoholic alike.

Powerlessness and unmanageability are the gateway to all authentic spiritual practice. For example, the Buddha began his teaching career with a discourse known as the "Four Noble Truths," the first of which is "the truth of suffering." To satisfy their curiosity, someone may read a self-help book, drop in on a yoga class, attend church, a Twelve Step meeting, or a spirituality workshop but they will not commit themselves to a course of action unless they honestly want transformation. Suffering is the impetus for change.

Spirituality is a vague word. It has nearly as many definitions as it has customers. In the chapters that follow, we will clarify the term, but for now it is enough to say that spirituality is more than the wishful anticipation of a better life. Such aspirations are one component of spirituality, but they are common to all suffering people. Thus, they do not define spirituality, unless we are prepared to admit the word is utterly meaningless. These aspirations must be joined by an actionable path that overcomes discontentment.

Action is a core characteristic of Twelve Step spirituality. "The spiritual life is not a theory," writes Bill Wilson. "We have to live it." If we do not live it, *it isn't real*. Work distinguishes true spirituality from wishful thinking. It is the mechanism by which motivation is transmuted into change. Only those who desire change in earnest will commit themselves to a life of self-reflection and rigorous honesty, or wake up an hour early to chisel into their day time for meditation, prayer, and study. Spirituality begins with suffering because suffering finances that desire. It brings us to the path and reconciles us to the work ahead.

Suffering itself is not the problem. It's a symptom of the problem. Unmanageability is like a flagpole that enables us to see the distant green from the tee box. The real target is not the flag but the hole, powerlessness. Pain and suffering are manifestations of powerlessness, which can be too subtle to detect without clear identifiers like alcoholism or drug addiction. Powerlessness is difficult to spot when the consequences do not *immediately* threaten our health, finances, or relationships. But if we look closely, we will see habits of thought and action that diminish our quality of life. These habits or patterns are a defining characteristic of suffering.

Powerlessness as Bondage

We must distinguish between pain and suffering. Pain is discomfort resulting from physical disease or tragedy. Replaying that pain is suffering. For example, it is natural to mourn the loss of a loved one. Reliving that loss is suffering.

The suffering addressed by spirituality is of a psychological variety. There is a relapsing or cyclic quality to this sort of suffering. The Buddha called this cycle "samsara." In modern times, we call it "addiction." This may not meet the clinical standards of an addiction, but it certainly adheres to the common sense definition. Practically speaking, an addiction is a behavior that produces suffering and is fated by choicelessness to repeat itself.

Thomas Jefferson tapped into something deeply human when he listed the pursuit of happiness among those inalienable rights in the Declaration of Independence. "That everyone desires happiness for himself or herself is an incontestable fact," the American philosopher Mortimer J. Adler states. "In everyone's vocabulary, the word 'happiness' stands for something always sought for its own sake and never as a means to anything beyond itself. No one can complete the sentence 'I want happiness because I want…' as one can complete the sentence 'I want wealth, or health, or freedom, or knowledge because I want to achieve happiness in this life.'"[1] We cannot want for anything but happiness; anything else would betray the idea of wanting, which is rooted in the pursuit of happiness.

In every form of addiction, the pursuit of happiness is thwarted by an attachment to suffering's causes. Addictions are not only incapable of bringing about true contentment, but once their fleeting pleasure is exhausted, they're revealed to be suffering in disguise. The short-lived comfort quickly turns to shame, stress, depression, anger, debt, and loneliness. Step One confronts us with this fact: We are powerless because our strategies for happiness carry the seeds of suffering.

The first Step forces us to acknowledge the wake of unmanageability trailing our pursuit of happiness. All along

---

[1] Mortimer J. Adler, *We Hold These Truths,* pg 52, 1987

we stalked love, prosperity, serenity, joy, fulfillment, and well-being; never did we intend to bring suffering upon ourselves or those we love. Despite our best intentions, we stand before Step One, admitting powerlessness and unmanageability. If our pursuit of happiness has brought us to Step One, then our strategies for happiness are not only ineffectual, they are counterproductive. We are way off the mark. Here, the words "powerlessness" and "addiction" find kinship with the much-maligned concept of "sin," which originally meant, "to miss the mark."

The spiritual path is populated by those who, time and again, have swore off alcohol, drugs, work-a-thons, binge eating, and pornography only to redeploy those forsaken vices much to their consternation. The consequences may not always be as drastic as those associated with alcoholism and drug addiction, but the inability to correct course is identical. When we recognize this, we acknowledge our powerlessness at the level called for by Step One. In this sense, we can all relate to the words of St. Paul, "I can will what is right, but I cannot do it."

When Paul says, "I can will what is right, but I cannot do it," he gives voice to the frustration of powerlessness, but he isn't talking about a coke habit or a drinking problem. He is addressing everyone who has struggled in vain to part ways with an unhealthy habit. Paul's words invite all of us into the experience of powerlessness.

Paul goes on to say, "For I do not do the good I want, but the evil I do not want is what I do." This is as concise a definition of powerlessness as one could hope to find. Next, he attributes that privation of power or freedom to sin: "If I do what I do not want it is no longer I that do it but sin that dwells within me."[2]

Admittedly, the word "sin" is damaged goods. It has certain implications we need to avoid, but none of these belong to the passages quoted above. Paul conceives of sin not as a failing of moral judgment or corrupt intent, but as a lack of power. He is essentially saying, "I know what is right, I want to do it, and I am trying as hard as I can, but damn it! I just can't make it happen."

Paul sees sin as a force that intrudes upon his sovereignty from within, causing him to "miss the mark." This mirrors the way alcoholics speak of "their disease"—an internal but foreign agent that compels them to act contrary to their best interests. Paul's "sin" and Wilson's "powerlessness" are, in effect, two ways of describing the experience of bondage. And we know from the previous chapter that bondage is a consequence of choicelessness.

I'm not suggesting that sex, alcohol, or even drugs are inherently sinful. I am suggesting that they run the risk of becoming compulsions when used as coping mechanisms, as does shopping, eating, and working. If the immediate gratification provided is mistaken for true happiness, these strategies will be increasingly exercised. This could lead to an anemic repertoire of coping skills, resulting in choicelessness. If the only available response to the stress of overworking is

---

[2] Romans 7:18-20, NSRV

to throw yourself into work, then that is bondage, which is the essence of both Paul's "sin" and our model of addiction.

If I desire to do one thing and not another, but find myself repeatedly engaged in the very act I reject, then I am not consciously willing the action. Something else compels the act. Paul calls this something else, "sin." Buddhists and Hindus call it "karma." For our purposes, it's "addiction." Whatever we call it, spirituality has been aware of it for centuries and has developed practices that combat it.

Action is an indispensable component of authentic spirituality because the application of spiritual principles installs new options, which resolves choicelessness. In this way, spiritual practice reinstates the power of choice and restores sanity. These practices will be covered in considerable detail throughout this book, but right now, we need to dive deeper into the choicelessness and insanity of typical addictions.

Bondage, Denial, and Insanity

Powerlessness is a controversial topic because it challenges free will. It's a particularly scandalous idea to the American mind, which celebrates individualism, competition, and unrestrained liberty. In this respect, powerlessness is the most un-American aspect of the Twelve Steps.

Free will is the most prized possession of every human being on this planet, which makes sense. It is difficult to imagine moving through life without faith in personal agency.

Therefore, we exhibit a natural preference for libertarianism and a resistance towards determinism. Practically speaking, this preference is helpful. It encourages us to give life our all, to live to the fullest. That said, unabridged free will is nothing more than a useful article of personal faith.

Freedom is inarguably constrained by environment, circumstances, resources, genetics, and upbringing. The degree to which the will is limited might be a matter for debate, but the fact that it is limited to some degree is incontestable.

Another force that constrains our liberty is addiction. It is impossible to fashion a definition of addiction that keeps free will intact. A compulsion is, by definition, a condition in which free will is suspended. No alcoholic would freely choose the suffering that inevitably follows the first drink if they were at liberty to choose otherwise. This bondage is a symptom of choicelessness. The addicted may confess an honest desire to change, but there is no practical alternative.

It is commonly thought that bondage is limited to those physically dependent upon illicit substances like meth, heroin, or alcohol, but bondage is not calculated in units of suffering alone. We also have to mark off the distance between our intentions and our actions. Freedom is annulled when compulsion vetoes our intentions and goals, forcing us to do what we do not want to do. This is true even if the compulsion does not result in unbearable suffering, like that produced by substance abuse.

Take Eric, for example. Like everyone else, he wants to be happy. Eric knows that meaningful interactions with his children are a better source of happiness than working extended hours, so he vows to invest more time and energy in the former. He promises to make the next tee-ball game, and he means it.

Unfortunately, Eric does not know how to manage stress effectively. All he knows is work, work, work. He uses the cause of his stress to manage his stress. When circumstances at the office trigger stress, he deploys the only coping mechanism he has, work. Eric is choiceless. If work is the only available means of coping with stress, you will find yourself caught in a cycle of working to deal with the stress of work. People like Eric are commonly called "workaholics" because they are addicted to their job. Unlike alcoholism, this compulsion may be masked by some positive consequences, like promotions and pay raises, but in the end, they turn out to be empty. They are not really promotions because they demote meaningful relationships, which leads to alienation, resentment, divorce, and loneliness.

Realistic alternatives are limited to those installed through practice. In addiction, there is one option that the mind obsesses over because it has practiced that one to the exclusion of all others. The behavior and its attendant suffering may be unwanted, but there just isn't any competitive circuitry. Therefore, the unwelcome outcome is realized time and time again. This continues on unabated because the mind willfully ignores the experience of powerlessness, filling in the gaps with disinformation. Here the mind's natural inclination to resist allegations of determinism and preserve the illusion of control manifests as addiction's primary weapon of defense, the infamous state of denial.

Denial preserves the appearance of choice in two ways. First, it maintains that other options were available and that they could have been implemented if we had chosen to or willed them with sufficient force. These alternatives are often perfectly reasonable. They exist as possibilities in the structure of reality but in the details of our life, they are purely hypothetical. They have not been practiced and, therefore, are not installed, which means they are not available. Hence, denial's gratuitous use of the word "if"—if only I'd said this or if only I'd done that. "If only" means "not really."

When recounting an outburst, for example, the mind prone to fits of rage might recall a recent sermon, which promoted turning the other cheek, instead of responding in kind. This is a perfectly reasonable alternative, but that cheek must be made familiar in the interval. "Turning the other cheek" lacks the weight or force required to counterbalance rage unless it has repeatedly been practiced. This is why Jesus instructs us to pray for our enemies. Prayer is a simulation that installs a new response towards antagonists. Merely hearing the sermon does not accomplish this feat, but that does not stop the rageful mind from wishfully regurgitating this idea to preserve the illusion of control. Denial clings to the belief that it could have taken the high road without ever accounting for the reasons it did not.

Second, denial works to rebrand the only *real* option. It dresses terrible ideas up with rationalizations and justifications until they seem desirable-ish. Denial polishes a turd, to put it crassly. It frantically swirls around those self-destructive behaviors until the suffering attached is minimized or explained away. For the addict, the only available option, the first drug, is unacceptable because it never stops with one. As the Narcotics Anonymous slogan goes, "One is too many, and a thousand is never enough." So the mind works to minimize the consequences of the impending first drug, claiming, "It's okay, this once" or "One won't hurt." It shaves off the binge in tow to make the obligatory first hit look like an acceptable option that was consciously chosen. It does this because the mind would rather be crazy than powerless! It would rather "choose" something wholly insane than forfeit the illusion of control. "The persistence of this illusion is astonishing," says Wilson. "Many pursue it into the gates of insanity or death."

This delusional thought process is obvious in the alcoholic and the addict because it is highlighted by catastrophic suffering, but the same patterns of thought are operable wherever addiction is concerned. The mind that binges on sugar dispels strife by whitewashing the candy bar with the pitiful line, "It is organic, all natural sugar." The spouse that compulsively seeks comfort in the arms of another subdues their conscience with "They'll never know." The mind goes the way of madness because it knows of no other way and because it is more comfortable with insanity than powerlessness.

The serial monogamist says, "I know the plan was to not jump into the next relationship, but I think they are the one." The mind spins the only available option until it reaches the minimum threshold of acceptability and then pretends to choose that course, but this choice is an illusion. There was no other *real* option presented. They were destined to enter that relationship because they do not know how to be alone.

Buying Time and Time Well Spent

The Twelve Steps occupy the space between the philosophical extremes of determinism and libertarianism. "The alcoholic *at certain times* has no effective mental defense against the first drink," writes Wilson. The key phrase is "at certain times," suggesting that at other times the will is (reasonably) free. This is important. On the one hand, addiction suspends free-will; whereas recovery restores it.

Willpower has its place in spirituality and recovery. Its exact role, however, is a matter of discussion reserved for later chapters. For now, it is sufficient to say we are at liberty to cultivate alternatives, when free of temptation. In the presence of temptation, the mind is pressured to issue a response. Where addiction is concerned, this pressure is too great to resist. Therefore, we are not free to think through the predicament or to invent a new solution. The response issued is largely automatic.

New alternatives can be built-in during intervals by practicing new responses. Just as athletes use practice to introduce and fine-tune skills automatically employed in games, during lulls we can use spiritual practice to upload and calibrate healthy reactions to fear, stress, anger, grief, and boredom. A straightforward example of this is when recovering alcoholics and addicts regularly call people in their support group, even though they have nothing of substance to talk about. This exercise establishes the habit of phoning others, which turns out to be an invaluable lifeline when temptation does arise.

Recovery communities also encourage newcomers to make "ninety meetings in ninety days" and to "change people, places, and things." Both suggestions possess a measure of common sense. In the early stages of recovery from a food addiction, meeting a friend at a pizza buffet with the aim of eating just a salad is no less foolish than a newly sober alcoholic stopping by a favorite watering hole to watch the game with old drinking buddies. As the old adage goes, sit in a barbershop long enough and you will get a haircut. Whatever our compulsion, early in recovery, it is wise to avoid the proverbial barbershop.

Those of us without a group to fall back on can create a support system by sharing our struggles, goals, and progress with caring friends. We can seek counsel from a priest, minister, rabbi, imam, spiritual mentor, or therapist. We can pick up one of the countless books containing time-tested spiritual instruction from the library or bookstore. Rather than sitting on our hands, we can proactively structure our days around esteemable activities like spiritual practice, housekeeping, work, physical exercise, and fellowship with supportive peers. Such commitments steer clear of temptation, cultivate self-worth, and place our thinking on a higher plane. If we are members of a religious or spiritual community, the readymade networks make this transition easier. But it must be remembered: This is borrowed time.

Avoidance is only half the battle. Evasion is not a long-term solution. These suggestions are short-term fixes, aimed at sidestepping early bouts with temptation that the newcomer is ill-equipped to handle. The required equipment, so to speak, is installed through spiritual practice, i.e., the Twelve Steps. The Steps are the long-term solution, but they take time to complete. These short-term measures effectively avoid temptation and in a pinch, can escape its grasps, buying the individual the time needed to complete the Steps and bring about lasting change. Long-term recovery is not about buying time, but what the individual does with the time purchased.

Suffering brings people to spirituality, but we mustn't confuse the aspirational spell cast after our most recent debacle with lasting transformation. Our brains have not miraculously been remapped. Such a change requires effort. The pink cloud, as it is often called in recovery communities, is a gift of inspiration that should be used to fuel our efforts. Along these lines, the honeymoon phase weds the aspirant to spiritual practices, which install new coping skills and promote long-term success.

This wave of inspiration is squandered in bare-knuckle bouts with our addiction. Will power cannot push through temptation indefinitely. It may win a fight or two, filling us with faux-confidence but in the end, resolve always gives way to temptation. This is one of the most disheartening facts about recovery. "All of us felt at times that we were regaining control," writes Wilson, "but such intervals—usually brief—were inevitably followed by still less control, which led in time to pitiful and incomprehensible demoralization."[3] I suspect everyone who has struggled to part ways with a self-defeating behavior has experienced this swing between the illusion of control and despair, even if their plight has not descended into incomprehensible levels of demoralization. For instance, this oscillation more or less defines the pop culture narrative about diets and exercise: it's easy to get started but difficult to stick with it—which raises a critical point. We need to address relapse and recovery with more common addictions before continuing.

Alcoholics, drug addicts, and gambling addicts can practice complete abstinence. This is not a viable long-term strategy for those suffering from food, sex, or shopping addictions. They can renounce particular foods or certain types of behavior, but in general still have to reckon with eating, sexuality, and shopping. This undoubtedly complicates matters. What follows is intended to help minimize those complications.

It is important to remember that complete abstinence is not the only measure of progress. Such perfectionism translates slips into shame, which becomes fodder for the addiction. If we take two steps toward our goal of abstaining from sugary foods, then one step back, one hundred days later that is fifty steps in the right direction. Beating ourselves up for the step back undermines the balance of progress.

---

[3] Bill Wilson, *Alcoholics Anonymous,* pg 30, 1939

Tipping the Scales in our Favor

Despite our best efforts to avoid temptation, there are sure to be sporadic bouts of craving that must be dealt with on the spot. To this end, willpower is most effective when it's pitted against lower level allurements. Relapse is a process—not an event—and the process consists of distinct stages. Understanding your pattern is critical, regardless of whether that pattern leads to a drink, drug, or tub of ice cream. Identifying a relapse as it builds up and intervening early may be the only way to survive those initial days, weeks, or months.

At first glance, the mind appears to weigh options on the scale of reason before selecting a course. Reason definitely plays a role, but in point of fact, feeling tips the scales. We do not choose who we are attracted to, who we loathe, or what types of food we want. We do not decide to desire pizza more than salad, and therefore cannot be said to freely choose pizza over salad. These preferences and aversions come to us. Reason rationalizes and announces a verdict rendered subconsciously. Making matters worse, addictions are organized around behaviors that elicit immediate gratification, so they're accompanied by intense cravings. The stronger these urges are, the more likely we are to receive an irrational verdict.

If relapse is a process and not an event, multiple judgments must be rendered in route. It is like an appellate court system that issues numerous rulings before reaching the landmark case of *Recovery v. Relapse*. Craving intensifies with each passing judgment until alas, we pick up that first drink or embark upon another unfinanced shopping spree. If we are aware of the lesser battles along the way, we can intervene before temptation reaches fever pitch.

Willpower rests on a sliding scale of craving. When craving is maxed out, there is no choice. Without choice there is no freedom, so peak craving is complete bondage. When craving is in remission, the mind is at liberty to elect a new course. Therefore, it stands to reason that when urges are faint, the will is still capable of exerting itself.

For example, when assailed by the ripened urge to watch pornography, the addicted mind is without defense. But when confronted by the lesser urge to idly indulge a sexual fantasy, willpower can divert that energy toward a more productive outcome. It can romantically engage a partner or complete a task on today's chore list. Instead of daydreaming about an illicit affair, it can redirect that energy toward physical exercise, prayer, or meditation. There may be a sincere desire to avoid pornography, but if this lower level lust is not quickly addressed, that is where it will lead.

Suppressing temptation seldom works because that energy compounds until action is taken. Unless a viable alternative is willed, the energy will follow the path of least resistance—the path carved out by the compulsion. The less-than-pornographic materials consumed early in the process—gawking, daydreams, suggestive images—trigger the release of a cocktail consisting of norepinephrine, dopamine, and sex hormones. This cocktail is experienced as "lust," which surges through the well-worn pathways in route to a pornography binge.

At peak craving, willpower is practically obsolete. It does not matter whether we are talking about sex, cinnamon rolls, or schnapps. The newly sober alcoholic who starts out with a desire to watch the basketball game at a local sports bar is likely to become fixated on the drinks others are enjoying. Before they know it, this fixation morphs into action, and they're ordering their second beer. Similarly, the afternoon coffee run is unmasked as a front only after we scarf down a half-dozen Dunkin' donuts. These lower level allurements could have been managed with a little awareness and preparation. Sadly, it is in hindsight that the basketball game and coffee run are realized to be carrots dangled by the addiction. Relapse is a subtle, seductive process that we must be on guard against.

The pathways of compulsion are highly trafficked, well-worn slippery slopes that connect triggers and pleasure centers with unhealthy behavior. There is so little resistance in these pathways that the stages of relapse are passed without much thought. This is one reason mindfulness meditation is effective in treating addiction. It cultivates a finely tuned awareness capable of identifying these early stages. This slows the process down, putting space between the individual and their cravings. Still, taken alone, such strategies have little enduring value. Recovery is not about fighting off temptation. It is about transcending temptation.

If we are forced to fight our addictions every day, the day will come when we suffer defeat. Moreover, this is a miserable way to live. *That's why the Twelve Steps promote surrender, rather than self-defense.* They encourage practitioners to cease "fighting anything or anyone—even alcohol." Surrender is more than bowing out. It rises above conflict. The Twelve Steps are a high road that leads to a higher plane, placing us above the fray. Ascending this path takes effort. This effort is spiritual practice.

Spiritus contra Spiritum

Addiction is described in Twelve Step literature as a "spiritual malady." A spiritual malady is a condition ultimately rooted in patterns of thought and behavior that fail to tap into the ground of meaning and being. Since they are disconnected from meaning and being, they lack purpose and value. This is what it means to be "dis-contented"—devoid of content or meaning.

Addictions are disconnected from meaning and being because they are predicated upon deceptions, namely the illusion of instant gratification. These obsessions are organized around non-being. They draw on nothing that is real or true and are therefore devoid of power and vitality. In fact, addictions feed on our self-worth, leaving us morally and spiritually bankrupt. When we have nothing to turn to but the causes of our discontentment, we are spiritually bankrupt.

Hopelessness crowds out the possibility of freedom, when fleeing to the next relationship is the only way to escape the heartache of the last; or more busyness is the only available response to the pain and suffering brought on ourselves and our family by our slavish devotion to work. When another drink is the only way to medicate the sorrow of the last, despair consumes us. The point of no return is reached, when the only available solution to a problem is that which created the problem in the first place. Then life is lived to fill a void, to worshipfully feed a belly, as St. Paul says.[4]

This belly is stuffed with all manner of narcotics: food, sex, drugs, money, philosophical codes, and belief systems. But in the end, all prove to be nothing more than anesthetics. If we are to be happy and free, we need something with deeper roots, a way of life that draws from the truth of our being.

To admit powerlessness is to hit bottom. Hitting bottom has nothing to do with losing a car, job, house, husband, or wife. It is about seeing through the illusion of control. At the bottom, there is no plan B, no exit strategy. When we hit bottom, we forfeit our schemes. This opens the door to spiritual practice. When we see that our ideas do not work, that our plans and strategies for happiness—rooted as they are in instant gratification—are ill-equipped for an adult world, then the adoption of a new way of life makes sense. The nail comes into sight.

The concept of bottoming out comes from the Greek word *krisis.* A crisis, according to Hippocrates, the founder of Western medicine, is "the turning point of a disease." A spiritual crisis is that critical, decisive moment where the motivation to change emerges, but the question remains: Will

---

[4] Philippians 3:19, NRSV

we capitalize on it? Will we redirect that energy toward the formation of a new life? Will we use it to fuel our journey? Or get wrapped up in the sentimentality of it all, splurging on another fleeting bit of solace?

There is an interesting relationship between rock bottom and transformation. What we are looking for is hidden in the one place we have been unwilling to look, our suffering. The only way out is to turn into our powerlessness. Deep down in every man, woman, and child is a thirst for meaning and vitality. The saint prays for the same reason the alcoholic drinks. Upon the cross, Jesus said, "I thirst." In point of fact, we all thirst. The question is from which well will we drink. "Everyone who drinks of this water will be thirsty again," Jesus counsels the Samaritan woman at the well.[5] This is the basic mechanism of addiction. We drink from a well that only makes us thirstier. We look to the bottle, to jobs, relationships, and material wealth for meaning and value, only to be disappointed, which, in turn, intensifies our thirst. However depraved our addictions might be, they are, in the final analysis, a search for fulfillment.

At the core of every addiction is thirst, but strangely enough, this thirst is also the source of meaning and being. It is the womb from which new life is born. This is why the spiritual path begins with the recognition of powerlessness. St. Augustine famously said, "You have made us for yourself, O Lord, and our heart is restless until it finds its rest in you." This restlessness, this thirst will be quenched one way or

---

[5] John 4:7-15, NRSV

another. It will either be the basis of our spirituality or the belly of our addiction.

When I moved out of my parent's house and got my first apartment, I, like so many bachelors, was completely helpless. I did not know how to do laundry—or maybe I just didn't want to do it—and I ate like a complete idiot. My diet consisted of frozen pizza, various types of sausage, chips, and sodas. One day, a friend encouraged me to eat a salad. There I was, reluctantly hunched over a bowl of lettuce adorned with vegetables—and I loved it! I made several trips to the salad bar that day, and over the next few weeks, found myself searching out restaurants with the best salad bars. I went from being opposed to salad to utterly obsessed with it.

As chance would have it, my doctor was my roommate's father. One day we were watching a football game at their house and I asked my doctor, "Are there any addictive properties in salad?" He looked puzzled and said, "Not that I am aware of...." I told him of my new, insatiable appetite for salads. Disinterested, he continued to water his lawn, but I pressed on: "Why in the world am I suddenly obsessed with salad? I don't want to go to a restaurant unless they have a good salad bar." In an effort to shut me up, he asked, "Are you drinking enough water?" I laughed and said, "Enough? I don't drink any. I only drink sodas." He shook his head and replied, "Well, you probably want salad because your body isn't getting enough water. Start drinking water and your weird obsession with salad will probably subside." And so it did. I started drinking water and my obsession faded.

We all thirst. The only question is how will we quench that thirst. Will we satisfy it directly? Or will we unconsciously yield to the forces of addiction and seek to quench our thirst for meaning in a perverted way? Will we hydrate with a bowl of salad or get a glass of water?

In 1926, Dr. Carl Jung treated Roland Hazard, the man who introduced Ebby Thatcher to the Oxford Group. In a letter to Bill Wilson, Jung said of Hazard, "His craving for alcohol was the equivalent on a low level to the spiritual thirst of our being for wholeness, expressed in medieval language: the union with God." Jung concludes his correspondence with Wilson by offering a most useful slogan. "You see, alcohol in Latin is *'spiritus'* and you use the same word for the highest religious experience as well as for the most depraving poison. The helpful formula therefore is: *spiritus contra spiritum.*" The formula is spirit over spirits; that is, spirituality over addiction.

The Twelve Steps begin with the admission of powerlessness. Powerlessness is more visible from the vantage point of alcoholism and drug addiction, but it is a condition that touches us all. The Twelve Steps are relevant to everyone because they meet us in our powerlessness, where we thirst. They are a system of principles conveyed along the lines of action and practice, which require no dogmatic allegiance whatsoever and stand to benefit anyone wishing to enlarge their spiritual life. This is why they are not just a significant contribution to the field of substance abuse treatment, but to the world of spirituality as well.

Next, we examine the centrality of religious liberty in American thought and how it impacted the development of the Twelve Steps.

5 LIBERTY OF CONSCIENCE

"If every one is left to judge of his own religion, there is no such thing as a religion that is wrong; but if they are to judge of each other's religion, there is no such thing as a religion that is right; and therefore all the world is right, or all the world is wrong. " ~ Thomas Paine

In colonial America, church and state were intertwined. People were forced to subsidize beliefs with which they did not agree, and certain denominations were not permitted to preach in public. "I have felt the effects of the ecclesiastical establishment, and have been told by the Judge from his seat, 'You shall lay in jail until you rot,' when my only crime was no other than that of preaching the Gospel of Jesus Christ," laments Jeremiah Moore.

Once a lay reader in the Anglican Church, Jeremiah Moore became a Baptist and in this way, a criminal. Moore and his Baptist brethren were held in contempt not only by the "ecclesiastical establishment," but by the House of Burgesses.

Their convictions were not merely unpopular, they were illegal.

The journey through American history that connects Jeremiah Moore and Bill Wilson is not as the crow flies, but it is relevant to our inquiry. Wilson knew nothing about Moore. His name is a footnote in a larger story. He is one of many who dedicated their lives to the cause of religious liberty. There is no Alcoholics Anonymous or Bill Wilson without Jeremiah Moore and his co-conspirators. Their efforts established the spiritual marketplace that one hundred and forty-eight years later hatched the Twelve Steps. Moreover, this struggle planted a pluralistic seed in the American psyche that later blossomed into the defining characteristic of Twelve Step spirituality: "God as we understand Him."

In 18th century Virginia, the Anglican Church was the State church. Baptist ministers often refused to pay taxes that financed Anglican beliefs and disobeyed laws that prohibited preaching in public. In 1773, Moore was arrested for bootlegging Baptist theology. By the next year, approximately half of Virginia's Baptist clergy had been arrested for defying the religious laws of the colony.

Jeremiah Moore's persistent preaching made him a frequent target of the Anglican establishment. He was incarcerated several times but continued to preach even as crowds gathered outside his jail cell. Moore, along with his colleagues and sympathizers, grew impatient with this harassment. In October of 1776, a petition was submitted to the House of Delegates that called for the end of state-sponsored religion.

"The Baptist Petition," as it came to be known, won the support of an articulate and powerful Virginian who, three months earlier, carved his name into history with those immortal words: "We hold these truths to be self-evident, that all men are created equal, that they are endowed by their Creator with certain unalienable Rights, that among these are Life, Liberty and the pursuit of Happiness."

Thomas Jefferson was, at that time, a member of the Virginia Assembly, and he devoutly believed that religious liberty was vital to a just government. The petition before the Assembly bore the signatures of over 10,000 people. Jefferson, an astute politician, capitalized on this opportunity to advance his cause.

The Wall of Separation

In the "Sage of Monticello" the Baptists found a powerful ally and a more than capable advocate. It is worth mentioning, however, that Jefferson was not sympathetic to their brand of religion. He was not a champion of their faith; rather, he was an ardent defender of their right to practice it freely. True to his liberal sensibilities, Jefferson believed that right was a natural endowment of humankind. And above all else, he wanted that belief to pervade the emerging Republic. It is on the principle of the matter that Jefferson finds common cause with the Baptists, not in their theology.

"I hold (without appeal to revelation) that when we take a view of the Universe, in its parts general or particular, it is impossible for the human mind not to perceive and feel a conviction of design, consummate skill, and indefinite power in every atom of its composition," Jefferson confessed to his friend, John Adams, in the Spring of 1823. But the force of Jefferson's conviction in a prime mover is matched only by his disdain for those who, like the Baptists, conflate Jesus with that Creator, inserting "a second pre-existing being, and ascribe to him, and not to God, the creation of the universe." This "unmeaning jargon," as Jefferson calls it, advances the view of atheism because, in his estimation, it promotes a senseless God, easily rebutted by the "simpler hypothesis of a self-existent universe." Jefferson then concludes his letter to Adams, "The truth is that the greatest enemies to the doctrines of Jesus are those calling themselves the expositors of them, who have perverted them for the structure of a system of fancy absolutely incomprehensible, and without any foundation in his genuine words. And the day will come," he continues, "when the mystical generation of Jesus, by the supreme being as his father in the womb of a virgin will be classed with the fable of the generation of Minerva in the brain of Jupiter."[1]

In matters of theology, Jefferson has little in common with the Baptists. He rejects any element of scripture or dogma that does not withstand rational inspection, which, in his estimation, makes for a truncated account of Christianity, as the *Jefferson Bible* attests. However, he believed "the dawn of reason and freedom of thought" to be the appropriate countermeasures, not government coercion.

---

[1] From Thomas Jefferson to John Adams, 11 April 1823, Founders Online, National Archives

Jefferson introduced the Virginia Statute for Religious *Freedom* in 1777. Therein he argues that "Almighty God hath created the mind free," thus the State must not infringe upon the right to believe or not believe as logic and conviction dictates. "The legitimate powers of government extend to such acts only as are injurious to others," he asserts. "But it does me no injury for my neighbour to say there are twenty gods, or no god. It neither picks my pocket nor breaks my leg." Jefferson goes on to declare that "to compel a man to furnish contributions of money for the propagation of opinions, which he disbelieves, is sinful and tyrannical." In short, government is just only when it prohibits the establishment of any religion and recognizes the right of all to practice their religion freely. These interlocking axioms erected what Jefferson later called a "wall of separation between Church and State."[2]

The Virginia Statute for Religious Freedom became law on January 16, 1786, more than a decade after its introduction to the House of Delegates. It guaranteed Virginians "the freedom to profess and by argument to maintain their opinions in matters of religion," while also ensuring that "no man shall be compelled to frequent or support any religious worship, place, or ministry whatsoever." Five years later, those sentiments were echoed by Jefferson's friend and collaborator, James Madison, who, in the First Amendment wrote, "Congress shall make no law respecting an establishment of religion, or prohibiting the free exercise

---

[2] Thomas Jefferson, Letter to the Baptists of Danbury, CT, 1802 *Worth noting that the wall of separation stands between "Church" and "State," but does not prevent religion and politics from intermingling.

thereof." When the book on Jefferson's life closed, the former President, Vice President, Secretary of State, Governor of Virginia, and Minister to France, counted the Virginia Statute, along with the Declaration of Independence and the University of Virginia, as his greatest accomplishments.

America's God

The First Amendment did not immediately dissolve the long-established bonds between church and state. The phrase "wall of separation" first appears in a letter penned by then-President Jefferson—more than a decade after the Bill of Rights was ratified. An association of Baptist ministers in Danbury, Connecticut, wrote him expressing their concerns with Connecticut's Constitution, which still considered religion "the first object of legislation." In reply, Jefferson wrote, "I contemplate with sovereign reverence that act of the whole American people which declared that their legislature should 'make no law respecting an establishment of religion, or prohibiting the free exercise thereof,' thus establishing a *wall of separation* between Church and State."

The Danbury letter is best known for Jefferson's "wall of separation," but it includes another interesting concept. The ministers made a passing reference to "America's God." They wanted to preemptively arrest Jefferson's trademark skepticism and assure him their sentiments were "uniformly on the side of religious liberty," not Christianity. This distinction is even more forcefully drawn by John Leland, another prominent Jeffersonian-Baptist, who declared, "Pagans, Turks, Jews, and Christians should be equally protected in their rights." America's God was born of liberty and is, therefore, inherently pluralistic. It is God as every American understands It.

As Baptists, they obviously worshipped a Christian God in private, but "America's God" points to the public domain. It consecrates a kingdom that is "broad, roomy, all inclusive." In a word, "democratized." America's God is interchangeable with "Nature's God," coined by Jefferson in the Declaration of Independence. It is a public God, a transcendent symbol of mankind's innate right to self-determination called forth by an unbroken lineage of Americans starting with Jefferson, continuing with Thoreau, Douglass, Lincoln, Anthony, and King. This is the God of America, and in the Twelve Steps, this democratized God is united with a spiritual path of practice.

"The Religion then of every man must be left to the conviction and conscience of every man," writes Madison. "It is the right of every man to exercise it as these may dictate." In a similar tone, Bill Wilson says, "The full liberty to practice any creed or principle or therapy should be a first consideration. Hence let us not pressure anyone with individual or even collective views. Let us instead accord to each other the respect that is due to every human being as he tries to make his way towards the light."[3] On another occasion, he adds, "This should be an entirely personal affair which each one decides for himself in the light of past associations, or his present choice."

---

[3] Bill Wilson, General Service Conference, 1965

Bill Wilson isn't digging through the archives, searching for catchy bits of patriotic rhetoric with which to pitch his case. He isn't parroting Jefferson, Madison, or any other American statesmen; nor is he intentionally modeling Twelve Step spirituality after the First Amendment. It's simpler than that; it comes to him naturally. The principle of religious liberty is so deeply ingrained in the American psyche that Wilson instinctively channels it when charting A.A.'s course.

The jewel of the Twelve Steps is "God as we understand him." It leaves the contents of faith "to the conviction and conscience of every man," allowing them to proceed with one God or twenty. "God as we understand him" is flanked by the phrases "Power greater than ourselves" and "Higher Power," which permit the individual to conceive of God in personal or impersonal terms. These three phrases enshrine religious liberty in the Twelve Steps. They lay the groundwork for an actionable system of spiritual practice that is accessible to any religious devotee, as well as the spiritual but not religious aspirant. In the coming chapters, we will see that this berth is wide enough to accommodate even agnostics and atheists. Such an all-inclusive and practicable path is peerless in the world of spirituality.

Pragmatic Spirituality

It is no accident of history that the Twelve Steps hail from the United States. They could come only from a culture that holds religious liberty in the highest esteem, but this freedom is only part of the balance due. Americans are not bound by race, religion, or ethnicity. The United States is a pluralistic nation of immigrants that consists of Protestants, Catholics, Jews,

Hindus, Muslims, Buddhists, and atheists. American philosophy has, therefore, always grappled with viewpoint diversity. This pluralism frustrates any attempt to settle on an orthodoxy. As a result, philosophers developed an orthopraxic approach to truth called "pragmatism," which is another decidedly American feature of the Twelve Steps. Pragmatism sees each hue in the kaleidoscopic tapestry of beliefs as "a syllable in human nature's total message," with it taking "the whole of us to spell the meaning out completely."[4]

Pragmatism was first conceived by Charles Sanders Peirce, then further developed and popularized by his friend, William James. It not only stands as the nation's greatest achievement in the field of philosophy but manages to capture the essence of American thought. For these reasons, it is the consummate American philosophy.

"Pragmatism" takes its name from the Latin word *pragmaticus*, meaning "concerned with practical results." In short, pragmatism judges ideas by their "influences and effects." William James applied this theory of truth to the field of spirituality, most notably in his book *Varieties of Religious Experience*, which profoundly influenced both Bill Wilson and the Twelve Steps.

In *Varieties,* James argues that "the gods we stand by are the gods we need and can use."[5] This is "America's God," and it is the God of the Twelve Steps, but James did not invent it.

---

[4] William James, *Varieties of Religious Experience,* Lecture XX, "Conclusions"

[5] William James, *Varieties of Religious Experience,* pg 324, 1929

He captured it.[6] James seized the Spirit of the American mind. If there is one man who deserves credit for inventing American thought, that man is the "The First American," Benjamin Franklin.

Ben Franklin is rivaled only by Washington and Lincoln in the annals of American history, but as a statesman, inventor, scientist, publisher, and philosopher, Franklin's influence eclipses civic life. His mystique and international celebrity made him the original symbol of *Americana*. Franklin's cultural impact continues to the present day. His *Poor Richard's* aphorisms are among the first viral memes, some are still in circulation: "A penny saved is a penny earned" and "Early to bed, early to rise, makes a man healthy, wealthy and wise." Franklin's industriousness, wit, and practical genius portend America's work ethic, satirical humor, and common-sense philosophy. Moreover, William James' pragmatic treatment of spirituality is prefigured in the way Franklin thought about God and religion.

In response to his probing parents, who fretted over his unorthodox ways, the thirty-two-year-old Franklin bluntly replied, "I think vital Religion has always suffer'd, when orthodoxy is more regarded than virtue. And the scripture assures me, that at the last day, we shall not be examin'd (by) what we thought, but what we did." The Twelve Steps concur with Franklin, focusing not on what practitioners believe but how they believe it. More to the point, Franklin told his worried parents, "I think Opinions should be judg'd of by their

---

[6] James knew as much, calling *Pragmatism* "a new name for some old ways of thinking."

influences and effects; and if a man holds none that tend to make him less virtuous or more vicious, it may be concluded he holds none that are dangerous; which I hope is the case with me."[7] In this retort, his pragmatism is on full display—beholden to no orthodoxy, anchored instead in actions and results. For this reason, it is easy to imagine him delighting in the spirituality proffered by Alcoholics Anonymous.

Another window into Franklin's character comes from the always opinionated John Adams, who quipped, "The Catholics thought him almost a Catholic. The Church of England claimed him as one of them. The Presbyterians thought him half a Presbyterian, and the Friends believed him a wet Quaker." Franklin effortlessly negotiates the volatile fault lines of sectarianism by appropriating virtues and practices from each denomination that are useful to him and leaving the rest. Similarly, the Twelve Steps allow those traversing their path to bring along any idea or belief that aids them on the journey while refusing to saddle travelers with the weight of opinions they disbelieve. Both Franklin and the Steps are poignant examples of the double-helix that forms America's pragmatic and pluralistic DNA.

The American experiment has long been driven by a particular line of inquiry: What works? The stated objective of the book *Alcoholics Anonymous* is to introduce the reader

---

[7] "From Benjamin Franklin to Josiah and Abiah Franklin, 13 April 1738," Founders Online, National Archives, last modified February 1, 2018, http://founders.archives.gov/documents/Franklin/01-02-02-0037. [Original source: The Papers of Benjamin Franklin, vol. 2, January 1, 1735, through December 31, 1744, ed. Leonard W. Labaree. New Haven: Yale University Press, 1961, pgs. 202–204.]

to a Power greater than themselves that will solve their problem.[8] Each individual, however, occupies a unique vantage point and must, therefore, conceive of that Power in a way that works for them. Since there is no one size fits all God in the Twelve Steps, we find neither theology nor dogma therein; instead, we find a spiritual marketplace that emphasizes action, direct experience, and results over orthodoxy. This marketplace is constructed in Step Two.

---

[8] Bill Wilson, *Alcoholics Anonymous,* pg 45, 1939

6 TRIED & TRUE

> "Never violate the sacredness of your individual self-respect. Be true to your own mind and conscience, your heart and your soul. So only can you be true to God." ~ Theodore Parker[1]

"A very tough-minded prospect was taken to his first A.A. meeting. The first speaker majored on his own drinking pattern. The prospect seemed impressed. The next two speakers (or maybe lecturers) each themed their talks on 'God as *I* understand Him.' This could have been good, too, but it certainly wasn't. The trouble was their attitude, the way they presented their experience. They did ooze arrogance. In fact, the final speaker got far overboard on some of his personal theological convictions."[2] This "sorry and unusual episode," remembered by Bill Wilson, begs an interesting question: What exactly do the Twelve Steps require *us* to believe?

---

[1] Theodore Parker, "Of the Position and Duty of a Minister," (1853)

[2] Bill Wilson, *The Language of the Heart*, pg 252, AA Grapevine, 1988

In retelling this story, Bill emphasizes the phrase "God as *I* understand him," which on the surface differs only slightly from the phrase "God as *we* understand him," but those differences are profound and far-reaching. The italicized *"I"* indicates that each speaker painted a rigid portrait of God. According to Wilson, the arrogance with which they oozed those ideas reeked of "do as I do, believe as I believe." He called it an "unusual episode" because it runs contrary to the ethos of Twelve Step spirituality, which is unabashedly pluralistic. The Steps celebrate the many paths that lead to God. This pluralism is exemplified by the word "we," not "I."

"The phrase 'God as we understand him' is perhaps the most important expression to be found in our whole A.A. vocabulary," Wilson writes. "Within the compass of these five significant words there can be included every kind and degree of faith, together with the positive assurance that each of us may choose his own." This assurance means the Steps advocate no particular brand of faith.

The Twelve Steps encourage practitioners to pursue a God of their understanding. Thus, they have no understanding of their own. The "Higher Power" of the Twelve Steps is generic enough to align with any of the world's religions or none of them. As Bill points out, they permit us to believe "that we have tapped the resources of God as he exists in us and in the cosmos," or we can claim to "have tapped a hidden or unused inner resource," if we prefer.[3] The choice is ours.

---

[3] Bill Wilson, "Where Will Power Comes In," The Grapevine, 1962

The Steps cannot win converts because they have no ideology to which people can convert. They have no belief system to defend or religious doctrine to promote. This position of neutrality is as practical as it is judicious. A.A.'s founders wanted their message of recovery to spread far and wide. Religious affiliations only stood to limit their reach. "We question very much whether our Buddhist members in Japan would ever have joined this Society had A.A. officially stamped itself a strictly Christian movement," writes Wilson. "You can easily convince yourself of this by imagining that A.A. started among the Buddhists and that they told you you couldn't join them unless you became a Buddhist, too."[4]

The Steps lack a sanctioned dogma about which to be scrupulous, but neither are they a free-for-all. The Steps are a "design for living." Therefore, they require the application of certain practices, instead of the adoption of certain beliefs. In short, the Steps are an *orthopraxic* (right practice) approach to spirituality. They are not interested in what you believe, rather how you believe it.

The Steps employ a practical theory of truth, judging the contents of a belief by its corresponding results in the field of action. As a result, Twelve Step spirituality is shaped more by William James' pragmatics than propositional religion.

---

[4] A.A.World Service, *As Bill Sees It,* "Not Allied With Any Sect," pg 34

James and the Twelve Steps

William James was born into America's intelligentsia. His father, Henry Sr., was a Princeton-trained theologian who subscribed to the mystical teachings of Emanuel Swedenborg. Henry Jr. is perhaps the most celebrated novelist in American history. William's godfather, Ralph Waldo Emerson, elevated individual liberty to the status of spirituality and is therefore, widely regarded as the architect of American philosophy. William also grappled with questions of consciousness and spiritual experience, but he grappled with those questions in the more rigorous domain of science.

William James is the "Father of American Psychology" and one of America's foremost philosophers. He is a titan in the intellectual world, and Bill Wilson is, perhaps, his most influential admirer. I say that because no one outside Wilson's personal orbit contributed more to the development of the Twelve Steps than did James, and those Steps are now practiced by millions of people the world over. Moreover, *Alcoholics Anonymous* is one of the best-selling books of all-time. "Bill W.'s" monumental impact is obscured by the anonymous nature of his work but in that work, James' pragmatics find its most effective vehicle.

Varieties of Religious Experience is James' masterstroke. It has been in print for more than a century. The text itself is transcribed from the prestigious *Gifford Lectures* delivered by James at the University of Edinburgh in 1901. In these lectures, the visiting Harvard professor applied his pragmatic theory of truth to religion and spirituality.

Varieties of Religious Experience is the only book cited by Bill Wilson in *Alcoholics Anonymous*. Bill first read *Varieties* in the wake of his own spiritual experience at Towns Hospital, which, it must be remembered, is the most formative event of his adult life. *Varieties* framed Wilson's outlook on spirituality. It helped him better understand his own experience and shed much scholarly light on the subject in general. More importantly, pragmatism supplied A.A.'s founders with the philosophical backbone needed to chart a nonsectarian course that does not succumb to miasmic fluff. *Varieties of Religious Experience* will, therefore, be cited throughout this book, as will other works by William James.

The Pragmatic Method

The Twelve Steps meld James' treatment of spirituality with a system of practice, creating a pragmatic path structure. The practices are standard spiritual fare: self-reflection, confession, restitution, prayer, meditation, and service to others. Much more will be said about the history, theory, and application of these practices in later chapters. First, we will focus on the philosophical view that supports them.

It is impossible to navigate the Twelve Steps without a standard of truth. "God as we understand him" quickly degenerates into nonsensical claims like, "Your Higher Power can be a light bulb or a doorknob" without guiding principles. These are admittedly silly examples but, nevertheless, common misinterpretations of Step Two in recovery communities. The Steps have no orthodoxic guiding star, so we need a principle of truth to tether us to reality. This principle comes from pragmatism.

Pragmatism is, first and foremost, a theory of truth. It doesn't seek to displace conventional theories of truth; rather it is another way of approaching truth. Science uncovers the nature of reality; whereas pragmatism is concerned with the meaning or value of reality. Pragmatism states that "truth in our ideas means their power to work," or as another *Jamesian* iteration has it: "You can say of (an idea) either that 'it is useful because it is true' or that 'it is true because it is useful.' Both these phrases mean exactly the same thing."[5] In short, when an idea functionally maps onto reality, it is useful or true.

It is important to note that utility and opportunism are not the same thing. Utility serves quality of life. Opportunism serves instant gratification, which is often more harmful than helpful. Pragmatism demands that the applied idea increase meaning and well-being to be considered useful.

When a proposition agrees with the facts, it is true. When the application of an idea increases our quality of life, it agrees with our nature. Pragmatism suggests this state of agreeableness is one form of truth; that the applied idea is true *for us*. Since it's insane to reject truth, we are obligated to strive after any manner of living that corresponds to our higher nature.

---

[5] William James, *Pragmatism,* pg 30, 1995, Dover Publications

We are called by duty to pursue the higher path. This dictum is reminiscent of Emerson's *Transcendentalism*[6], but it isn't explicitly spiritual. James takes it a step further, when he adds to the equation, "If there be any idea which, if believed in, would help us to lead that life, then it would be really better for us to believe in that idea."[7] It would be better for us to believe that idea because it facilitates a way of life that agrees with our nature. The idea fits us, so it is a fit idea. It is true. How does this tie into Twelve Step spirituality? Step Two initiates the search for a fit idea, "a Power greater than ourselves."

The second Step reads, "Came to believe that a Power greater than ourselves could restore us to sanity." Sanity is the better life we are obliged to pursue, and a Power greater than ourselves is the idea that aligns with our higher nature.

Step Two is not saying, "You must now believe in God." We are not even talking about God. We aren't there yet. At this point, Wilson says, we need to ask ourselves only one question: "Do I now believe, or am I even willing to believe, that there is a Power greater than myself?" Not an intervening deity or a creator of the universe, but "a Power greater than ourselves." That's it.

"The pragmatic method is primarily a method of settling metaphysical disputes," says James. It is a sensible way of

---

[6] Emersonian Transcendentalism is an American philosophical system that posits divinity pervades all of nature, including humanity, and that individuation is achieved by the aspirant experiencing their original connection to the universe.

[7] William James, *Pragmatism,* pg 30, 1995, Dover Publications

determining what is and is not meaningful. Consciousness is a spectrum, and its default mode is more attuned to instant gratification than meaning, but there is a dimension of experience above and beyond what we presently think. This dimension is the unknown. The term "Higher Power" is a placeholder for this transcendent realm. It represents the world of possibilities, and the Twelve Steps are a means of exploring that space.

The second Step is not a declaration of faith. *It is a hypothesis.* The word "could" indicates possibilities that have to be verified through a process of experimentation. Hence the phrase, "Came to." Belief is not a precondition of Step Two. Belief concludes the process initiated by Step Two. We experiment with the "Higher Power" idea in Steps Four through Nine. The verification event is called, in Twelve, a "spiritual awakening." If practicing the "Higher Power" idea ushers in a better life, then it is true for us. It agrees with our nature and realizing this is the essence of a spiritual awakening. Once we've had a spiritual experience, we can configure our beliefs to it. This is the meaning of "Came to believe."

Believing does not mean we are accepting metaphysical claims that are disagreeable to us. In fact, it means the opposite. If the claim does not agree with our nature, it is not true for us. If a particular concept complicates life, rather than facilitating a better life, then it is a hindrance, not an aid, and should be discarded. In the next chapter, we will explore the relationship between skepticism and Twelve Step spirituality. For now, suffice it to say that the Steps do not pressure us to adopt opinions we disbelieve. For that reason, they are incompatible only with those who are unwilling to experiment with spiritual practices.

The sole objective of the Steps, according to the twelfth, is to evoke a transformative experience. Every nut and bolt, every idea and practice therein, is part of a greater assembly, the spiritual awakening. The Higher Power idea is introduced not to win converts, but to aid in the production of that awakening, and that is the standard by which it and all other spiritual terms must be judged.[8]

Solving Names

Now that we have a working theory of truth, we can define our terms. How do we define terms while preserving the individual's liberty to choose the conception that best suits them? Pragmatism focuses on the functionality of an idea. It swats away light bulbs and doorknobs because they are incapable of functioning as a Higher Power, not because they are unorthodox. Unconventional views are championed by the Twelve Steps, so long as they work. Conversely, conventional ideas are rejected if they do not. We are going to define *the role* that concepts like "God" and "belief" play in the Steps, not particular beliefs about God. This will lay the foundations for the next chapter, where we will examine religiosity, agnosticism, and atheism in light of the Twelve Steps.

---

[8] James isn't suggesting that we believe in spite of evidence to the contrary. He also notes that beliefs mustn't clash with other vital ideas, like scientific law. This is omitted because it is superfluous to our discussion.

The God of the Twelve Steps is famously flexible, but it does come with fine print. It has to pass the pragmatic scratch test. The objective it is measured against is laid down by Step One. God has to solve the problem of powerlessness.

Twelve Step spirituality sees God as a solution to the problem of powerlessness, not as a theological proposition. This means that the Steps are not satisfied by affirmations of God's existence; nor are they interested in theological proofs. The Steps do not care whether a particular theory of God accounts for the origins of the universe. They care only that our God-idea works to improve our lives. Does our Higher Power usher in a way of life replete with useful alternatives that restore the power of choice, thereby solving the problem of powerlessness? This is the only question that matters.

Resolving powerlessness is not an intellectual exercise. The Steps deal in the concrete details of our life, imploring us to "practice these principles in all of our affairs." For God to break through our compartmentalized life, and find its place at the center of all our concerns, God must be our ultimate concern. Our Higher Power must—not in theory but in practice—be our highest Power, a concern so fundamental that all other affairs are subordinate to it.

"The universe has always appeared to the natural mind as a kind of enigma, of which the key must be sought in the shape of some illuminating or power-bringing word or name. That word names the universe's principle," says James, "and to possess it is after a fashion to possess the universe itself." A useful conception gives us a handle, something to grab on to. It enables us to possess or wrap our mind around the transcendent mystery, transforming that Higher Power into an actionable idea. This empowers us to practice that ultimate Principle in all of our affairs.

The label we choose is a personal matter. "'God,' 'Matter,' 'Reason,' 'the Absolute,' 'Energy' are so many solving names," writes James.[9] The term that unlocks our mind and opens us up to a Higher Power is our "solving name." It is our conception of God. It matters not one iota what others think or what we were taught to believe growing up. The only criterion is whether or not our name deciphers the mystery, rendering it intelligible and actionable for us. Each mind occupies a unique vantage point, requiring a different key. All that matters is that our key unlocks our mind, reconciling us to a Higher Power.

Haggling over what to call our Higher Power is a fatuous debate that persists only when extraneous influences are permitted to weigh in on a personal matter. This is where pragmatism intervenes. It asks, 'What difference does it make to call it by one name or the other?' To quote James again, "If no practical difference whatever can be traced, then the alternatives mean practically the same thing, and all dispute is idle." On the other hand, if one name orients our mind to the import of an experience and the other does not, then a practical difference is made, and pragmatism settles the dispute.

What if none of the options are appealing? That is not a problem. Actually, at this stage, it is to be expected. We have not yet had a direct experience of the reality to which those

---

[9] William James, *Pragmatism,* pgs 18-21, 1995, Dover Publications

words point, so our language is undefined and imprecise. Clarity comes later, as a result of following through with the process. The process either concludes with an experience that justifies continuing on the spiritual path or it doesn't. Either way, clarity comes. Remember, Step Two begins, "Came to believe." We have to start the process before we can "come to." So let's turn our attention to the role that belief plays in process.

Coming to Believe...

In common usage, the word belief is synonymous with "opinion" or "think." It is typically used in a manner consistent with the statement, "I believe in God," which upon careful examination means, "I think God exists" or "In my opinion, God exists." Such sentiments are detached from experience, and consequently of little help in the production of a spiritual awakening. Therefore, this is not the way "believe" is used in Step Two.

"Think" is a less commanding word than "believe." If the second Step were rewritten, "Came to *think* that a Power greater than ourselves could restore us to sanity," the meaning of the Step would be altered. "Think" lacks the conviction that "belief" takes from direct experience.

Opinions are ideas that fail to compel action in ourselves or others. My recommendation of a restaurant I've never been to isn't worth the time it takes to vocalize. It fails to persuade you or I because it isn't rooted in experience. It's pure speculation.

At the other end of the spectrum is knowledge, which is truth clearly demonstrated and beyond dispute. Knowledge is sufficient to compel action in both self and other. We know from experience not to touch a hot stove because we will get burned. It's common knowledge.

Belief falls between opinion and knowledge. Beliefs do not compel action in others, but they do compel action in ourselves. This is because they're based on private, rather than shared, experiences. Beliefs are personal truths. Consequently, their sphere of influence is limited to the individual that holds them. While beliefs fall short of knowledge, they are imbued with personal experience, which grants them an air of authority that reliably guides our actions. Thus, belief eclipses opinion.

Once again, beliefs are not knowledge. They are based on personal experience and as a result, their authority is limited to the person who had the experience. When religious beliefs are confused with knowledge, fundamentalism is the result. Personal experience is projected onto others, and ideas that work for the individual are mistaken for orthodoxic nuggets of wisdom to which everyone must subscribe. "God as *we* understand him" is usurped by "God as *I* understand him," and the resulting attitude is one of "do as I do, believe as I believe." This is entirely inconsistent with Twelve Step spirituality, which tempers belief with a dose of agnosticism. This agnosticism is administered by phrases like "Higher Power" and "God as we understand him." In fact, Wilson says A.A.'s trademark phrases are "the great contribution of our atheists and agnostics."[10] These phrases ensure that no one is pressured with "individual or even collective views," inviting each practitioner to clothe their spiritual experience with beliefs that work for them.

Since belief is rooted in subjective experience, it cannot satisfy objective questions. A spiritual awakening does not, for example, provide proof or knowledge of God's existence. It reveals a dimension of our experience that we may deem worthy of the label "God," but that does not preclude others from labeling it "Atman," "Allah," "Buddha-nature," or "Universal Consciousness." Nor does it prohibit more humanistic conceptions like "True Self" or the "Ground of Being." These solving names trade in a private economy, so none of them hold absolute value. Their value is derived from their ability to decipher our experience and assimilate our life to the power of that experience.

The distinction between belief and opinion is also important. Action is the threshold an opinion must pass to attain the status of belief. The force that ripens opinion into belief is experience, which is a product of experimentation. Step Two announces the experimental process that matures our ideas into proper beliefs. This is tantamount to saying that our ideas must be made real, which is another feature of Twelve Step spirituality that is consistent with pragmatism.

"The truth of an idea is not a stagnant property inherent in it," according to James. "It becomes true, is made true by

---

[10] Bill Wilson, *Alcoholics Anonymous Comes of Age*, pg. 167, 1957

events."[11] In other words, beliefs are not disembodied propositions that hold intrinsic value; nor are they cashed in upon intellectual adoption. We have to realize our beliefs or make them real.

In the Twelve Steps, opinions are tested in the laboratory of spiritual practice. Some ideas ring hollow, whereas others are hallowed by direct experience. When ideas are practiced and they resonate, they become true. These ideas form our belief system—the constellation of ideas that lead us to a meaningful life. Our beliefs may not be facts, but they are true for us. And we live as if they're true because, for us, they're tried and true. This *living as if* is what it means to believe.

The function of belief in Twelve Step spirituality is to mobilize and inform action. The Steps are disinterested in theology and abstract philosophies. Remember, they were conceived with the suffering alcoholic in mind. The addict cannot afford to be seduced by saccharine conceptions of God, or by highbrow philosophical systems that leave one paralyzed in thought. Such ideas are impotent. They are powerlessness masquerading as a Higher Power, which, by Twelve Step standards, is idolatrous.

"Truth" describes the relationship of an idea to reality. If we believe something, we live as if it's true. Conversely, if we do not live as if it's true, we don't actually believe it. The idea in question might be philosophically sound or aligned with religious orthodoxy, but if we don't *act* on it, we don't

---

[11] William James, *The Meaning of Truth: A Sequel to "Pragmatism,"* pg vi, 1909

actually believe it. Perhaps we haven't sufficiently practiced or cultivated the idea, or maybe it's a threadbare concept that doesn't resonate with our higher nature. In either case, it lacks "cash value," as Wilson and James liked to say. As we shall see in the next chapter, this is a problem with which fundamentalists and atheists must contend.

Conclusion

We have to *come to* our beliefs honestly. True beliefs can't be plucked from a book or ripped out of a Sunday sermon. We must carve them out of our experiences, or they aren't ours. Those approaching Step Two with plagiarized ideas are immediately rebuffed by common-sense. Their views cannot possess the Power they boast because they just took Step One. They just admitted their ideas were powerlessness.

The individual traversing the Steps may be well-versed in scripture or philosophy, but this is of no practical import whatsoever. This can be difficult for both the fundamentalist and the prideful intellectual to accept, but it is essential nonetheless. Nothing can be added to a cup that is full. The admission of not-knowing, the acknowledgment of the unknown, is crucial to the process. This acknowledgment creates the space needed for our Higher Power to reveal itself.

Those with religious convictions will find nothing in the Twelve Steps that interfere with their faith and those lacking such convictions find equal accommodation. Twelve Step spirituality is a melting pot, where Christians, Jews, Buddhist, Hindus, and Muslims, as well as unaffiliated people, walk shoulder to shoulder along the same path. The Steps are prepared to tolerate any idea or belief—and as we shall see, some measure of disbelief—so long as the idea in question binds us to a path of action that leads to a higher life.

Now we will turn our attention to the relationship between the Twelve Steps and religiosity, agnosticism, and atheism.

7 "WE AGNOSTICS" 2.0

"The only thing that [*Varieties of Religious Experience*] unequivocally testifies to is that we can experience union with something larger than ourselves and in that union find our greatest peace." ~ William James

The Twelve Steps are imbued with a common sense that scoffs at religious and philosophical systems that attempt to strip us of beliefs that arouse our better angels. Charles Sanders Peirce, the mastermind behind pragmatism, founded his philosophy upon this common sense: "Bad reasoning as well as good reasoning is possible; and this fact is the foundation of the practical side of logic."[1] The Twelve Steps use this fact to slice through fundamentalism and inflexible atheism, however well-reasoned. In *Alcoholics Anonymous*, Wilson treats atheism and fundamentalism with a dose of practical logic, though skeptics receive more attention.

---

[1] Charles Sanders Peirce, *Popular Science Monthly,* "The Fixation of Belief," November 1877

In the *Big Book,* there is an entire chapter devoted to the subject of disbelief entitled, "We Agnostics." On the other hand, Wilson speaks to fundamentalism only a handful of times. For example, he distinguishes between propositional religion and practical spirituality by citing Jung's counsel to Roland Hazard, who notes that Hazard's "religious convictions" fall short of the "vital spiritual experience."

Like philosophical views, religious sentiments frequently pose as sincere beliefs. Practical logic detects this insincerity by measuring the distance between thought and action. When convictions do not rise to the level of action—whether they be moral, religious, or philosophical—pragmatic spirituality calls their bluff. Wilson does not equivocate on this point, but he does spend far more time refuting claims that preclude belief than professions that masquerade as belief.

Wilson's caution toward atheism is not unfounded. Atheism is obviously problematic for any system of spirituality. However, fundamentalism is just as incompatible with the Twelve Steps. They both circumvent action. The reason Wilson spills so little ink on the subject of hyper-religiosity, I suspect, is simple: Atheism was the nuisance in Wilson's inner circle, not fundamentalism.

The early members of New York A.A. who formed Wilson's inner circle were not overly religious people. Mostly, they favored a spiritual but not religious program. The vast majority thought a purely Christian approach to the problem of alcoholism both divisive and ineffective. They were flanked by vocal minorities advocating the extremes. On one side stood Fitz Mayo and Paul Kellogg, lobbying for a Christian program. Opposite them were two pivotal figures in A.A.'s history, Hank Parkhurst and Jim Burwell, who campaigned for a program bereft of God.

Hank Parkhurst was a close friend of Wilson's who was instrumental in the publication of *Alcoholics Anonymous*. Burwell typically gets credit for the phrase "God as we understand Him," as well as founding Alcoholics Anonymous in Philadelphia and San Diego. In his early days, however, Jim was an agitator who openly denounced God at meetings. On one occasion, he criticized the personal beliefs of others, which according to Wilson, so enraged some members that they tried to vote him out. This scene is unfolding while Wilson is writing the book, which is collectively edited by those enduring this nuisance. Therefore, it comes as no surprise that *Alcoholics Anonymous* spends more time swatting at atheism than fundamentalism. It is the gadfly in the room, literally.

Whatever Wilson's grounds for focusing on skepticism more than hyper-religiosity, the fact remains that both can be stumbling blocks on the Twelve Step path, and he acknowledges as much. That does not mean atheists and fundamentalists can't use the Steps to effect a more fulfilling life. It merely means fundamentalism and atheism present unique challenges that we must face head-on.

Show Me Your Faith Apart from your Works

Fundamentalism views spirituality as a series of truth claims to be either accepted or rejected. It derives these claims from a literal interpretation of scripture, which fundamentalists believe to be inerrant. Therefore, the proposals hold absolute value. Their ideas do not become true; they are eternal facts—true for everyone, always—and as such, are expected to be believed by everyone even if they fail to effect transformation.

For example, Christian fundamentalism makes claims about God, creation, Jesus's birth and death, as well as the afterlife. The candidate is expected to adopt these propositions without reservation because they are sacred truths. The veracity of these claims rests entirely on their sanctity, which is another sacred claim in-and-of itself. Fundamentalists do not care whether these ideas affect meaningful change in the mind of the propositioned because fundamentalism does not employ pragmatic standards. Its tenets are judged by otherworldly standards.

Fundamentalist's claims are more like shibboleths that supposedly grant the candidate safe passage into the hereafter. They apply to the afterlife, not the here-and-now. When an idea does not correspond to this life and is unaccountable to results in this world, it is unactionable. An unactionable idea cannot be realized or made real. It cannot become true. Impracticable belief systems circumvent the process of coming to believe, putting them at odds with Twelve Step spirituality.

The Twelve Steps are prepared to accept members of any belief system, including those who maintain that God created the world or that Jesus died for the forgiveness of their sins. The Steps do not judge those belief systems unfit; instead, they reject the notion that affirming such propositions is tantamount to conversion. That may be all that is required to obtain a comfortable spot in the afterlife, as fundamentalists suggest, but that has nothing to do with this life, which is the sole concern of the Twelve Steps.

Transformation requires more than a profession of faith. Spiritual claims must correspond with daily life. We have to actualize them in our affairs. When dogma displaces practice, the Steps immediately counter, "Faith without works is dead."

In no way is this intended as a reproach of Christianity. In fact, "faith without works is dead" comes from the New Testament book of James (2:26). It was a popular slogan in the Oxford Group, and when Bill and Bob defected, they brought it with them.

"Faith without works is dead" means that beliefs unaccompanied by action are lifeless. They are not real. This attitude harmonizes with the standard of belief outlined in the previous chapter, which sees an idea graduate from the station of opinion to belief when lived out. When the apostle James says, "Show me your faith apart from your works, and I by my works will show you my faith,"[2] he foresees the pragmatics of William James. The apostle is effectively saying, "My faith is realized by my actions; whereas your

---

[2] James 2:14-26, NRSV

faith, lacking works, is unrealistic." If you cannot demonstrate your faith, it is not real.

Most religious people accept this axiom, but there is a tendency within some circles to overlook action, focusing instead on the profession of faith. Those approaching Step Two with this propositional mindset see no need to carry on with the remaining Steps. Spirituality is, for them, a ballot of theological propositions. Once each box is checked "Yes"—and perhaps a few prayers uttered—they've fulfilled their spiritual obligations. When the second Step mentions belief, they breathe easy. They are relieved because their religiosity misinterprets Step Two, confusing *"Came to believe that* a Power greater than ourselves *could"* with an entreaty to "believe *in* God." The former implies process and is accountable to results, whereas the latter appeals only to conjecture.

When the path concludes with believing in God and God's existence is pre-certified, the goal is accomplished before the process commences. This sleight of hand is an example of spiritual bypassing, which is inconsistent with the spirit of the Steps.

Open-mindedness is the active principle in Step Two. There can be no movement or progress in a mind hardened by preformed ideas. It is open-mindedness that facilitates the process of "coming to." This openness creates an internal space where beliefs are forced to compete for the individual's heart and mind, the most resonant gaining favor. James, in *Varieties of Religious Experience*, describes this dynamic in decidedly Darwinian terms: "It is but the elimination of the humanly unfit, and the survival of the humanly fittest, applied to religious beliefs."

The phrase "survival of the fittest" was coined by the famed social Darwinist, Herbert Spencer, to whom Wilson falsely attributes the following quotation: "There is a principle which is a bar against all information, which is proof against all arguments and which cannot fail to keep a man in everlasting ignorance—that principle is contempt prior to investigation."[3] The quote celebrates open-mindedness. It does not say that contempt condemns one to everlasting ignorance. Closed-mindedness or contempt prior to investigation carries that sentence.

Insight is born of direct experience, which is a product of experimentation. It is the investigative process that is critical. Skeptics are more prone to premeditated contempt because Step Two is spiritual in nature, but prejudice is just one way to sabotage honest inquiry. Fundamentalists take a different tack. Fundamentalists practice confirmation before investigation, but the outcome is the same.

Contempt prior to investigation and preemptive consent are opposite sides of the same coin, closed-mindedness. This closed-mindedness is particularly troublesome where spirituality is concerned. The substance of spiritual experience is meaning and intentionality, which are tapped by direct experience. Bypassing experimentation forestalls direct

---

[3] The quote is actually a hodgepodge quotation with attribution for the gist belonging to William Paley.

experience, resulting in an impotent belief system, instead of a Power greater than self.

If the individual presumes belief *in* God is the goal, and they already affirm God's existence, then the impetus for working the remaining Steps is subverted, and the process is sabotaged at its outset. "God" is played like a "get out of spiritual practice card," which enables the individual to neglect a personal inventory, take a hard pass on sharing their faults with another, skip making amends, and go onto Steps Eleven and Twelve, recasting them as rote accessories of a barren faith. Since these are the practices that install viable alternatives, the problem of powerlessness persists. Such a god is, in truth, no God at all. It is a "spoiler god," and this spoiler god begs the question, "How is that working out for you?"

The Steps honor any image of the divine that inspires growth and recovery, so they are axiomatically bound to reject any notion that suppresses either. When the pragmatic metric is inverted, you get the query, "How is that working out for you?"

Step Two assumes the individual admitted powerlessness and unmanageability in Step One. This admission implicates our presenting "beliefs," be they philosophical or religious. They too are powerless. These convictions went with us to the liquor store, the drug dealer's house, the casino. They overlapped our sick relationships, accompanied us on each spending spree, and watched from afar as we slipped into the oblivion of another food coma. These beliefs may mirror those required to curry God's favor in the afterlife, but the Twelve

Steps demand more. They insist upon beliefs that are capable of triumphing over suffering in this life, so we have to ask ourselves: *Are these ideas true for us? Do they work? Do they meet suffering with meaning and purpose?* Perhaps they will prove true, but to find out we have to proceed with an open mind.

The propositions fundamentalists affirm are not at odds with the Steps, but their relationship to those ideas are. The Steps are a path of practice. So inaction is irreconcilable with the Twelve Steps, and fundamentalism suppresses action. That said, fundamentalists do not have to discard their belief system to proceed with the Steps. They may need to recalibrate it for daily life or adopt actionable ideas that augment it, but the Steps do not strike at the substance of their beliefs.

Fundamentalism is present in all religions, and the Twelve Steps indiscriminately apply this practical standard to every belief system they encounter, whether it be Christian, Muslim, Hindu, Buddhist, or Jewish. It actually has nothing to do with religion. Mere ideation is the problem. When unactionable ideas pose as sacred beliefs, the Steps are obliged to confront them. They throw down the pragmatic gauntlet, "How is that working for you?"

Atheism and the Twelve Steps

The rationale that rebuts fundamentalists also cuts through the protestations of their rival, the atheist. "I do not need God," the skeptic says. "I believe the meaning of life and an understanding of the human condition is laid bare by reason and science alone." Without uttering a word of metaphysics or imposing a single supernatural belief, Step Two responds, "And yet, here you stand in the shadow of powerlessness—unable to reason through your pain and suffering; unable to bring about lasting change...So, how's that working for you?"

This condescending retort directly challenges the God of reason, so it may ruffle a few atheist's feathers. Nevertheless, it is a good starting point because it frames the ensuing discussion. The clash between skepticism and spirituality typically pits reason against blind faith. This dichotomy is false where the Twelve Steps are concerned. First, the object of faith is undefined in the Steps; the practitioner supplies their own Higher Power. Second, "faith" is not blind. Practical results support faith on the Twelve Step path. This point exposes the real conflict between skepticism and the Steps.

The conflict is between two distinct theories of truth. One analyzes and describes the material world. This is scientific, objective truth. The other is a useful approximation of reality that is scaled to the environment in which our brains evolved, namely the personal domain. This is the functional theory of truth espoused by pragmatism. An idea is functional when it resonates with the individual and informs their conduct.

Pragmatism tells us nothing about the origins of life, and the scientific method has little to say about how to live a meaningful life. Both the scientific and the pragmatic points of view are necessary. However, conflict results when these viewpoints trespass on each other's epistemological territory.

Religious claims lose value when they are presented as scientific facts because they do not meet science's standard of truth. Likewise, materialists deprive themselves of meaning and value when they observe private life through a scientific lens because science lacks a value systems and is generally disinterested in the experience of meaning. For example, science makes no ethical distinction between fidelity and promiscuity, and is therefore of no use to someone struggling to be faithful to their partner.

Science and spirituality occupy two different vantage points and have divergent interests. As a result, they represent unrelated ways of thinking about the universe and our place in it. The former concerns itself with knowledge and the latter with belief. When conflict arises, it is a consequence of malpractice, not competing theories of truth.

For their part, the Twelve Steps avoid this controversy. They do not advance metaphysical claims about the physical world. The Steps are entirely concerned with "the practical side of logic," as Charles Sanders Peirce called it. And they judge any idea that facilitates a meaningful life as true. The Steps ask materialists to cultivate adjacent values that reliably guide them toward a higher life; they do not ask aspirants to adopt a metaphysical worldview they disbelieve.

The distinction between knowledge and belief coupled with the freedom of conscience assures skeptics they can proceed along the path with their faith in logic intact. That's the good news. The bad news? They can't proceed with faith in *their* logic.

The first Step condemns the aspirant's presenting logic. It diagnoses their ideas "powerless" and their relationship to those ideas as "insane." This does not mean that the ideas the individual subscribes to are necessarily "untrue"—only that they are presently meaningless. Accepting this diagnosis is critical because the admission of powerlessness clears the way for a new logical edifice to be constructed. To this end, materialists must admit the possibility of a Higher Power—not a supernatural God, but higher order principles that transcend *their* logic, lest they confine themselves to those unavailing possibilities known to the current configuration of their consciousness. In short, the skeptic must be willing to explore the unknown, and this exploration is called spirituality.

The discussion is now properly framed but before we continue, a word about what follows. This endeavor is not an attempt to win skeptical converts. The Twelve Steps are a "design for living," not an ideology. If skeptics are disinterested in the Steps, that is their prerogative. The following serves two purposes: First, it is meant to assist those who aspire to spiritual practice but struggle to reconcile it with their materialistic worldview. Second, this discussion demonstrates the plasticity and usefulness of the Steps. These are the uniquely American traits that make the Twelve Steps one of the world's most effective systems of spiritual practice, capable of benefiting religionists and skeptics alike.

Two Sides of the Same Coin

Attempting to reconcile atheism and spirituality presumes they're hostile to one another. We need to correct this misunderstanding at the outset, which necessitates defining our terms. Atheism and the Twelve Steps have one essential thing in common: neither is a belief system. Atheism is the negation of theism, so an atheist is anyone who rejects the notion of an intervening, personal deity. No more, no less. Such a person may still identify as Buddhist or Taoist or subscribe to transcendentalist ideas. In short, atheism does not reject spirituality.

"Spirituality" is a vague word. Its definition is context dependent. In the Twelve Steps, spirituality refers to a way of life—a series of principles and practices that work to restore the individual's sanity, enabling them to live to greater effect. The Steps accommodate Catholics, Buddhists, Muslims, and Taoists, not to mention spiritual but not religious folks. At the level of belief, this community is divided. And the Steps do not try to overcome these differences of opinion. Instead, they unite this diverse group on a more basic level, the level of practice.

Twelve Step practitioners subscribe to different ideas but adhere in action to the same way of life. This way of life is the thrust of their Higher Power. When Twelve-Steppers seek counsel, their program offers practices, not metaphysical propositions. When readers search the pages of *Alcoholics Anonymous* for guidance, the book responds, "These are the steps we took," not "These are the ideas we subscribe to."

Spiritual practice is a means to an end on the Twelve Step path. The program of action aims to effect a spiritual experience, which is an awareness of a Power greater than self. Therefore, to reconcile atheism with Twelve Step spirituality, we have to square atheism with spiritual practice and the resulting spiritual awakening, not with metaphysics or theology.

The Twelve Steps take the term "spiritual experience" from *Varieties of Religious Experience,* replacing the catchword to avoid *religious* associations. Wilson defines the spiritual experience as "a personality change sufficient to bring about recovery." It is a transformational experience.

Lasting transformation is the touchstone that distinguishes what Wilson terms "spiritual experience" from neighboring phenomena that tend to be rapturous but fleeting in nature. Religious people are not alone in desiring transformation. Anyone stuck in the rut of suffering, wants to be free. Spiritual experience simply posits the possibility of freedom. It suggests that we can attain a higher life, and the historical fact that religion pioneered that life does not preclude atheists from pursuing it on terms more accommodating for them.

Similarly, atheists and skeptics are guilty of obstinacy when they dismiss spirituality outright because it is historically associated with religion. Dismissing spiritual practice due to its association with religion is no less absurd than denouncing medicine or education because the Catholic Church historically built hospitals and schools. These superficial judgements are based on ego, and transformation demands that we look past our false-self to a higher plane. We have to see through the historical relationship between religion and spirituality to discover the transformational value of spiritual practice.

"Most cultures have produced men and women who have found that certain deliberate uses of attention—meditation, yoga, prayer—can transform their perception of the world," writes Sam Harris, a neuroscientist, philosopher, and perhaps the most prominent atheist in the world. "Leaving aside the metaphysics, mythology, and sectarian dogma," he continues, "what contemplatives throughout history have discovered is that there is an alternative to being continuously spellbound by the conversation we are having with ourselves; there is an alternative to simply identifying with the next thought that pops into consciousness."[4] In his Buddhist-inspired vernacular, Harris is talking about seeing through the "illusion of the self," and self-transcendence is a "spiritual" goal. He refers to "freedom from self" as both "the goal and foundation of '*spiritual*' life."

Selfless awareness might not sound like much of a Higher Power but it is equal, in effect, to the concept of "conscious contact" introduced in Step Eleven. It offers a higher perspective, which squares with what Wilson calls the "spiritual angle." Religious people refer to this as "God-consciousness." Harris and Wilson, in their respective languages, are describing opposite sides of the same coin. In other words, the absence of self is the presence of God, as far as the Steps are concerned.

Their difference is not without distinction, but it is free of disagreement. Wilson describes what is present in the experience, while Harris focuses on what is conspicuously absent from it. One interprets music as the harmonious

---

[4] Sam Harris, Waking Up, Chapter One

arrangement of sound, whereas the other describes it as strategically placed moments of silence. Neither is wrong. What Harris calls "the phenomenon of self-transcendence," Wilson refers to as "a spiritual awakening." They are just approaching it from two different vantage points.

Skeptics are not obligated to agree with Harris just because he is a well-known atheist. However, the endorsement of spirituality by a conscientious nonbeliever is proof that reconciliation is possible. We find further agreement between Wilson and Harris in the most unsuspecting of places. Both see psychedelics as useful tools in the production of spiritual experience.

Obviously, dropping acid is not one of the Twelve Steps, so I'm not interested in the spiritual utility of psychedelics; instead, I'm interested in the underlying reasons for their shared enthusiasm for psychedelics. It strengthens the argument that Wilson's "spiritual experience" is equal to Harris' notion of "self-transcendence," which makes it easier for the skeptic to conceive of "a Power greater than ourselves" as a Power beyond ego.

"Psychedelics do not guarantee wisdom or a clear recognition of the selfless nature of consciousness," Harris cautions. Wilson agrees, saying that psychedelics do not produce the spiritual experience. Rather they seem, in his words, "to have the result of sharply reducing the forces of the ego—temporarily, of course." This diminishing effect is helpful, Wilson reasons, because "it is a generally acknowledged fact in spiritual development that ego reduction makes the influx of God's grace possible." Harris would undoubtedly reject to calling that influx "God's grace," but he agrees, in general, that as the spellbinding forces of ego retreat, the "depths of awe and understanding" dawn.[5]

Wilson and Harris are describing a psychic event characterized by self-transcendence. While both believe that psychedelics can be of "some value to some people,"[6] each concedes that spiritual practice is a more reliable method of ego deflation, which is the aim of Twelve Step spirituality.

"Do. Or do not. There is no try."

Wilson tries to reconcile the skeptic to Twelve Step spirituality at the level of ideas, which, in my opinion, misses the point. The Steps have no doctrine to defend or theology to promote, including theism. Since atheism is the rejection of theistic beliefs, and the Steps are not in league with theism, there is no irreconcilable conflict between the two. The Steps propose practices, not specific beliefs, and for that reason, the above quote from Yoda highlights the more pressing matter.

This book focuses on spiritual practice, rather than specific beliefs, because the former is non-negotiable and the latter is incredibly flexible in Twelve Step spirituality. Furthermore, the creation or adoption of a spiritual vocabulary follows spiritual experience chronologically on the Twelve Step path. We come to those ideas by way of practice and direct experience. Therefore, the question is not "Can an

---

[5] Sam Harris, "Drugs and the Meaning of Life," samharris.org/podcasts
[6] *Pass It On*, A.A. World Services, pg 370, 1984 (personal letter from Wilson to a friend)

atheist believe in God?" but "Can they pray and meditate?" Can an atheist actually work the Twelve Steps?

From the vantage point of atheism, there is nothing objectionable about self-analysis or restitution. Indeed, critical thinking is central to a scientific worldview, and these exercises do little more than apply critical thinking to our personal affairs. The value of meditation is evident to atheists hoping to escape the hypnotic chatter between their ears. But what about prayer? Why in the world would anyone pray if they do not believe someone or something is listening? Whether atheism accords with Twelve Step practice is largely dependent upon our answer to this question.

The question "Why would an atheist pray if they don't believe someone is listening?" assumes being heard is the point of prayer. This is a common assumption to be sure, but that assumption is part of an equally common belief, namely that God is a supreme being who listens and responds to prayers. While it is true that some, maybe even most, subscribe to this notion of God, remember: "We need not consider another's conception of God." This means we are not required to adopt anyone's ideas about God *or the manner in which they express those ideas.*

Petitional prayer is an accessory of theism, a particular God-idea that no one is compelled to adopt in theory or practice. Moreover, it is "only one department of prayer," as James notes in *Varieties*. "If we take the word (petitional) in the wider sense," prayer becomes "inward communion or conversation with the power recognized as divine." James concludes that this practice "is the very soul and essence of religion."[7]

At first glance, prayer seems pointless without an audience. However, asking, "Why would you pray if God isn't listening?" is tantamount to asking, "Why would you journal if no one is going to read it?" People journal all the time without an audience. Privacy is the magical ingredient that makes journaling an effective practice. It enables us to be honest with ourselves. Why can't prayer be practiced with the same degree of privacy? It is privacy that facilitates "inward communion or conversation with the power recognized as divine."

We only assume the point of prayer is to be heard and answered, but people pray all the time without expecting their prayers to be heard. Buddhists pray without any thought of a reply. Contemplative prayer, which has a long tradition in both Judaism and Christian monasticism, has more to do with listening than being heard. Our Higher Power provides a selfless outlook. Prayer practices that theory of mind, granting us a God's-eye view.

Moving beyond ego is the thrust of all contemplative spirituality, whether in God-centered traditions like Christianity, Judaism, Islam, or Hinduism or in non-theistic traditions like Taoism and Buddhism. Therefore, contemplatives see prayer as a vehicle of transcendence, not as a way of making requests or filing grievances. If the atheist is *willing* to use prayer as a vehicle of transcendence, then

---

[7] William James, *Varieties of Religious Experience*, pg 464, 1920

there is no conflict between atheism and working the Twelve Steps.

There are those who subscribe to a strict materialism, *in addition to their atheism*, which devalues trans-rational modes of intelligence. This mindset disposes of spiritual experience and invalidates all spiritual practice by condemning anything outside the normal waking state of consciousness. Thus, it is incompatible with all forms of spirituality, including the Twelve Steps. More will be said about this attitude later. However, there are no irreconcilable differences between spirituality and pure atheism, unless by spirituality you mean the belief in a theistic God—and the Twelve Steps do not.

Anybody at All

If the Steps are a means of experimentation that predicts a transformative experience, and that experience hinges on transcending self, then the testable hypothesis is that suffering increases and decreases proportionate to ego's involvement. Wilson confirms this in his Step Three commentary, which states: "Selfishness—self-centeredness! That, we think, is the root of our troubles."[8] Steps Four through Nine test this proposition. If the claim proves true, new life emerges. The practitioner is certainly free to ascribe theistic causes to that experience, and if those beliefs work for them, they are true for them. However, the process verifies that suffering is "basically of our own making," not the existence of a supreme

---

[8] Bill Wilson, *Alcoholics Anonymous*, pg 62, 1939

deity, so no one is compelled to adopt such language. The skeptic is at liberty to choose a more humanistic conception, as long as it effectively deciphers the experience, rendering it actionable for them.

Language does not threaten atheism on the Twelve Step path because the Steps insist that everyone describe their experience in terms that work for them. When Wilson says, "Our more religious members call it 'God-consciousness,'" he implies non-religious members call it something else, and the Steps afford them that liberty. The Power greater than self is often depicted non-theistically in Twelve Step literature. In addition to "Higher Power," phrases like "Spirit of the Universe" and "inner resource" abound. Of course, Wilson gratuitously uses the broad term "God" and even inserts it into the Steps. He also employs explicitly theistic language like "Father" and "Creator" in *Alcoholics Anonymous*. How could he not? Wilson is writing for a diverse audience, making overtures to each camp.

Moreover, Bill W. was an avid spiritualist whose agnosticism eventually gave way to a self-styled Christian mysticism. Far from orthodoxy, he still conceived of God in personal terms, as did most of his audience. Nevertheless, Bill emphatically states that "Step Two is the rallying point for all of us. Whether agnostic, atheist, or former believer, we can stand together on this Step." [9]

"I well remember the evening on which the Twelve Steps were written," Wilson recalls. "I was lying in bed quite

---

[9] Bill Wilson, *Twelve Steps and Twelve Traditions*, pg 33, 1953

dejected and suffering from one of my imaginary ulcer attacks. Four chapters of the book, *Alcoholics Anonymous*, had been roughed out and read in meetings at Akron and New York. We quickly found out that everybody wanted to be an author. The hassles as to what should go into our new book were terrific." The phrases that set Twelve Step spirituality apart from other paths were born of these struggles.

Every Tuesday night Wilson shared his latest efforts with the New York group at his Brooklyn home. The first chapter was his personal story. The second and third focused mainly on the alcoholic condition, only dabbling in spirituality. All this went over without a hitch. It was chapters four and five that struck a nerve. The fourth chapter waded into the question of God, and the fifth spelled out the Twelve Step program. But Wilson's initial draft did not result in *twelve* Steps.

Bill started with six proposals, "which his associates at the previous meeting agreed pretty well summed up what they had learned from the Oxford Group."[10] When Bill returned to the group with a draft of chapter five, the six-step procedure now numbered twelve and it was spelled out in a somewhat devotional tone. This led to a lively debate.

"I was greatly pleased with what I had written, and I read them the new version of the program, now the 'Twelve Steps.'" The Akron group liked the changes, "but in New York," Wilson said, "the hot debate about the Twelve Steps and the book's contents was doubled and redoubled." The warring factions consisted of "conservative, liberal, and

---

[10] Ernest Kurtz, *Not-God: A History of Alcoholics Anonymous*, 1991

radical viewpoints." The conservatives thought "the book ought to be Christian in the doctrinal sense of the word" and that it should profess as much. "The liberals were the largest contingent and they had no objection to the use of the word 'God' throughout the book, but they were dead set against any other theological proposition." In other words, "Spirituality, yes. But religion, no—*positively* no." The atheists and the agnostics, the "radical left wing," as Wilson called them, wanted the word God deleted from the text entirely, electing for a psychological text instead.

The theistic language in *Alcoholics Anonymous* is an apparent overture to the conservative camp. However, the liberals won the day as the final product is a spiritual but not religious text, though even this victory is measured, as some ground is ceded to disbelief. The "agnostic contingent," Bill says, "finally convinced us that we must make it easier for people like themselves by using such terms as 'a Higher Power' or 'God as we understand him.'"[11] These are the "concessions to those of little or no faith; this was the great contribution of our atheists and agnostics. They had widened our gateway so that all who suffer might pass through, regardless of their belief or lack of belief. God was certainly there in our Steps, but He was now expressed in terms that anybody— *anybody at all*— could accept and try."[12]

The gate is wide enough for believer and nonbeliever to pass through simultaneously. The Twelve Step path narrows only as principles and conscience dictate. It never bottlenecks

---

[11] Bill Wilson, *The Language of the Heart*, pg 201, AA Grapevine, 1988

[12] Bill Wilson, *Alcoholics Anonymous Comes of Age*, 161-67, 185

around a particular conception of God. A skeptical reader might reply: "Yeah, I follow what you're saying, but 'God,' smacks of a supernaturalism that forfeits my atheism." The lazy response is "You are not obligated to use that word," which is true, but there is a superior freedom offered. The Steps are a skeletal path that expects the individual to furnish their skins. They do not merely *allow* practitioners to form their conception of a Higher Power, they *insist* upon it.

The phrase "moment of clarity" is frequently substituted for "spiritual awakening" in Twelve Step circles. This phrase speaks to the purity of direct contact. William James calls this clarity the "noetic quality" of mystical experience. Spiritual experiences are, for James, "states of insight into depths of truth unplumbed by the discursive intellect." These insights are "full of significance and importance," though they remain "inarticulate." They are intuitive. This "ineffability" is another trait of spiritual experience identified by James.[13] The experience "defies expression." In Wilson's words, it is "impossible for any of us to fully define or comprehend that Power, which is God." In this context, "God" does not define that Power. It symbolizes that Power which escapes definition and comprehension.

According to James, "no adequate report" of spiritual experience "can be given in words." As a result, "it cannot be imparted or transferred to others." We cannot persuade others of its significance because experiences are "states of feeling,"

---

[13] The other two traits of spiritual experience James mentions are transiency and passivity or the feeling that event comes over the subject. *VSE*, pg 371 (1929)

not "states of intellect." Both secular terminology and orthodoxic conceptions of God are inadequate to this end. Interpersonal squabbling over humanistic or theistic terms is, therefore, a fatuous debate over varying degrees of inadequacy.

The significance of spiritual experience is limited to the individual in which it occurs. For this reason, we need not weigh our conception against another's. Our conception need only conform to the internal logic inspired by our moment of clarity. It must symbolize the significance of our experience. In this sense, "God as we understand him" is like a spiritual Rorschach blot splattered on our mind by the spiritual awakening.

"God" has a complex history. Its range of meaning is diverse and often conflicting. This conflict arises when the mind reaches for the word "God." For this reason, discarding the term may prove the simplest course, but there is a deeper point to make. When the mind reaches for "God," it's stating a preference for "God." It is choosing "God" as its solving name. Since a private experience summoned the term, outside viewpoints have no standing. This is the extent of Step Two's intellectual freedom, which is not always appreciated. When external naysayers gain representation in our head, we squander our personal liberty.

Attempting to reconcile our experience with the world's innumerable conceptions of "God" is a mistake. It opens a confidential matter to the court of public opinion, which destroys our intellectual freedom: "I believe the world is fourteen billion years old. This other guy thinks the world was created by God five thousand-years ago. Our intellectual lives cannot overlap!" The debate rages on until the mind vetoes our preferred solving name. But ask yourself, "Who cares what that other guy thinks?" Literally, *who* cares? When we choose to care, our beliefs are characterized by antipathy to what he thinks. Why cede intellectual freedom to someone with whom you disagree? More importantly, why sacrifice the meaning symbolized by your preferred term?

Spiritual symbols must point past themselves to a higher order, namely the transcendent realm that necessitates them. When we entangle our symbols in foreign affairs, we lead them away from the experience of meaning, and before long they become meaningless. The resulting belief system may correspond to our peer's opinions or a scientific view of the world, but it fails to map onto our daily life in a meaningful way. In Twelve Step spirituality, "God *as we understand Him*" is a personal reality, not a communal concept. It is beholden only to the private experience that invites it. If the mind reaches for "God," we should grab it with no concern for what others think because what they think is owed to their experience. If the mind reaches for another term, be it True Self or Buddha-nature, follow that prompting. It will not lead you astray, which is why the Steps grant that intuition illimitable freedom.

God as we understand IT

According to Wilson, "Higher Power" and "a Power greater than ourselves" are "supplemental expressions" that are "scarcely less valuable" than the keynote phrase, "God as we understand him." In each there is a hint of skepticism, which makes "God" accessible to believer and non-believer alike. But what does God look like to the atheist? The first answer that comes to mind is "Nothing!" Strangely, this retort does not dispose of "God." Ask any seasoned Buddhist or a Christian mystic like Meister Eckhart and they'd reply, "Couldn't have said it better myself!" because "nothing" is the preferred answer of contemplatives.

The famed mythologist, Joseph Campbell, once said, "God is a metaphor for that which transcends all levels of intellectual thought." Contemplatives prefer *apophatic* language because, for them, "God" points to a transcendent experience that is ineffable. They point to the transcendent by negating descriptions of the divine.[14] *Cataphatic* thinkers, such as Wilson, attempt to describe the experience or the attributes of God in positive terms. While they disagree about how to conceptualize the experience, both are pointing to the same panoramic reality.

Words have meaning to the extent that they correspond to real events. Words that do not correspond to reality are useless. This rule also applies to "God." Skeptics often see no value in spiritual terms because they lack the experiences that necessitate them. These experiences do not elude them; rather, their distrust of spirituality wards them off. Skeptics are suspicious of spiritual practices and intuitive states that do not conform to an intellectual framework. When skeptics experiment with spiritual practices like prayer or meditation,

---

[14] *Cataphatic* and *apophatic* are both traditional types of theology. The former is more orthodox; the latter is commonly aligned with mysticism.

they too have spiritual experiences, and these experiences are the real events to which those words point. They render spiritual terms useful.

The following discussion aims to demonstrate both the plasticity and value of those terms, as well as to disarm any prejudice that would prevent further investigation.

The utilization of spiritual symbols does not come with a subscription to creationism or any other form of supernaturalism. The atheist is still an atheist—only now, one who holds a selfless vantage point and spiritual practices that bring that perspective to bear in all their affairs. The atheist can employ "God" as a symbol without forfeiting their atheism because a symbol is not a truth claim about the physical world. Returning once more to Campbell, "a symbol is a sign that points past itself to a ground of meaning and being that is one with the consciousness of the beholder." Symbols are units of meaning. "God" points to the source of meaning within us, not outside of us to a supreme deity.

There is nothing in the Twelve Steps that says "God" is an obligatory symbol. Replacing it with "Higher Power" or any other workable notion is certainly permissible. The atheist may even prefer something more specific like "the Absolute." They might select something more religious like the non-theistic notion of Buddha-nature (*Tathāgatagarbha*). "That reality is 'independent' means that there is something in every experience that escapes our arbitrary control," writes William James.[15] Since reality escapes our control, the atheist is free to

---

[15] William James, *The Meaning of Truth*, pg 69, 1909

take Truth (with a capital 'T') as their higher power, which conveniently harmonizes with the Step's goal of restoring sanity. The atheist is also free to repurpose "God," using it to symbolize an impersonal, psychological experience that is devoid of any metaphysics. In brief, "God" does not have to signify the existence of a supreme being. It can be a symbol that derives value from its capacity to invoke and convey that transcendent meaning and purpose.

This way of thinking is problematic only in a mind with one theory of truth. Remember, both scientific and pragmatic truth are necessary. The value of scientific truth is demonstrated all around us: The computer this book was written with and the tablets it's being read on are obvious examples, but even they pale in comparison to penicillin, vaccines, and special relativity. That said, the picture painted by modern science is worlds removed from the evolutionary environment of our ancestors.

Atheism rejects intelligent design. Therefore, it must admit that reality is not configured to human beings. If there is no creator, then the world was not designed with humans in mind. To the contrary, humans struggled to adapt to reality, which is the gist of evolutionary theory. Consequently, consciousness endeavors to configure itself to reality—most of which is undetectable without modern instrumentation. Present-day physicists, chemists, and biologists see worlds that were invisible to our pre-scientific ancestors. Since these worlds were not part of our evolutionary environment, they did not guide the evolution of consciousness. As the old saying goes, "Out of sight, out of mind."

The human mind is not designed to think scientifically or to perceive science's exacting truths. Instead, humans developed a practical standard of truth that concentrates on immediate, perceptible realities and aims to put us in working contact with our surroundings. This common sense developed in relation to our external environment, but it can also be used to navigate our inner world. Pragmatism codifies these navigational principles, and our beliefs serve as a map of our inner world.

Science is not at odds with pragmatics or spirituality. Science is a system of testing and collecting knowledge about the universe. Pragmatism and spirituality focus on useful and meaningful ideas that agree with the individual's nature and fit, like a missing puzzle piece, into their moral landscape. Therefore, the skeptic can entertain humanistic conceptions of spirituality, while maintaining a scientific worldview.

"Humanism is often identified with unbelief and contrasted with faith," writes the distinguished theologian, Paul Tillich. "This is possible only if faith is defined as belief in the existence and actions of divine beings," which is certainly not the case in the Twelve Steps. "If faith is understood as the state of being ultimately concerned about the ultimate, humanism implies faith," Tillich claims. "For humanism the divine is manifest in the human; the ultimate concern of man is man. All this, of course, refers to man in his essence: the true man, the man of the idea, not the actual man, nor the man in estrangement from his true nature."[16]

---

[16] Paul Tillich, *Dynamics of Faith,* pg 72, 2001

God, *as the humanist understands It*, is the embodiment of humankind's highest Self in every phase of life. This may seem contrary to the notion of a Power greater than self, but it accords with the conclusion drawn by James in *Varieties of Religious Experience*, whence the Steps derive much of their understanding of a Higher Power and the spiritual experience. There, James plainly states that "anything larger will do," including "a larger and more godlike self, of which the present self would then be but the mutilated expression."[17]

Humanists can find much in the transcendentalism of Emerson and Thoreau, which not only discloses richness and depth but entreats us to "suck the marrow out of life." In my opinion, an open-minded atheist can even find useful material in certain Christian thinkers.

Tillich, for example, is one of the most influential religious thinkers of the 20th century. He argued that God cannot be the name of *a* being because *a* being, however supreme or powerful, is still limited. Since God cannot be subjected to finitude, Tillich joins atheists in rejecting the notion of *a* supreme being. He saw God not as the name of a being, but as a symbol for Being-itself. From this angle, "God" does not exist, but signifies existence itself, which we participate in through conscious contact.

All this is mentioned not to advocate for or to reject a particular conception of God, but to showcase conceptions that are meaningful and agreeable with atheistic spirituality. There are innumerable ways to conceive of a Higher Power.

---

[17] William James, *Varieties of Religious Experience*, Lecture XX, 1902

Language is not something to fret over. If using the term "God" complicates things, and "Truth" or "the Absolute" avoids these complications without sacrificing substance, the latter is our obvious choice. If the term "God" is more meaningful and does not trigger a cerebral traffic jam, then once again the choice is obvious: "God" should be employed with no attention paid to what others think.

"Not-God"

The Twelve Steps may not insist upon a theistic God, but they do require belief in a Power greater than self. They demand that we get out of self, and our Higher Power is a selfless vantage point. In Step Three, we surrender our self-centered worldview. Steps Four through Nine, execute the terms of that surrender, bringing about an experience of self-transcendence. This experience transforms Step Two's hypothesized Higher Power into a reality, "conscious contact." Step Twelve makes conscious contact the center around which all our other ideas and concerns are organized.

"There is a God, and I am not it" is a popular Twelve Step slogan. Ernest Kurtz, the preeminent A.A. historian, took the title of his seminal work on the history of Alcoholics Anonymous (*Not-God)* from this slogan because he believed "there is a God, and I am not it" captured the essence of Twelve Step spirituality. However, this slogan doesn't mean that God is an external deity, since Wilson states in the "Spiritual Appendix" that most conceive of their Higher Power as an "unsuspected inner resource."

The Steps propose a Higher Power that is "not I," yet reconcilable with an "inner resource." This leads to the unavoidable conclusion that "greater than ourselves" means "a Power superior to ego," not necessarily a supernatural being. Egoless reference points are found at both ends of the transcendental spectrum. We can *apophatically* plumb our depths or *cataphatically* reach for the heavens, losing ourselves in the glory of God or the mystery of silence.

For some, the axis of transcendence surpasses the infinite reaches of outer space; for others it stretches the expanse of inner space; and for still others, it does both. In any event, the God idea represents a reality too vast for ego to occupy its center—and yet, this reality is at the center of our being. It is both far-reaching and close at hand. This is consistent with James' verdict in *Varieties of Religious Experience*: "Let me then propose, as a hypothesis, that whatever it may be on its *farther* side, the 'more' [or greater] with which in religious experience we feel ourselves connected is on its *hither* side the subconscious continuation of our conscious life."[18]

Spiritual experience, by definition, introduces a greater power, which, on its farther side may be conceived of as an external deity, but on its hither side, is an internal connection called "conscious contact" in the Twelve Steps. Conscious contact is an ecstatic experience, coming from the Greek *ekstasis,* which means "standing outside oneself." Whether the state of ecstasy is believed to be brought about by an external God or conceived of as an out-of-ego experience is a matter for each person to decide. As long as the experience

---

[18] William James, *Varieties of Religious Experience*, Lecture XX, 1902

exposes a plane higher than self-consciousness, the Steps are satisfied.

God of Reason

Ego is our thinking mind personified. Obviously, there is no little tyrant in there pulling the levers. In brief, the ego is an anthropomorphic illusion held over our habits, self-centered ideas, fears, and expectations. The next chapter will elaborate upon the selfish nature of ego. For now, it is sufficient to say that ego is less than eager to relinquish control. It is a collection of habitual attitudes and behaviors, which, by definition, are entrenched. This entrenchment is the boundary we must transcend.

"There is a God and ego ain't it" captures the only precondition placed on our Higher Power by the Twelve Steps. This is a standard everyone should be able to tolerate, but atheism stops at the water's edge when it worships reason. It approaches the unknown, then turns around. The Steps are not hostile toward reason, but they stand firm in their conviction that reason is a means to an end, not an end in and of itself. Once a possibility is reasoned out, a subsequent leap of faith is required.

The skeptic isn't required to blindly believe anything, but they are expected to act blindly. There is no other mode of exploration. When, instead, they cling to reason, the skeptic remains stuck between their ears. Disembodied beliefs tether fundamentalists to the shore, and sterile logic keeps the skeptic on ego's short leash. Both defy the only non-negotiable.

Wilson identifies the veneration of reason as the obstacle that bars the skeptic from the spiritual realm. In the chapter "We Agnostics," when the word "Reason" is used to describe an end rather than a means, Wilson capitalizes it, suggesting "Reason" has achieved God-like status.[19]

By now, it should be evident that the Steps do not pressure the skeptic with metaphysics or religiosity. They do, however, subordinate reason to a more intuitive form of intelligence, which makes some skeptics uncomfortable.[20] Those who have placed the "God of Reason" on their altar see the journey from the head to the heart outlined by the Steps as sacrilege. The Steps cannot abide this degree of intellectualization because, in practice, it amounts to worshipping thought, which Step One indicted.

The goal of the Steps is to restore sanity, which they aim to do by anchoring the mind in first principles. The ability to logically examine the evidence of our senses and draw conclusions is one of man's greatest attributes, as Wilson points out.[21] But it is only *one* of man's great attributes—not the only one and certainly not the principal one.

---

[19] Bill Wilson, *Alcoholics Anonymous,* pg 53, 1939

[20] This subordination refers exclusively to daily living; obviously, the Steps do not subordinate medicine, chemistry, biology, physics, or even philosophy to intuition. The spiritual experience is confined to those domains afflicted by personal powerlessness.

[21] Bill Wilson, Alcoholics Anonymous, pgs 53-54, 1939

In mathematics and science, reason should reign supreme, but when we pass into the spiritual realm—the world of meaning, values, and purpose—epistemology is democratized. Reason is just another instrument in our spiritual toolbox. Basic awareness apprehends reality as-it-is, whereas reason works back through experience to convert that awareness into a meaningful and functional model that maps onto our present circumstances. When reason is mistaken as the *Alpha* and *Omega*, the range of possibilities shrinks to those already cataloged by thought. This narrowing of the mind is especially problematic where addiction is concerned.

"We have no imagination, whereof we have not formerly had sense, in whole or in parts," writes the philosopher, Thomas Hobbes. "So we have no transition from one imagination to another whereof we never had the like before in our senses."[22] Thought is memory set in motion. It draws from previous sense impressions and uses reason to arrange a creative and useful perspective. When the thinking mind is the sole arbiter, only those possibilities that square with our predetermined ideas are permitted. Step One condemns this inbred state of mind, calling it insanity. The Steps cannot tolerate this sort of thinking because it creates a loop, realizing the same undesirable outcomes over and over again.

In addiction, the "mental states that precede a relapse" are "the crux of the problem."[23] Since the mind cannot realize what it has no recollection of, thought is incapable of overcoming addiction. This is true whether the addiction is to

---

[22] Thomas Hobbes, *The Leviathan*, Chapter Three
[23] Bill Wilson, *Alcoholics Anonymous,* pg 37, 1939

alcohol, drugs, sex, gambling, work, or food. In each case, denial corrupts reason. The thinking mind endlessly generates rationalizations and justifications that announce relapse. Sure, the mind may wax rationally in the absence of temptation, but reason does the addiction's bidding when the inevitable button is pressed. It advertises a drink, drug, or half-gallon of ice cream. We cannot rely upon the thinking mind to reason us out of a problem that it is actively thinking us into, and for this reason, Twelve Step spirituality is irreconcilable with any worldview—atheistic or religious—that keeps the individual beholden to thought. Freedom from self is synonymous with freedom from thought.

Einstein famously remarked, "We can't solve problems by using the same kind of thinking we used when we created them." The believer and the nonbeliever alike are prone to fall back on their old ways of thinking. This isn't due to belief or disbelief. It is just a feature of addiction. The addicted mind is always working towards the object of its addiction. Ego is more than capable of shrewdly using religious convictions and skepticism to justify inaction, which protects the *status quo* and guarantees relapse.

The common denominator between fundamentalism and militant atheism is intellectual certainty; both are equally certain about the truth of their claims. The addicted mind uses this certainty to dispose of countermeasures. The believer can disregard an inventory or the confession of shortcomings because *they know* God will deliver them from their addiction if they just ask and believe. Likewise, the non-believer can do the same (nothing) because *they know* such pious displays are hogwash. All the while, the addiction knows—and I mean, really knows, as in, from past experience—that both these intellectual strands lead to inaction, which ensures relapse. This deranged thinking is so prevalent in recovery communities that many Twelve Steppers have adopted this modified version of Einstein's quote as a definition of insanity: "Insanity is doing the same thing over and over again expecting different results."

Conclusion

The Twelve Steps are a path of action, not a spellbound adherence to unsubstantiated ideas that amount to wishful thinking. They are a process of coming to believe, where religious and secular ideas alike are verified by direct experience. It would be a mistake, however, to assume this verification event installs a static, unchanging worldview.

Intellectual certainty boasts unsurpassed understanding. It arrogantly claims that nature and nature's God have divulged themselves of mystery. Moreover, our "Higher Power" cannot serve as a higher power unless it is beyond thought. "God" is not greater than thought, if it is apprehended by a thinker.

Our beliefs are true for us because they fit our lives, but our lives continue to unfold. The beliefs that are tailored to today may not work tomorrow. Pragmatic truth is not an immutable property, so the conclusion announced by certainty is an illusion. The Twelve Steps are ultimately about process, not ideas. They are a way of life, not a belief system. Coming to believe is an unending process.

For our spirituality to remain vital and adaptable to daily living, the God-idea mustn't retreat to the hills of settled dogma. Day-to-day, "possibilities, not finished facts, are the realities with which we have actively to deal," writes William James.[24] Solid, inviolable facts are too bulky and awkward to deal with the shifting, pressing terrain of daily life. "Every time this dubious principle of religious rightness takes a firm grip on men's minds," Wilson says, "there is hell to pay, literally."[25] When rightness solidifies the God-idea, understanding is mistaken for the reality it is meant to symbolize. From there, we slip back into ego's silo, closing ourselves off to the realm of possibility.

In this chapter, we explored the intersection between religiosity, skepticism, and a Higher Power. We saw that the God of the Twelve Steps begins where ego ends; that there is no ideological requirement; and that we come to this Higher Power through an experiential process. We will now shift from the view of Twelve Step spirituality to its application. The remaining chapters make frequent use of terms like God, Higher Power, and True Self. In each instance, they accord with the above standards.

---

[24] "Is Life Worth Living," The Will to Believe and Other Essays in Popular Philosophy, William James, pg 62, 1907

[25] A.A. World Services, *Pass It On,* pg 283, 1984

8 WILL AND LIFE

"Grace is always sufficient, provided we are ready to cooperate with it. If we fail to do our share, but rather choose to rely on self-will and self-direction, we shall not only get no help from the graces bestowed on us, we shall actually make it impossible for further graces to be given." ~ Aldous Huxley

We admit that we are powerless in Step One. If "I" am powerless, then so too are the thoughts and behaviors that constitute "I." In other words, ego is powerless. The admission of ego's powerlessness introduces the possibility of a Power greater than self, which is explored in the second Step.

In Step Two, we have a choice to make: We can continue to bemoan suffering while clinging to its causes, or we can exercise those transcendent possibilities not yet realized. We must choose between ego and a Higher Power. If we are at Step Three, we chose the latter.

Open-mindedness doesn't weigh every silly proposal advanced, and it certainly doesn't abandon reason or discernment. It investigates realistic possibilities. A possibility is any option not ruled out by facts. When facts actually support a possibility, it is realistic.

The second Step submits a realistic possibility. It posits a spiritual awakening, which is supported by testimonials now numbering in the millions. This witnessing is one of the primary roles of Twelve Step storytelling. It adds practical weight to an otherwise unworldly notion. If practicing the God-idea can restore sanity to the most desperate of alcoholic minds, then surely it holds promise for higher bottom cases.

Reports of spiritual experiences are as old as the historical record itself. For millennia, people have testified to their transformative effects. Bill W. and his troop of alcoholics are a continuation of this tradition. The metaphysical claims that accompany these reports are speculative, but the experiences they encase are phenomena. Indeed, *Varieties of Religious Experience* is a scientific effort to look past the metaphysics and assess the veracity of these experiences.

Radical empiricism is a function of William James' pragmatics. It states that the subjective is, from another vantage point, objective. Spiritual experiences are psychic events, and the impact of these events is verifiable. Their metaphysical accoutrements are not testable, but we can gauge the experience's effects upon the believing individual. When we compare the spiritual awakening to a stated goal, we can judge it as adequate or inadequate, true or false. The spiritual experience either sobers the alcoholic up or it does not. It either pacifies the shopaholic's impulsivity and calms the rageaholic's fury, or it does not.

In the Twelve Steps, the verifiable proposition is not the existence of a supreme being or any other metaphysical configuration of a Higher Power. The testable hypothesis is that practicing the God-idea brings about a spiritual awakening, which restores soundness to both mind and body.

Insanity and addiction are auto-repeating patterns of thought and behavior that realize unwanted outcomes. Step Two proposes a method of transcending this circuitry. The very existence of Alcoholics Anonymous demonstrates the utility of this method. There is no lineage of continuous sobriety, no meetings, no fellowship unless the Steps are capable of freeing the most addicted minds. Once again, if practicing the God-idea works under these extreme conditions, it stands to reason that it can work for all of us. In Step Three, we decide to test this reasoning for ourselves.

Made a Decision

"The more closely I scrutinize my states," observes James, "the more persuaded I become, that whatever moods, affections, and passions I have, are in very truth constituted by, and made up of, those bodily changes we ordinarily call their expression or consequence." In short, mental states are not disembodied ideals. They are physical.

Take anger, for example: "Can one fancy the state of rage and picture no ebullition of it in the chest, no flushing of the face, no dilation of the nostrils, no clenching of the teeth, no impulse to vigorous action, but in their stead limp muscles, calm breathing, and a placid face?"[1] No, obviously, we cannot. What we call "rage" *is* the offense, the increased heart rate, the clenched fist, the elevated tone of voice, and ensuing tantrum. Anger cannot be separated from the expression. They are one and the same.

Moreover, every mental state "tells the same story"—not just anger, affection, fear, and joy, but ideas too. This pragmatism is baked into the Twelve Steps, wherein ideas are characterized by the acts they engender. For example, let's look at gratitude. A.A.'s routinely say that "gratitude" is "a verb not a noun." For them, gratitude ripens when its hallmark feelings of abundance blossom into acts that demonstrate appreciation. "Belief" is another good example. In the Twelve Steps, belief doesn't ratify an idea but adopts the acts implied by that idea. Similarly, the Steps do not see spirituality as a theory of life, but as a way of life marked by the application of transcendent principles.

Pragmatism states that ideas become real when they take on physical characteristics. This physicality is the first order of their verity. It establishes their presence in the real world. These ideas become true if they produce positive outcomes in the real world. The Twelve Steps employ this method of verification.

---

[1] William James, "What is an Emotion?," 1884

Speculative evidence is inadmissible in the court of Twelve Step spirituality. Only practical results are allowed. Our God-idea has to be a working concept. Our Higher Power must enter the world of responsibility and struggle against the demands of life—that is where it proves itself. Step Three is the point on our journey where we begin to press the God-idea out into the field of action.

The third Step reads, "Made a decision to turn our will and our lives over to the care of God as we understood Him." To understand Step Three, we need to unpack the word decision. "Three frogs are sitting on a log. One frog decides to jump off. How many frogs are left on the log?" This cute little riddle is often used by Twelve-Steppers to draw attention to the need for action. The prescribed answer is, "There are three frogs left on the log because the one frog just decided. It did not jump." Though the story conveys the character of the Steps, it grossly underestimates the word "decide."

The word "decision" either implies action or it is synonymous with "consider," which for our purposes is untenable. Swapping "decision" with "consider" drastically alters the meaning of the third Step. We consider our options in Step Two. Step Three is the time to act.

In Three, we decide to turn our will and life over to a Higher Power, then execute that decision in the remaining Steps. The process of actualization commences with Step Three. Applying the principles of self-reflection, honesty, ethical behavior, prayer, and meditation in all of our affairs is *how we practice the God-idea*. This is what *turning over our will and life* means.

"Step Three calls for affirmative action," says Wilson, "for it is only by action that we can cut away the self-will which has always blocked the entry of God—or, if you like, a Higher Power—into our lives." The mutual exclusivity of God and ego is the basis of Wilson's logic. He is effectively saying "God and ego cannot dwell together in the same space." If we cling to ego, we refuse God. Consequently, letting go of ego triggers a spiritual experience. This axiom is best captured by Oliver Wendell Holmes, Jr., the legendary Supreme Court Justice, who once told his friend, William James, "The great act of faith is when a man decides that he is not God."

The Steps have no theology to espouse. They do not test ego by affirming a particular conception of God. Instead, they take the *via negativa* or the path of negation. The Steps reduce ego. They wager that a spiritual awakening results from dismantling the false-self. Step Three serves two purposes. As stated above, it commits us to the ego-deflating work of Four through Nine, but it also outlines the terms and conditions of this trial.

Willing vs. Willful

This call to action raises the question of willpower, which the first Step seemingly invalidated. So why is willpower resuscitated in Step Three? In point of fact, Step One did not invalidate willpower. Rather, it suggested that addiction is a state of mind in which willpower has no viable options to support. Step One determined that the addicted mind improperly utilizes willpower to launch what Wilson calls the "full frontal attack by the will."

The first Step considers this headstrong strategy improper because it attempts to resist the forces of addiction with grit and fortitude alone. It tries to hunker down in a fortress of inaction, rather than using willpower to finance healthy, actionable alternatives. In a word, this ill-advised strategy can be categorized as "willfulness." Step Three reintroduces willpower under the heading of "willingness" and counts it as indispensable. To understand the importance of Step Three, we need to hash out the differences between willfulness and willingness.

"Willingness and willfulness become possibilities every time we truly engage life," writes Dr. Gerald May,[2] himself a spiritual director and psychiatrist specializing in addiction. Willingness and willfulness are attitudes staked at opposite ends of the spectrum of willpower. Willingness deals with things-as-they-are; whereas willfulness stubbornly clings to predetermined outcomes.

Willingness is a state of mind that is open and responsive to the changing terrain of the present moment. In the words of Dr. May, "Willingness implies a surrendering of one's self-separateness, an entering-into, an immersion in the deepest process of life itself."[3] Willingness *consents to* and *participates in* a larger process, which is ego deflating.

---

[2] Dr. May was a Psychiatrist, chief of inpatient services at Andrews AFB, and a senior fellow at the Shalem Institute for Spiritual Formation.

[3] Gerald May, *Will and Spirit*, pg 5, 1982

Ego is, by definition, a self-centered worldview. It is a perspective that revolves around self. Step Two inserts the notion of a Power greater than ego, which serves as a selfless reference point. This reference point issues a call to adventure, inviting us to explore the unknown. Willingness answers that call. It broadens our horizons by acting on ideas that correspond to a higher vantage point.

The call to adventure is equal to Wilson's call for "affirmative action." It announces "the self-searching, the leveling of our pride, the confession of shortcomings" that the Twelve Step "process requires for its successful consummation."[4] Such work is challenging and, at times, uncomfortable, so willingness is essential.

Willingness marches into the unknown without the comfort of understanding. It never clings to preordained ideas. In fact, such expectations are a dead giveaway that we are dealing with willfulness. According to May, "Willfulness is the setting of oneself apart from the fundamental essence of life in an attempt to master, direct, control, or otherwise manipulate existence."[5] This separation or disembodiment, is the bedrock of ego. It establishes an inbred sense of self that is unaccountable to reality; that is judged not by the content of its character but by what it thinks about itself. The ego willfully manufactures, exploits, and suppresses the truth to protect this persona. It lies to itself, omits facts, and ignores reality. In a word, willfulness is insanity.

---

[4] Bill Wilson, *Alcoholics Anonymous,* pg 25, 1939
[5] Gerald May, *Will and Spirit*, pg 6, 1982

Willfulness is an attempt to be something we are not. This effort is not just the cause of our suffering; it is the reason for its perpetuation. An impostor is attempting to draw on power it lacks to effect change where it has no jurisdiction. The ego is powerless because it isn't real. It's an apparition. When we set ourselves apart from life to "master, direct, control, and manipulate," we reject the truth of who we are. In Twelve Step shorthand, this is called "playing God."

Outgrowing the God-Complex

Playing God is ego's *modus operandi*. In his third Step commentary, Wilson offers the following pith instruction: "We had to quit playing God. It didn't work."[6] These nine words outline the parameters of the Twelve Step experiment. We have to suspend ego's truth distorting operations to glimpse sanity. Practically speaking, we have to turn over our "will" and "life."

The terms "will" and "life" refer to perception and behavior, respectively. The third Step asks us to surrender these faculties because our perception and behavior are distorted by ego. Our perception is self-centered, and our behavior is selfish. For this reason, Wilson declares selfishness and self-centeredness "the root of our troubles."[7]

---

[6] Bill Wilson, *Alcoholics Anonymous*, pg 62, 1939
[7] Ibid, pg 62

Self-centeredness is a perceptual filter that bends reality to ego's liking. Selfishness presses that warped perception out into the world of time and space. Together, self-centeredness and selfishness constitute insanity, the willful complex that prevents a Higher Power from entering our lives.

The common denominator between selfishness and self-centeredness is "self." In this context, "self" refers to our *persona*, not our person. Our persona is the mask we hold over our True Self. It is a psychological self, an ego. This distinction is important for a couple of reasons.

First, it reminds us that spirituality embraces our humanity; it does not reject it. The Steps do no eradicate anger or sadness, for instance. They anticipate them. Twelve Step spirituality prepares us for these human emotions. It does not suppress emotion in pursuit of an inhumane ideal. We are rational *and* emotional organisms. There is nothing wrong with that. It is not a problem to be overcome; that we confuse what we think and feel with a reality to which others must conform, that is the problem—that is insanity.

Second, the distinction between person and persona further clarifies the basic requirements of a Higher Power. As stated in the previous chapter, this power must be higher than self. Now, we know that means this Power must go beyond self-consciousness and override self-serving impulses. This basic requirement is plucked from *Varieties of Religious Experience*, which says, "The power should be both other and larger than our conscious selves."[8] The "conscious self" is not our person. It is our persona or ego. Self-centered perception and selfish behavior form the ego complex, and unpacking these components sheds more light on the role of our Higher Power.

Self-Centered Perception

Self-centeredness means "self" is at the "center," which implies 'I' is the measure of all things. In a self-centered mind, ego is the metric that determines the value of every person we meet and every object we encounter. If something makes us feel good, it receives positive marks. If something makes us feel bad, its evaluation is negative. The fact that bystanders who fail to elicit a positive or negative response from us are quickly forgotten evinces this mode of perception.

Self-centeredness mistakes our feeling about something for the essence of that something. It sees people as objects, denying them an existence that is independent of our fears and desires. It reduces them to a function in our life: an ally, adversary, or passerby.

When we arrive at the office for our first day on the job, we enter the conference room a stranger. Let's say we try to break the ice with a joke. There are those who do not notice our humor. We dismiss them. Then, there are those who laugh and engage with us. They make us feel welcomed, so we cultivate those relationships. Perhaps others find our humor

---

[8] William James, *Varieties of Religious Experience*, Lecture XX, 1902

off-putting or inappropriate. In them, we find no safe harbor and steer clear. All this is normal enough. It becomes problematic when our evaluation of these characters is mistaken for the truth of who they are.

Alarm bells go off when Tom, the resident stick-in-the-mud, denounces our nervous attempt to lubricate the conference room with humor as "inappropriate in a professional setting." Being singled out alienates us. Stress arises, followed by anxiety and anger. Our thoughts search for a justification that transfers those uncomfortable feelings to Tom: "I can't believe that bastard. That's why nobody likes him. He's miserable as hell!" In reality, those feelings belong to us, not Tom. Thus, blame is the habit of a foolish mind. It tries to transfer non-transferable emotions. This triggers a malfunction or an obsession: "Who the hell does he think he is?! I tell you what, let him say something else…I'm going to let him have it in front of God-and-everybody…Tell me I'm inappropriate—whatever dude. You're inappropriate!" And so we obsessively brood for hours on end.

This embittered dialogue attempts to blame our agitation on Tom, but at great expense to our well-being. Stress, fear, and anger pour adrenaline on the carburetor between our ears, hastening our thoughts. The mind hurries from a comfortable stroll to a jog, then to an outright sprint. In minutes, we are twenty, forty, sixty thoughts removed from the present moment. Our thoughts harden as their pace quickens, turning our rant into an alternative reality—much like the accelerating blades of an airplane propeller appear to be a solid disk. Eventually, the mind reaches that critical speed where we cannot differentiate the true from the false. The hallucination is too thick to see through. At this point, the whirling chorus between our ears proclaims, "Tom is an asshole!"

Our feelings about Tom crystallize our perception of Tom. "Asshole" is the role ego assigns him in this self-centered drama. This label measures his worth relative to our ego. It casts him as the antagonist, which conveniently makes us the protagonist. This valuation says nothing about who he is; it is a ploy to unburden ourselves of those negative emotions. Of course, this projection doesn't actually transfer the mass of negativity over to Tom. That is an illusion. However, blame does transfer power. It places our happiness and well-being in the hands of someone we cannot control, rendering us powerless over our suffering.

"Tom is an asshole" means, "Tom was born with the all the hallmarks of an asshole." He emits bad vibes but in point of fact, those bad vibes are our feelings, which reside within us. Unfortunately, we no longer see Tom for who he is; we only see what we think about Tom, which signifies how we feel. "Tom makes me feel bad; therefore, Tom is bad." This way of thinking becomes apparent when we share our thoughts about Tom with one of our friends, who responds: "Oh, I like him. He is nice." There is a glitch at that moment. When someone we like is fond of someone we dislike, it doesn't compute. Self-centeredness malfunctions.

Self-centeredness is a curtain hung over the mind's eye that dims the light of reality. It throws shade on truth. In this case, the truth of Tom. He actually exists from his side, independent of what we think. Tom has friends and a family that loves him, but we are incapable of seeing this. Our thoughts and feelings about Tom are negative, so he is thought to be an inherently negative person. He is the villain in our story, and so he remains—unless, of course, mutual disdain for another co-worker forces us to play the "enemy of my enemy is my friend" card. Then, we buddy up with Tom. Self-centeredness is, after all, endlessly opportunistic!

Self-centered perception swings both ways. During the honeymoon phase of a relationship, for example, the image of our partner is forged by the intoxicating passions that pervade the budding affair. They are "our soulmate," "other half," or "true love," and there is nothing our friends can say to convince us otherwise. Attempts to persuade us that our "soulmate" is toxic will fall on deaf ears because when we see them, all we see is how they make us feel *right now,* which is head-over-heels in love. We write off their past indiscretions with the one-liner "people change" to protect and possess the immediate gratification squeezed from the relationship. Once again, we do not see them, but what we think about them, which is colored by our bubbly feelings.

As previously stated, perhaps the clearest example of self-centeredness is the cold treatment paid to those nameless multitudes that fail to move ego's needle one way or the other. This slew of anonymous faces fall to the wayside because they neither arouse our affections nor invoke our wrath. They do not affect the plot, so they are extras in ego's narration. It's like they aren't even there.

Selfish Behavior

Self-centeredness tells a story. This story is a work of fiction—propaganda, to be more precise. The author is a false-self. Since it is false, this self has no authority, no power, no creativity. The ego cannot create, so it manipulates. It uses fear and expectations as propaganda to bend the truth to its point of view. But concocting a story is not enough. The ego has to publish this story. It has to print, distribute, and promote the falsehood to give it the appearance of life.

The ego's distorted world rests on two pillars. The first is self-centeredness, which is a monumental feat of self-aggrandizement that envisions a planet populated with characters who exist solely to serve the ego's agenda. The second pillar is selfishness. Selfishness publishes self-centeredness. It prints the lie. Selfishness lives as if the story is real and it expects others to do the same.

Selfishness acts out self-centeredness. It treats people in a manner that is consistent with ego's appraisal of them. Selfishness takes those who elicit positive feelings as hostages, and it treats those with whom we disagree like hostile combatants. In both cases, it fails to afford either the dignity or autonomy they are owed. Self-centeredness casts friend and enemy as supporting characters in ego's drama, while selfishness orders them around.

When we label someone an "asshole," we treat them as such. We talk about them behind their back and plot against them, taking verbal, emotional, and occasionally physical jabs at them. Ultimately, the ego is trying to manage negative emotions. It pushes adversaries around because they are projections of unwanted feelings.

Self-centeredness casts our negative emotions onto rivals, while selfishness works to keep those emotions at bay by pushing our rivals away. This strategy is problematic for many reasons. For starters, it is unethical and delusional, but it is also ineffective. No one wants to be ridiculed, attacked, or singled out. Thus, our adversaries reply in kind. They fight back and with each tit-for-tat, the tension escalates. This escalation has the unintended consequence of bringing our foes even closer. Before long, they are living in our heads as resentments.

Moreover, this course becomes a self-fulfilling prophecy. Our selfish behavior begs retaliation, which reinforces the self-centered notion that our negative emotions emanate from our foes. This strategy binds us to the causes of our misery.

Selfishness is no less unavailing at the other end of the spectrum. The impulse to "complete ourselves" is so great when we meet our "other half" that we become possessive. Self-centeredness believes the significance of our "significant other" is measured by their effect upon us. It only sees the void-filling passions they ignite in us because ego sees the world through the lens of its own inadequacies. As a result, ego is constantly agonizing over whether an individual threatens to expose its weaknesses or compensate for them. In this case, ego sees the other as a missing piece of itself. It believes that they fit the "hole in our soul," so selfishness takes them as a "soul-mate."

Selfishness carries out the will of self-centeredness. It does not love; it treats the lover like property. Selfishness tries to possess them by clinging to the feelings they invoke. We smother our lover because we want to protect and control the bliss they arouse. In all this, we forget they are a person. Instead of taking on a partner, we take a hostage, which backfires.

Healthy, independent people need breathing room, so they push back. This space scares ego. It threatens the loss of something ego depends upon. As a result, we squeeze tighter, inadvertently pushing away those we want to bring closer. The friction and conflict continue to mount until our other half escapes, leaving us feeling broken. At which point, they're reclassified: "The love of our life" becomes an "asshole" we have to defend ourselves against.

"So our troubles, we think, are basically of our own making," writes Wilson. "Driven by a hundred forms of fear, self-delusion, self-seeking, and self-pity, we step on the toes of our fellows and they retaliate. Sometimes they hurt us, seemingly without provocation, but we invariably find that at some time in the past we have made decisions based on self which later placed us in a position to be hurt."[9] To further illustrate his point, Wilson offers a helpful analogy: "Each person is like an actor who wants to run the whole show; is

---

[9] Bill Wilson, *Alcoholics Anonymous,* pg 62, 1939

forever trying to arrange the lights, the ballet, the scenery and the rest of the players in his own way. If his arrangements would only stay put, if only people would do as he wished, the show would be great. Everybody, including himself, would be pleased. Life would be wonderful." Of course, "the show doesn't come off very well," as evidenced by the unmanageability that brought us to the spiritual path in the first place.[10]

Selfishness is an attempt to impose order. These edicts appear rational if self-centeredness is the basis of your rationale. Hence the saying, "You can't solve a problem with the same way of thinking that created it." Selfishness feels like righteousness because it is consistent with our self-centered value system. For this reason, our Higher Power must serve as a moral check against selfish behavior and as the basis for a higher theory of mind that gaurds against self-centered perception.

Turning Over Our Will and Life

Self-centeredness sees the world through the distorted lens of our false-self, which is stained by insecurity, fear, anger, and attachment. It forgets that we are part of the show. From self-centeredness' make-believe director's chair, selfishness barks orders at everyone on stage. We are pretending to be God and this ego trip is what we are asked to forfeit in Step Three.

---

[10] Bill Wilson, *Alcoholics Anonymous,* pg 60-61, 1939

We have to quit playing God; it does not work. We have to subordinate our will (perception) to selfless awareness, which requires practices like inventory, confession, amends, prayer, and meditation. Once established, this selfless reference point becomes the center around which our life (behaviors) is organized.

The execution of Step Three begins with a prayer. "The Third Step Prayer" is a practice that taps the heartfelt longing to transcend ego and reconnect with the vitality of our true life. When practiced daily, this prayer helps relieve our minds of "the bondage of self." However, we must strive to embody the principles embedded in this prayer. Insight destroys delusion, but only work can uproot the defects of character that persist as forces of habit. When we are ready to take this Step, we mindfully say the following:

> "God, I offer myself to Thee—to build with me and to do with me as Thou wilt. Relieve me of the bondage of self, that I may better do Thy will. Take away my difficulties, that victory over them may bear witness to those I would help of Thy Power, Thy Love, and Thy Way of life. May I do Thy will always!"[11]

The prayer's wording is optional, but prayer itself is necessary. For agnostics and atheists, this is where the test of willingness begins. The only way forward is to transmute open-mindedness into investigative action. There is no requirement that you believe anyone or anything is listening,

---

[11] Bill Wilson, *Alcoholics Anonymous,* pg 63, 1939

but you must be willing to work with the practice of prayer to advance in the Steps. Why pray, if no one is listening? Once again, this question assumes being heard is the point of prayer. Lama Govinda, a Buddhist teacher, defines prayer as "a calling up of the highest forces of our mind, of our highest ideals, and the remembrance of those who realized them (Buddhas), coupled with the firm resolution or vow to follow their example and to put into practice our aspirations."[12] From this angle, prayer calls forth a higher order motivation from within, not without.

Petitional prayer is symptomatic of a particular conception of God, which no one is obliged to consider. If praying the "Third Step Prayer" in that format works for you, then by all means. If it does not work for you, ask yourself what value the words prayed hold for you. What is the "bondage of self?" Is freedom from ego not the epitome of freedom? What does it mean to live a life that bears witness to those I would help? Search yourself for the underlying meaning of those words, for the realities they signify within you.

This sort of inquiry is another form of prayer. Even if you do not believe in God, as a matter of experimentation, assume there is an order of truth higher than the present arrangement of your conscious mind and send the prayer in that direction. Imagine the word "God" points to a greater reality and ask yourself, 'Where is it leading me?' Where does my mind turn when it thinks of a Higher Power? Bring your awareness into

---

[12] Lama Anagarika Govinda, *Foundations of Mysticism,* pg 124 (footnote 1), 1969

that space. This is a type of prayer that anyone can practice, but we cannot stop there. We cannot give up something we are unaware of, so Step Three demands more action.

Conclusion

We have discussed the nature of self-centeredness and selfishness in theory, but Step Three calls for affirmative action. A theory of selfishness and self-centeredness is useless unless applied to the details of our life. We cannot part with selfishness and self-centeredness unless we know how they manifest in our lives. Therefore, the next step is to turn the light of awareness on ourselves. Steps Four and Five facilitate this introspective turn. Before we dive into the fourth and fifth Steps, let's return to early 20th century America and examine the Oxford Group, A.A.'s predecessor and the originators of Steps Four through Nine.

9 THE OXFORD GROUP

> "I think the [Oxford] 'group' proper disowned Bill when he proceeded on his guidance to create a special group for A.A.'s. At that time, if you were associated with the 'group,' your guidance seemed to be of questionable worth unless okayed by Sam Shoemaker or Frankie Buchman or one of his accredited representatives." ~ John Ryder (New York Oxford Group Member)[1]

Frank Buchman came to Northern England lacking purpose. The recently unemployed minister wandered into a small, stone chapel in Keswick, England, and claimed one of that Sunday's many vacant pews. There he sat transfixed, as Jessie Penn-Lewis, a Welsh Evangelist, painted a portrait of Christ crucified. "I saw the nails in the palms of His hands, I saw the bigger nail which held His feet," recalled Buchman. "I saw the spear thrust in His side, and I saw the look of sorrow and

---

[1] A.A. World Services, *Pass It On,* pg*178*

infinite suffering in His face. I knew that I had wounded Him, that there was a great distance between myself and Him, and I knew that it was my sin of nursing ill-will."[2] Buchman left that chapel determined.

This sermon was not Frank Buchman's first on the suffering and death of Jesus, nor was it the first time he contemplated the reconciliation therein. Nevertheless, Jessie Penn-Lewis shook him to his core. She managed to press upon him certain themes that he previously overlooked. Suddenly, atonement ceased to be a theoretical matter and became, for him, an experience.

Before coming to Keswick, Buchman operated a homeless shelter for young men in Philadelphia. He was slavishly devoted to this work, which on the surface epitomized Christian charity. The hospice's success outpaced his budget, so he appealed to the board of trustees for more money. When the board refused his demands, Buchman tendered his resignation.

Frank Buchman identified with his work, and without it, he fell into a deep depression. Under the auspice of "doctor's orders" and on the dime of his father, he took a trip abroad. In July of 1908, his tour of Europe stopped in Keswick.

The thirty-year-old Buchman might have come to England without purpose, but he did come for a reason. He was there for the annual "Keswick Convention." He hoped to meet Frederick Meyer, a British preacher and author he

---

[2] Garth Lean, *Frank Buchman: A Life*, pg 30, 1985

admired. Meyer was a regular speaker at the Keswick Convention, but was unable to attend that year. Buchman was disappointed. Nevertheless, he immersed himself in the week-long event.

The Keswick Convention is an international gathering of Christian evangelicals. The convention began in 1875 and in its one hundred and forty three year history, Keswick has hosted the likes of Billy Graham, who drew more than 15,000 people. In Buchman's day, the convention didn't attract Graham-sized crowds, but the small country town was still teeming. When the convention came to town, Keswick's population more than doubled, swelling from 4,000 to roughly 10,000 inhabitants. This influx exhausted the town's minimal lodging, which left hundreds gleefully camped amidst the picturesque countryside. "The scenery of its lakes and dales, hills and mountains, is lovely beyond description," an American attendee told a paper covering the 1908 event. As for the convention itself, the singing was "tender, sweet, supplicatory, and often subdued." The meetings were "quiet and undemonstrative."[3]

When he arrived, Frank Buchman's emotional state did not comport with this charming environment. By his own admission, he was self-centered and full of resentment when he wandered into Lewis' service. The image of the crucified Christ she outlined served as a looking glass for Buchman. "I don't know how you explain it, I can only tell you I sat there and realized how my sin, my pride, my selfishness and my ill-will, had eclipsed me from God in Christ. I was in Christian

---

[3] *Otago Witness*, "Keswick Convention," Issue 2853, 11/18/1908

work, I had given my life to those poor boys and many people might have said 'how wonderful,' but I did not have victory because I was not in touch with God. My work had become my idol."[4]

Buchman's thoughts wandered from the little stone chapel in Keswick, across the Atlantic, settling on those he loathed. Buchman resented the hospice's trustees for refusing his demands, but at Keswick he had a change of heart. "I thought of those six men back in Philadelphia who I felt had wronged me. They probably had, but I'd got so mixed up in the wrong that I was the seventh wrong man," he realized. "Right in my conviction, I was wrong in harbouring ill-will."[5] This element of Buchman's "Keswick experience" informs not only the Oxford Group but Twelve Step spirituality. It echoes forth when Wilson writes, "If somebody hurts us and we are sore, we are in the wrong also."[6]

The Keswick experience had an immediate and lasting impact on Buchman. As soon as Jessie Penn-Lewis concluded, the repentant minister returned to his quarters and put pen to pad. "I have harboured an unkind feeling toward you—at times I conquered it but it always came back," Buchman wrote Dr. Ohl, the presiding trustee. "Our views may differ but as brothers we must love. I write to ask your forgiveness and to assure that I love you and trust by God's grace I shall never more speak unkindly or disparagingly of you." All six were to receive such a letter. In this practice of

---

[4] Garth Lean, *Frank Buchman: A Life,* pg 30, 1985
[5] Ibid, pg 30
[6] Bill Wilson, *Twelve Steps and Twelve Traditions,* pg 90, 1953

self-reflection and restitution, one sees the prefiguration of Steps Four through Nine.

Collegiate Ministry

Frank Buchman wanted to change the world—of this, there can be no doubt. Whether Buchman's virtue or narcissism guided him is another matter, but his ambition cannot be questioned. He always sought to position himself on the highest perch. Throughout his controversial career, Buchman hobnobbed with Kings, Queens, Princes, and Prime Ministers. He dined with tycoons and courted Nazis. In the end, his habit of stalking fame and power dogged both his reputation and his legacy project, the Oxford Group.

Mundane tasks and incremental progress tempered Buchman's megalomania immediately after his Keswick experience. In 1909, he became the YMCA Secretary at Penn State. The Young Men's Christian Association was founded in 1844 by an English philanthropist named George Williams. They melded evangelism, Christian virtues, and athleticism to create a "muscular Christianity." Their collegiate ministries were particularly successful in the latter half of the 19th century and early into the 20th century. They held campus revivals called "decision nights," where students professed Christ their savior. Buchman's style of evangelism enabled him to thrive in this environment.

As YMCA Secretary at Penn State, Buchman employed a mixed bag of tactics. He packed auditoriums and cultivated personal relationships, especially with influential men about campus. In public venues and private interviews, his message focused on the themes of his Keswick experience: the individual's relationship with God, the shortcomings that frustrate it, and the process of reconciliation. This message was generally well received.

Under his leadership, YMCA membership skyrocketed in Happy Valley. Of Penn State's 809 eligible students, only 166 were members of the YMCA in 1906. "Two years after he arrived, it had jumped to 1,200 out of a total of 1,620."[7] But this was of little consolation to Buchman. He constantly questioned the veracity of these conversions. Did they mirror the transformation he experienced in Keswick or were they conversions in name only? Was he racking up impressionable young men on decision night or true converts? These questions haunted Buchman.

Buchman shared these concerns with Frederick Meyer, who, in 1912, visited Penn State while on a U.S. speaking tour. Like other Baptists of the day, Meyer railed against social ails like drunkenness and prostitution, but his message was multifaceted. He wasn't just a teetotaling moralizer. He was a man of practical religion, possessing a subtler, more spiritual side. In *The Secret of Guidance*, he writes, "The Spirit of God within thee and the presence of God without thee cannot be discerned whilst the senses are occupied with pleasure, or the pulse beats quickly, or the brain is filled with the tread of many hurrying thoughts." Meyer concludes with the following instruction: "Let no day pass without its season of silent waiting before God." During his Penn State visit, he

---

[7] Philip Boobbyer, *The Spiritual Vision of Frank Buchman*, pg 14, 2013

offered Buchman similar advice, which forever changed his pastoral practice. It also planted seeds that later bloomed into an Oxford Group hallmark that inspired one of A.A.'s twelve Steps.

When Buchman raised his concerns about conversions, the reflective Meyer asked, "Do you let the Holy Spirit guide you in all you are doing?" Buchman tepidly replied that he read the Bible and prayed daily, and would, from time to time, receive inspiration. His mentor found this response wanting.

Deeply influenced by Quakerism, Meyer was an advocate of silent meditation. He thought "guidance" threadbare unless it was combined with active listening. "But do you give God enough uninterrupted time really to tell you what to do?" he asked Buchman. This exchange was a pivotal point in Buchman's career. From this point on, periods of silence became a fixture of his daily routine.[8] These periods of silence later developed into an Oxford Group staple called "quiet time," which Bill and Bob utilized in their own way.

Forming the Oxford Group

Buchman left Penn State in 1915. He became a YMCA missionary in Asia, meeting both Rabindranath Tagore and Mahatma Gandhi during his travels. In China, he also made the acquaintance of Samuel Shoemaker, who, for our purposes, is of greater consequence than the two giants of the Indian subcontinent. Sam is the critical link connecting the

---

[8] Garth Lean, *Frank Buchman: A Life*, pg 36, 1985

Oxford Group to Alcoholics Anonymous. "The early A.A. got its ideas of self-examination, acknowledgment of character defects, restitution for harm done, and working with others straight from the Oxford Group," says Wilson, "and directly from Sam Shoemaker," who not only mentored Bill, but served as the Oxford Group's "leader in America."[9]

In 1917, Sam Shoemaker was a twenty-four-year-old Princeton student interested in mission work. He satisfied this curiosity with a trip to China. Shoemaker taught business at a campus satellite in China and helped open a new YMCA chapter while there. This is also where he met Buchman. The young missionary was impressed with Buchman's style of evangelism and the two became fast friends.

Buchman juggled his missionary work with his collegiate ministry, which included frequent stops at Princeton, where Shoemaker had returned from China to finish his studies. Buchman's message centered on the "moral and spiritual needs of individuals," instead of the "mastery of theological minutiae."[10] This approach appealed to Shoemaker, who after completing seminary became an Episcopal priest. It also worked well on college campuses, especially Oxford University in England.

The group formed at Oxford University was so lively and well received that it became the namesake of Buchman's movement. However, his following quickly outgrew its

---

[9] Bill Wilson, *A.A. Comes of Age,* pg 39, 1985

[10] Ibid, pg 49

collegiate skins and morphed into an international, evangelical movement. In North America, operations were managed by Dr. Shoemaker, who was recently named rector of Calvary Episcopal in Manhattan. Nearly a decade later, Bill Wilson stumbled down the aisles of Calvary looking for the promised reprieve his friend Ebby found in Buchman's movement, "the Oxford Group."

The Backstory of Alcoholics Anonymous

On January 20, 1933, the front page of the *Akron Beacon Journal* read, "Akron's leading citizens were at the Mayflower hotel Thursday night, welcoming members of the Oxford Group to the city." Among them was the tire tycoon Harvey Firestone, whose son, Russell, suffered from alcoholism. Firestone's former aide, Jim Newton, took Russell to an Oxford Group conference in Denver where he met Sam Shoemaker. Following the conference, Russell found some measure of relief and his grateful father extended an invitation to the Oxford Group. Buchman's penchant for power and publicity made him all too eager to accept the magnate's invitation.

This event came to be known as the "Dinner Jacket Revival." When Buchman arrived he was greeted by Firestone and Frank Seiberling, co-founder of Goodyear Tire—and as fate would have it, Henrietta Seiberling's father-in-law. Nearly two years later, Bill Wilson paced the same hotel's lobby before phoning Walter Tunks, who just so happened to be Firestone's minister. It was Tunks who referred Wilson to Mrs. Seiberling, setting up the now famous meeting between

Bill W. and Dr. Bob. Without this tightly woven web of Oxford Group connections, it is unlikely that Bill W. would have met Dr. Bob. However, the relationship between Alcoholics Anonymous and the Oxford Group is deeper and more complicated than a rolodex.

Standing next to Shoemaker, roughly twenty years later, Bill told the crowd gathered for A.A.'s World Convention, "It is what Ebby learned from Sam and what Ebby told me that makes up the linkage between Sam, the man of religion, and ourselves." He was careful never to mention Buchman's controversial name. Following his death in 1961, Bill privately expressed regret for not squaring A.A.'s debt with the Oxford Group founder—still, he made no public overture. For reasons yet to be disclosed, Buchman's name was too toxic. Instead, Wilson linked A.A. to the Oxford Group through Ebby and Sam.

Ebby Thacher is, of course, Bill's childhood friend. Like Bill, Ebby suffered from alcoholism. In fact, before he came to Wilson's aid, Ebby was rescued from his alcoholic hell by a couple of Oxford Groupers.

Ebby Thacher was born into a prominent New England family with ties back to the American Revolution. Dr. James Thacher was a surgeon in George Washington's Army who witnessed the hanging of Benedict Arnold's accomplice, Major John André, at West Point. The surgeon's oft-cited war journal provides posterity with an invaluable account of this dramatic scene.

The Thacher family fortune began with Ebby's grandfather, George, who manufactured railroad car wheels. George also served as Albany's mayor during the Civil War, welcoming the newly elected Lincoln to town in 1861. Ebby's father and uncle inherited the family business after their father passed. His uncle also served as Mayor of Albany and as a New York state Senator. Ebby's brother, John Thacher, boasts the fourth-longest mayoral tenure in Albany history and the distinct honor of being nominated to succeed Franklin Roosevelt as Governor of New York. Ebby, to put it delicately, was less distinguished.

John Thacher's rise to prominence coincides with his younger brother's descent into alcoholic despair. Ebby was an eyesore the family needed to hide from public view, so he retreated to the family's home in Manchester, Vermont—ten minutes from Dorset, the birthplace of Bill Wilson. There Ebby's drunken debauchery drew the ire of local law enforcement on two occasions, one of which found his car parked in a neighbor's kitchen. The judge agreed to release Thacher into the care of several Oxford Group members, including Roland Hazard, recently released from the care of Dr. Carl Jung.

Hazard brought Ebby to the Calvary Mission in New York, and introduced him to the Rev. Sam Shoemaker. Rev. Shoemaker was known for his non-denominational ecumenism, which rings forth in Ebby's now fabled retort to Wilson, "Why don't you choose your own conception of God?" This is the message Shoemaker passed onto Alcoholics Anonymous through Ebby Thacher.

Ebby's encouraging advice to Bill is a step towards A.A.'s "spiritual but not religious" brand, but it is only a foot in the door. Later, this door is flung open by Wilson's disbelieving colleagues. The Oxford Group never sought to sever ties with Christianity, as did Alcoholics Anonymous. Buchman saw the movement as "an organic fellowship of Jesus Christ."[11] He did reach out in earnest to non-Christians but always couched his message in a Christian motif.

Thacher is influenced by Shoemaker's Christian ecumenism. When Ebby said "choose your own conception," he did not mean a Hindu or a Muslim God. He meant whatever version of the Judeo-Christian God best suited Bill—be it a Methodist, Baptist, Catholic, or a non-denominational variety. This intrafaith approach was standard fare in the Oxford Groups. It was the liberal bunch of early A.A.'s who insisted upon no religious affiliation. More specifically, it was the atheists and agnostics who broadened the tent with inclusive terms like, "Higher Power" and "Power greater than ourselves," bringing the seed planted by Ebby to full bloom.

The Four Absolutes

Bill Wilson and Dr. Bob were not trying to convert people. Their efforts were exclusively focused on carrying the message to suffering alcoholics. For this reason, they chose action as their shibboleth, rather than a rote profession of faith. This shift was made easier for them by the Oxford Group's practices, which united faith and works.

---

[11] Philip Boobbyer, *The Spiritual Vision of Frank Buchman*, pg 91, 2013

Buchman primarily focused on the practical side of faith. He had little interest in the details of theology, which he found more "theoretical" than "vital."[12] "His emphasis on spiritual practices rather than beliefs meant that his message could easily be adapted to non-Christians," writes historian, Dr. Philip Boobbyer.[13] And this is precisely what Bill Wilson did. He adapted Oxford Group practices to serve his spiritual but not religious purposes. He stripped them of their Christian vestiges and engineered an actionable path structure organized around the personal experience of a Power greater than self. This path permitted the individual to conceive of their Higher Power in terms befitting them. Therefore, the debt Wilson failed to square with Buchman was in the amount of practices, not beliefs.

Spiritual practice in the Oxford Group revolved around a quartet of moral principles known as the "Four Absolutes." Buchman believed these absolutes epitomized the Sermon on the Mount. The Four Absolutes were honesty, purity, unselfishness, and love. They were presented not as "misty ideals" but "practical standards" cultivated by four adjoining "spiritual activities." When Bill Wilson said, "A.A. got its ideas of self-examination, acknowledgment of character defects, restitution for harm done, and working with others straight from the Oxford Group," he was referring to these activities. These four practices are described as follows in the anonymously penned text, *What is the Oxford Group?*

---

[12] Garth lean, *Frank Buchman: A Life,* pg 49, 1985

[13] Philip Boobbyer, *The Spiritual Vision of Frank Buchman*, pg 90, 2013

1. "The Sharing of our sins and temptations with another Christian life given to God, and to use Sharing as Witness to help others, still unchanged, to recognize and acknowledge their sins.
2. Surrender of our life, past, present, and future, into God's keeping and direction.
3. Restitution to all whom we have wronged directly or indirectly.
4. Listening to, accepting, relying on God's Guidance and carrying it out in everything we do or say, great or small."[14]

Wilson and his team of collaborators compiled a list, similar to the one above, which enumerated the practices they thought were indispensable to their sobriety. In December of 1938, Bill carried this list to his upstairs office, took out his notepad, and started writing. "Uninspired as I felt," he later recounted, "I was surprised that in a short time, perhaps half an hour, I had set down certain principles which, on being counted, turned out to be twelve in number." It didn't take long to arrive at twelve because he chiseled those principles from the Oxford Group's existing four-part program.

Wilson massaged the Oxford Group's "Four Absolutes" and "Spiritual Activities" into what we now call the Twelve Steps. He dropped the Christian language, inserting in the final draft, "Power greater than ourselves" and "God as understand Him." Wilson scrapped the word "absolute" and

---

[14] Anonymous, *What is the Oxford Group?*, pgs 8-9, 1933, Oxford University Press

replaced "sin" with "shortcomings" and "character defects." These edits relieved the program of rigidity and religiosity.

Next, Wilson fleshed out the practical details, which enlarged the list. "Sharing our sins and temptations with another Christian life" became Steps Four and Five respectively. "Restitution" was divided into Eight and Nine. Then, he added Step Ten to overscore the process, stating in no uncertain terms that this is a ceaseless way of life, not a curriculum from which one graduates. After that, "listening to God's guidance" was recast as Step Eleven's *improving our conscious contact through prayer and meditation.* Finally, "carrying that guidance out in everything we do" was rendered "practice these principles in all of our affairs," which he joined with selfless service in the twelfth Step. In this way, Bill and his alcoholic colleagues carved Twelve *spiritual but not religious* Steps out of the prototype provided by their Christian forerunners.

The Schism

Alcoholics Anonymous' debt to the Oxford Group is considerable, but it is important to remember that they parted ways for a reason. The Oxford Group was a Christian evangelical movement at heart. Yes, their "faith without works" approach was adaptable to a non-Christian audience, but the Twelve Steps are innately non-religious. They are not a Christian path that others must adapt to; the Steps are an independent program of action to which religion must adapt. In other words, A.A.'s program is amenable to Christianity, just as it is amenable to Buddhism, Judaism, Islam, Hinduism, and Humanism. The Steps are entirely unaffiliated, which makes them accessible to more suffering alcoholics. Accessibility, not conversion, was the main objective of Bill and Bob. Thus, their work subverted the Oxford Group's agenda.

For example, the Oxford Group practiced witnessing. This witnessing amounted to "sharing with others the main reasons and the concrete results of surrender to God."[15] Oxford Group house parties gave members a space to share these reasons and results with others. When members spoke, they set their experience in a Christian context, just as Buchman framed his in Keswick. Christianity was their common denominator. They gathered to support each other in their efforts to live a higher Christian life. This was not true for A.A.'s co-founders. They were there to recover from alcoholism.

Bill and Bob shared their struggles with alcohol when they "witnessed" at Oxford Group meetings, as did their followers. Non-alcoholic Oxford Groupers tried in vain to relate. The alcoholics knew from personal experience that talking powerlessness, not God, was the best way to secure the trust of another alcoholic. It is part of A.A.'s origin story, dating back to Dr. Silkworth's parting advice to Bill—advice that turned Wilson's encounter with Dr. Bob into an international fellowship of recovering alcoholics. However practical the advice was for the alcoholics, it put them at odds with the Oxford Group. It undermined their meeting format. This subversion frustrated mainstays, and understandably so.

---

[15] Anonymous, *What is the Oxford Group?*, 1933, Oxford University Press

The Oxford Group was a Christian movement with Christian objectives that Bill Wilson was trying to repurpose.

Bill and Bob favored a meeting format that facilitated recovery, not religion. The alcoholics were frustrated by the periods of quiet time and the testimony that dominated Oxford Group house meetings. They were not personally opposed to prayer or quiet time, and certainly not God or spirituality. They just had different objectives and prioritized all of this differently.

"I don't think we should talk too much about religion or God," Bill and Bob confessed to Henrietta Seiberling. Henrietta's son, John Seiberling, served sixteen years in the U.S. House of Representatives. He taped his mother's account of A.A.'s early history and entered the transcript into the Congressional record in 1973. The transcript records this exchange between A.A.'s co-founders and Henrietta. When Bill and Bob questioned all the God-talk at Oxford Group meetings, she shot back, "Well, we're not out to please the alcoholics! They have been pleasing themselves all these years. We are out to please God. And if you don't talk about what God does, and your faith, and your guidance, then you might as well be the Rotary Club." This sharp-tongued response reveals the grievances non-alcoholic Oxford Groupers in Akron and New York lodged against their alcoholic counterparts.

Another impasse was the absolute value Christian belief possessed in Oxford Group culture. Since the Oxford Group was a Christian movement, Christian tenets were non-negotiable. The Twelve Steps, on the other hand, are organized around recovery. Thus, beliefs hold no absolute value. They are measured by the effects produced. This practical standard clashed with the evangelical culture in Oxford Groups house parties, which exhibited less ecumenism than did Rev. Shoemaker. Bill and Bob's pragmatic perspective further divided the two groups.

The Twelve Steps join Dr. James Leuba who, in *Varieties of Religious Experience,* William James quotes as saying, "God is not known, he is not understood; he is used. If he proves himself useful, the religious consciousness asks for no more than that. 'Does God really exist? How does he exist? What is he?' are so many irrelevant questions. Not God, but life, more life, a larger, richer, more satisfying life, is, in the last analysis, the end of religion."[16] This sentiment squares perfectly with the Twelve Steps, particularly Step Two, which sees belief as a means to an end, namely the restoration of sanity. For this reason, the pragmatics of William James, particularly the presentation in *Varieties,* exhibits more influence over the function of belief in the Twelve Steps than does the Oxford Group.

Bill and Bob were always respectful of Oxford Group norms. Although, the same couldn't be said of all their compatriots. As the ring of sober alcoholics widened, so did the disunity between the two camps. New alcoholic members felt no personal loyalty to the likes of Henrietta because they joined the group through Bill, Bob, and in some cases, second and third-generation alcoholics. They ignored the group's wishes and talked recovery over religion. In response, Oxford

---

[16] William James, *Varieties of Religious Experience,* pg 497, 1929

Group leaders in Akron and New York extended the duration of quiet time to smother the excessive talk of alcoholism with silence. Before long, Oxford Group mainstays viewed Bill's work with suspicion. Even his closest friends tried to sabotage his movement.

Bill's ally and mentor, Sam Shoemaker, later admitted to undermining his efforts. "If you ever write the story of A.A.'s early connection with Calvary, I think it ought to be said in all honesty that we were coached in the feeling that you were off on your own spur, trying to do something by yourself, and out of the mainstream of the work," he confessed. Though not mentioned, it's hard to imagine anyone other than Buchman coaching Shoemaker, the Oxford Group's North American leader.

Another one of those "coached" was the associate pastor at Calvary who, in 1937, delivered a sermon about "the divergent work of a secret, ashamed sub-group."[17] This sermon proved to be the straw that broke the camel's back. It convinced Wilson that the time had come to take his "sub-group" and their "divergent work" elsewhere. Soon thereafter, work began on the book *Alcoholics Anonymous*.

The Weight of Controversy

Other factors also contributed to the split. Buchman and his close followers saw themselves as "Holy Crusaders in modern dress," and their crusade became increasingly well dressed. Over the years, Buchman focused more and more on heads of

---

[17] Ernest Kurtz, *Not-God: A History of Alcoholics Anonymous*, pg 45, 1991

state and magnates, and less on average people. The practice of converting persons of influence was always part of Buchman's repertoire but by the 1930s and 40s, his reputation afforded him audiences with titans of industry and preeminent politicians. His proximity to power transformed the Oxford Group into a quasi-non-governmental organization hell bent on establishing a "New World Order for Christ, the King."[18]

"We know that until God is the deciding factor in the negotiations for Peace among Nations, the League of Nations will remain earth-bound," a widely circulated Oxford Group pamphlet read. "Practical Christianity is the only possible solution to the economic and peace problems of the world. There is no other solution."[19] This naïve take on politics and human nature suggests the Oxford Group is humanity's last hope and effectively designates Buchman as God's promised vicar. This sort of nonsense won the Oxford Group notable critics, like Reinhold Niebuhr.

Reinhold Niebuhr was a prominent theologian and towering intellectual in 20th century America. Niebuhr condemned Buchman and his followers for running "to Geneva, the seat of the League of Nations," to "Prince Starhemberg," "Hitler," and to "any seat of power" in search of converts. The idea Niebuhr condemns, "is that if the man of power can be converted God will be able to control a larger area of human life through his power than if a little man were converted."[20] Niebuhr thought Buchman was trying to save

---

[18] *What is the Oxford Group?*, 1933, Oxford University Press

[19] Ibid

[20] Reinhold Niebuhr, *Christianity and Power Politics*, pg 160, 1969

the world "by bringing the people who control the world under God-control." This effort, however, was a thinly-veiled ruse. More accurately, Buchman wanted to bring the world under Oxford Group control, which was a front for his control, and Niebuhr knew it.

The great German theologian and Nazi dissident, Dietrich Bonhoeffer, offered a similar critique. He said that Buchman's "naïve" attempts to convert Hitler were grounded in a "laughable" misunderstanding of German politics: "It is we who ought to be converted, not Hitler."[21]

Dating back to his days at the Philadelphia hospice, Buchman sought total control. When events did not unfold favorably, he reacted petulantly. Now the religious leader was grasping at power, real power, and with each lunge, the controversy grew. He twice attended the annual Nazi rally in Nuremberg, Germany. One journal from the period has him "heiling Hitler" after an hour.[22] He also attended the Berlin Olympics in 1936, where he dined with Heinrich Himmler, the leader of the SS.[23] On two occasions, he unsuccessfully sought a meeting with Hitler. In interviews, he appeared to be either adoring of the German Führer or attempting to win him over with praise. Neither was a good look, and he was labeled a Nazi sympathizer.

If the Oxford Group "would content itself with preaching repentance to drunkards and adulterers one might be willing

---

[21] Eberhard Bethge, *Dietrich Bonhoeffer: A Biography*, pg 358, 2000

[22] Henry Williamson, *Goodbye West Country,* pg 247, 1938

[23] Garth Lean, *Frank Buchman: A Life,* pg 239

to respect it as a religious revival method which knows how to confront the sinner with God," Niebuhr wrote. Needless to say, Buchman did not heed his advice. Bill Wilson did, however.

A.A.'s "singleness of purpose" institutionalized the renowned theologian's counsel. In Alcoholics Anonymous, Niebuhr saw none of the "decadent individualism" he decried in the Oxford Group movement; rather he praised A.A. for their achievements, which he believed "tremendous both in the history of religion and in the history of therapeutic medicine." He was especially impressed with the way A.A. uses "people who have themselves come through the experience of alcoholism to help other people" because "it prevents self-righteousness which so frequently, mars the life of Christians."[24] Reinhold Niebuhr's contribution to Alcoholics Anonymous and Twelve Step spirituality does not stop with a few flattering lines, however. He also authored the *de facto* prelude to Twelve Step meetings heard around the world, the "Serenity Prayer."

The Impasse of Anonymity

Buchman claimed to be interested in people, not numbers. This claim is difficult to reconcile with his pursuit of power and celebrity, as well as his love of the limelight. This criticism isn't restricted to Frank Buchman's personality. It is part of the Oxford Group's structure. Its members were encouraged to seek out influential people. This vulgar

---

[24] Reinhold Niebuhr, "A.A. Grapevine," June 1960

evangelism did not square with the needs of their alcoholic detachment. It forced them to part ways with the Oxford Group.

Buchman's public controversies certainly widened the rift, but the biggest obstacle to reconciliation was the Oxford Group's brand of evangelism. Their pyramid-like outreach scheme presented unique problems for rehabbing drunks. Recovering alcoholics treasure anonymity because alcoholism is heavily stigmatized. This stigma was especially harsh in the early 20th century. Alcoholic members of the Oxford Group wanted to secure gainful employment, guard their families against ridicule, and protect what good reputation they had left. Running around town professing themselves drunks, especially to prominent people, as the Oxford Group would have them do, was not in their best interest. This policy forced their hand. They had no future in the Oxford Group. The only option was to break away and form a new movement that protected their anonymity.

The Way Out

Alcoholics Anonymous was published in 1939. This text came to be known as the A.A. "Big Book" because of its girth, not its biblical-like importance to the movement. The fellowship takes its name from the book, which is fitting because without the book there is no fellowship. The fellowship, Alcoholics Anonymous, is unified by the text, *Alcoholics Anonymous*. The book outlined a solution they could all agree upon. It provided them with "a way out" of both alcoholic despair and the Oxford Group. Interestingly enough, the book was nearly titled *The Way Out*.

Years later, Wilson formulated "Twelve Traditions" that serve as guiding principles for the A.A. organization. Aldous Huxley believed these Traditions were Wilson's highest accomplishment, calling him "the greatest social architect of the 20th century." In effect, these Traditions inverted the Oxford Group power structure, concentrating power in the membership. The Oxford Group never eclipsed the personality of their controversial leader; whereas A.A.'s Traditions guaranteed that no individual, not even Wilson, would rise above the whole.

A.A. is not a self-help group, as is often thought. It is a mutual-aid organization. In the first of his Twelve Traditions, Wilson identifies "unity" as the fellowship's foundation: "Our common welfare should come first; personal recovery depends upon A.A. unity." The individual depends upon the group, so unity is of paramount importance. Groups are unified by a common purpose. The fifth Tradition states A.A.'s purpose: "Each group has but one primary purpose—to carry its message to the alcoholic who still suffers."

The *Big Book's* message brings A.A. groups together. "We have *a way out* on which we can absolutely agree and upon which we can join in brotherly and harmonious action," Wilson writes in *Alcoholics Anonymous*. "This is the great news this book carries to those who suffer from alcoholism."[25] A.A. takes its primary purpose from the pages of *Alcoholics Anonymous*.

---

[25] Bill Wilson, *Alcoholics Anonymous,* pg 17, 1939

Alcoholics Anonymous supplied its namesake with the unity and purpose required to wean off its parent organization. The message therein contained the hard-earned wisdom of the first class of men and women to recover. Yes, Bill Wilson authored the *Big Book*, but it was a collaborative project that included input from those around him. The collective wisdom found in *Alcoholics Anonymous* and the "Twelve Traditions" is a product of trial and error. They knew that leading with powerlessness was key to gaining the confidence of newcomers because preaching failed to gain them the confidence of anyone. They learned the hard way that kinship in suffering always precedes a shared solution. This insight is the most basic unit of knowledge in Twelve Step culture. Without it, Bill and Bob's initial meeting lasts only fifteen minutes, and there is no fellowship.

Sales of *Alcoholics Anonymous* were scarce for two years. Then, Jack Alexander's catalytic article in the *Saturday Evening Post* introduced A.A. to the general public and the book began its assent to over thirty-million sold. One of the few who purchased an early copy was Dr. Dilworth Lupton, a Unitarian minister in Ohio. He immediately saw the Twelve Steps as a remarkable contribution to the spirituality of humankind.

"Beauty knows no particular age or school. Beauty is never exclusive and provincial; it is inclusive and universal," Dilworth observed. "So, too, in the field of religion. We are beginning to recognize the substantial unity of all religious faiths. Back of all religions is religion itself. This universality of religion is recognized by Alcoholics Anonymous. Their meetings are attended by Catholics, Protestants, Jews, near-agnostics, and near-atheists," Lupton said in November of 1939. "Perhaps these laymen in Alcoholics Anonymous are laying foundations for a new universal movement in religion."

It is difficult to argue with Dr. Lupton's assessment. In the Twelve Steps, we see the "foundations for a new universal movement in religion," a system of spiritual practice characterized by pluralism and pragmatism, rather than dogmatism.

Dr. Lupton's remarks come from a sermon he delivered at the Unitarian Church in Cleveland entitled, "Mr. X and Alcoholics Anonymous." Mr. X is his friend, Clarence Snyder, one of Dr. Bob's many protégés. In May of 1939, one month after the book was published, Snyder announced his resignation from the Oxford Group and organized the first meeting under the heading "Alcoholics Anonymous." Clarence did not start A.A. as he liked to claim. He did, however, finalize the divorce, taking the name for his splinter group from the text upon which it was founded.

The conflicting interests of the Oxford Group and what was to become Alcoholics Anonymous were immediately apparent. Over the years this gulf widened, resulting in a clean break. The publication of *Alcoholics Anonymous* set forth the ideas, principles, and practices that distinguished Twelve Step spirituality from the Oxford Group. This book enabled Snyder to start *a meeting* in Cleveland and take for its name "Alcoholics Anonymous," but both the fellowship and the program predate Snyder's efforts. Those seeds were planted when Henrietta Seiberling introduced Bill W. to Dr. Bob in June of 1935.

10 BIG CHUNKS OF TRUTH

"No man's really any good till he knows how bad he is, or might be; till he's realised exactly how much right he has to all this snobbery, and sneering, and talking about 'criminals,' as if they were apes in a forest ten thousand miles away; till he's got rid of all the dirty self-deception of talking about low types and deficient skulls; till he's squeezed out of his soul the last drop of the oil of the Pharisees; till his only hope is somehow or other to have captured one criminal, and kept him safe and sane under his own hat." ~ G.K.Chesterton

"I got dressed up, fixed my hair, and put on some cologne, before going to my first A.A. meeting," a long-time member of A.A. recalled. "The meeting was at a clubhouse. There must have been thirty or forty people there. I obviously spent more time getting ready for the meeting than anyone else. It was very casual. Not at all like church, which is what I expected. I weaved through the crowd, found an empty seat, and sat there quietly waiting for the meeting to start."

> "Finally, the speaker took the podium. He opened the meeting with the Serenity Prayer, which I knew was coming from TV and movies. When the prayer was over, I noticed a large, framed copy of the Twelve Steps on the wall behind him. Oblivious to the speaker, I analyzed each:
> 'Step One: Admitted we were powerless over alcohol—that our lives had become unmanageable?'
> 'Yeah, of course,' I thought. 'That's why I am here! Done with Step One.'
> Then, I proceeded to Step Two. 'Sure, I believe in God'—after all, I was raised in the Church. This was easy, so I kept going.
> 'Turn my will and life over to God?' Come on....I've been baptized for years—next!
> Then, came Step Four: 'Made a searching and fearless moral inventory of ourselves.' And there my sprint through the Twelve Steps came to a halt."

The aversion to Step Four reported in this story is quite common. Steps One, Two, and Three imply action. Bill labors this point in his commentary on each. However, this is not obvious to the unstudied mind reading them off a placard. At first glance, they appear to be propositions, not principles, and therefore demand consent, not practice. Step Four is immune to such confusion.

Step Four trades purely in an economy of action. There is no idea to affirm, no belief to profess, and no theory to ponder. It is all business. The measure of progress is self-evident: Have you completed a moral inventory or not?

Inaction is the surest guarantor of the *status quo*. Step Four is disinterested in our excuses, philosophical ramblings, or pie-in-the-sky rhetoric. Here, our head-spun rationalizations collide with the testimony of our still-capped pen and empty notebook. The blank pages blunt the force of self-deception. They refute the claim, "I want a more meaningful life and am willing to work for it." For this reason, Wilson says, Step Four is the "first *tangible* evidence of our complete willingness to move forward."[1]

The Will to a Higher Power

Step Three invites us to turn our will and life over to a Higher Power. This directive is not uncommon. People frequently advise friends and family, "Let go, give it to God." The question is, "How? How do I turn my will and life over to God?" The Steps, beginning with Four, answer that question. The fourth Step is the first item on Step Three's to-do list.

"Turn it over to God" is not a vague platitude in Twelve Step spirituality. It is a call to action—a procedure consisting of personal inventory, moral introspection, restitution, prayer, and meditation. Step Three proposes turning our will and life over to a Higher Power, but you cannot turn over what you do not possess. Personal inventory takes possession of our thoughts and actions.

---

[1] Bill Wilson, *Twelve Steps and Twelve Traditions*, pg 54, 1953

In *Alcoholics Anonymous,* Step Three ends and Four begins, when Wilson writes, "Being convinced that self, manifested in various ways, was what had defeated us, we considered its common manifestations." In Step Three, we find a model of ego, which is comprised of self-centered perception and selfish action. Step Four applies this model to the details of *our* life.

A mere theory of ego is not sufficient. We must identify the ways ego influences our will and life, which is to say our thoughts, words, and deeds. Step Four inventories these influences. It indexes the patterns of self-centered perception and selfish behavior that form our character defects, which Steps Six and Seven forfeit.

The transition from Three to Four may be simple, but it is not easy. This transition isn't made until pen is in hand, and often that pen weighs a thousand pounds. This thousand-pound pen is the dead weight of a psychological toddler going boneless in protest.

The first three Steps do not vanquish the ego. It is alive and well when we arrive at Step Four. Needless to say, ego isn't a connoisseur of self-reflection. It is programmed to look at everyone and everything, except itself. Moreover, selfishness and self-centeredness are modes of perception and behavior coded by immediate gratification. The ego takes one look at a "searching and fearless moral inventory" and exclaims, "No thank you!" And it is unreasonable to expect anything else.

The problem is ego. The solution is spiritual practice. We cannot expect the problem to subside before the solution is applied. Therefore, we have to complete our inventory in spite of ego's protestations. We can't wait for ego to fancy a fourth Step because that day isn't coming. The ego is not going to examine itself. We have to find motivation elsewhere.

The ego is not going to sign off on acts of transcendence because it is the object that spiritual practice seeks to transcend. We must price this fact into our spirituality. Ego's resistance is the primary obstacle to spiritual practice. As such, it is one of the practical objectives that we have to measure our conception of God against: Does our Higher Power actually overpower ego? Does it provide us with a higher order motivation that encourages us to proceed with the process?

Experience is a result of experimentation and practice. So reason will have to supply our inspiration on the frontend, not experience. The rationale may be religious: "The Steps can bring closer to God and help me live in accord with His will." It might also be humanistic: "I want to live a deeper, more principled life, and not realize on my deathbed that I have not lived at all." In either case, it probably includes a little self-interest: "I do not want to suffer. I owe it to myself and my family to live the best life I can." Whatever the rationale, it must extend a line of motivational credit.

The initial deposit of inspiration is only seed money. It is not a long-term solution. This burst of inspiration provides us with just enough capital to launch our venture. Spiritual experience purchases the inspiration needed to make a lifelong journey. But we have to invest action before we can expect to see a return. We have to do what we do not want to do, namely examine ourselves.

Self-Examination as the Way Out

At first, there is little chance of *wanting* to do a fourth Step. Searching and fearless moral inventories just aren't fun. However, "wanting" is not a prerequisite of action. We don't have to want to do something before we can do it; that is a false notion belonging to ego. And it is this *wanting* that binds us to ego. A selfish person, simply, is someone who cannot turn away from what they want or into what they do not. When we act contrary to the wishes of ego, we step outside the envelope of self into the unknown. This is how we encounter a Power greater than ourselves. Each step away from ego is one in the direction of a Higher Power.

The self-centered mind is fenced in by fear and expectation. These base motivations make our life superficial and claustrophobic. We transcend ego when we act in accord with higher order principles. These principles lead us into uncharted territory. For this reason, willingness is indispensable.

People often portray the fourth Step as the bogeyman, which is understandable. "Moral," "fearless," and "searching" are scare words to many. On the other hand, the fourth Step is frequently described (in retrospect) as liberating and redeeming. People fear it on the front-end but sing its praises in hindsight. Why?

Suffering brings us to spirituality, but no one commits themselves to a transformative path of action because they had a bad day. Suffering is a process, not an event. It is the cyclic nature of suffering that delivers us to the path. We are bogged down and willing to do anything to get out. The fourth Step is liberating because it shows us the way out. It directs our attention to where we have been most neglectful.

Blame and projection are standard features of ego. As a result, the self-centered mind is hyper-focused on the faults of others. This extroverted gaze focuses on what we can't control. Self-centeredness is, therefore, disempowering. The Dalai Lama once said, "Being aware of a single shortcoming within yourself is far more useful than being aware of a thousand in someone else." The faults of others, whether they be real or fancied, lie outside our jurisdiction. We can't do anything about them. When we fixate on what we cannot control, we spin our wheels in misery.

It might feel stuck, but "stuck" is actually an illusion. Honest self-appraisal shatters this illusion. The Dalai Lama's adage is true because our flaws are workable. When we discover a single shortcoming in ourselves, we discover an opportunity to grow. We find a stepping stone, a lifeline, something to pull ourselves up from the pit of despair. For this reason, those who approach Steps Four and Five with trepidation, sing its praises in retrospect.

"We thought 'conditions' drove us to drink, and when we tried to correct these conditions and found that we couldn't to our entire satisfaction, our drinking went out of hand and we became alcoholics," explains Wilson. We can substitute "drink" for any number of bedevilments and watch as the same story unfolds. Attempts to quell stress, fear, or anger with countermeasures like sex, shopping, or ice cream are bound to end where they began: Frustrated by the suffering we set out to remedy. "It never occurred to us that we needed to change ourselves to meet conditions, whatever they were."[2]

Obstacles are the Path

In Plato's *Apology,* Socrates famously states that "the unexamined life is not worth living." It's not that we find worth in the examination of ourselves, but that the process of examination promotes consistency between character and action, which cultivates self-worth. In short, when we are true to our Self, self-worth follows. Hence the Twelve Step slogan, "Self-esteem is the result of esteemable acts."

Being true to your Self is the way of contentment. It is the defining characteristic of what the Greeks called *eudemonia,* "the good life." We cannot, however, do right by something we are ignorant of, so self-examination is essential to a meaningful life.

The happiness we seek evades us because it is too often dependent upon the world complying with our demands. Arranging the world to our liking is an impossible task. We can identify every fault in others and tirelessly try to correct

---

[2] Bill Wilson, *Twelve Steps and Twelve Traditions*, pg 47, 1953

them, but fail to make even an inch of progress. This fool's errand creates the illusion that we are stuck. However, if we identify one fault within ourselves, we begin to make progress, because in that fault we find something we can change.

Surprisingly, true happiness is found where we refuse to look, namely in our faults. When the mind that is obsessed with the defects of others turns inward, it sees more than just flaws. It sees potential. Our flaws differ from the faults of others because they are in our jurisdiction. They are workable. There are possibilities hidden within them, so when we look upon our faults with a constructive gaze, we see hope, rather than despair.

Shortcomings are areas where we fail to bring forth the fullness of our person. The gulf separating our true life and the life we are living is the realm of potentiality. Spiritual practice invades this space with the aim of actualizing that potential.

The basic structure of spirituality is generic. The facts of our life fill the mold. When we identify a shortcoming, we disclose the next leg of our journey, which is an interior trek to the summit of our highest Self. We reach this peak in those moments lived honestly and completely. The fourth Step outlines the path before us by inventorying our shortcomings.

Step Four is a kind of spiritual cartography. It maps out our path. Stress, insecurity, fear, and anger are not obstacles to the path; they are the path. "What stands in the way becomes the way," says the philosopher-king Marcus

Aurelius. What is spirituality but the effort to be more open-minded, patient, loving, and ethical? Where should our efforts be focused, if not where we are narrow-minded, intolerant, resentful, and self-serving?

Spirituality is just daydreaming without introspection. Shortcomings are the only opportunities we get to practice spirituality. Where there is no account of our faults, there is no path, only theory—and we cannot advance on a virtual path.

Moreover, we cannot advance from an imagined starting place. It does us no good to pretend we are further along than we are. Pretending we're above stress, fear, and anger does not bring peace, courage, and compassion; only the burden of concealing these shortcomings from ourselves and others. We sell ourselves short when we purport to be above the fray. This is arrogance pretending to be maturity. We have to start where we are, and the fourth Step pinpoints our location.

Writing Off Blame

The fourth Step is a formal exercise that aims to install the habit of self-reflection. The columns, categories, and specific questions found in Step Four are necessary for a couple of reasons. First, they get at the causes of our discontentment, shining light on the conditions our addictions seek to remedy.

The fourth Step reveals ego's strategies for what they are: Jerry-rigged coping mechanisms. This insight deflates the force of craving and paints the addiction as an immature exercise in futility. In the short-term, this makes it easier to forsake temptation. In the long-run, it informs a healthy and direct response to suffering.

Finally, Step Four's rigid structure wards off blame. It keeps ego at bay, forcing the mind to adopt the habit of self-inquiry. This habit comes in two waves, immersion and repetition. Step Four is the immersive wave. It is a comprehensive personal inventory that scours our past for overdue resentments. This approach not only supplies us with a long list of unresolved grievances but guides us to healthy resolutions. It helps us work through each of our identified faults, one after the other, planting the seeds of self-reflection. The tenth Step uses repetition to ingrain the principles of introspection. It is a daily effort to be more self-aware and less inclined to blame others.

Blame is disempowering. It projects our shortcomings onto others. Since our shortcomings are where we find room to grow, we reject our potential when we blame others. Moreover, this untapped potential is the inner resource that blossoms into an experience of our Higher Power. Therefore, blame denies the possibility of a Higher Power. When blame puts our responsibilities onto others, it places our well-being in the hands of others, effectively making them our higher power.

"Where other people were concerned," says Wilson, "we had to drop the word 'blame' from our speech and thought."[3]

---

[3] Ibid, pg 47

Blame might be disempowering, but it is a powerful habit. The mind reverts back to this habit unless tethered to spiritual principles. The fourth Step's format is no mere formality. It is our leash.

Step Four wrests blame from ego's hands by leaving no room for finger pointing. It turns the page into a mirror that reflects only our insecurity, stress, fear, anger, and resentment—those elements that cut us off from "the sunlight of the spirit." In this way, the format imposes a selfless angle. It insists on a viewpoint larger than ego, binding us to principles that are greater than our fears and expectations.

The Steps do not establish contact with a Higher Power. They make us conscious of the built-in point of contact at the center of our being. In other words, they *restore* us to our original condition. As the clouds of selfishness and self-centeredness part, the brilliant light of conscious contact shines forth. We do not have to seduce God with worship or manufacture a Higher Power out of highfalutin theology. God is a self-emergent experience. It arises when the mind is free of egoic debris, which begins with clearing away the wreckage of our past. In this way, Twelve Step spirituality resurrects God-consciousness.

How to do a Fourth Step

Step Four consists of three inventories: resentment, fear, and sex. Each section asks specific questions. The following commentary elaborates on these questions. When doing a fourth Step, honesty and thoroughness are what count. It is all for nothing if the final product is lazy or if it willfully withholds information. There is no need to be obsessive-compulsive about the style or appearance of your inventory; that your efforts are exhaustive and sincere is more important.

Bill offers two formats. Since a user-friendly layout comprised of simple questions and only enough space to answer those questions directly best facilitates an honest, thoroughgoing inventory, the format Bill outlines in the book *Alcoholics Anonymous* is preferable to the one offered in *Twelve Steps and Twelve Traditions*. The latter method is ambiguous and meandering; whereas the former is clear and concise. For this reason, we will utilize the format found in *Alcoholics Anonymous*.

Inventory One: Resentment

The Steps are concerned with cultivating practical knowledge about everything from God to ego. They are focused on the reality underlying spiritual terms, the point where these terms meet with our experience. Consequently, Wilson's model of ego in Step Three is followed by the directive in Four to "consider its [ego model] common manifestations." The fourth Step is looking for evidence of ego in our life. According to Wilson, resentment is the "number one" symptom of ego, so this is where our moral inventory begins.[4]

Resentment is commonly thought to be synonymous with animosity. This is only half-true. In resentment, there is always fear and in fear, resentment. Resentment isn't just

---

[4] Bill Wilson, *Alcoholics Anonymous*, pg 64, 1939

aggressive, it is also oppressive. Resentment prohibits a full and honest life. As a result, there is pent-up energy, which festers until it becomes putrid. This rot often takes the shape of animus that is projected onto the supposed oppressor, but not always. It may also take the form of depression, envy, arrogance, lust, gluttony, or shame. What appears to be resentment on the surface is always rooted in fear.

Longevity is another trait that sets resentment apart from garden-variety anger. Resentment has a long lifespan. It is *re-sent* information. The extroverted orientation of ego ignores the underlying causes, blaming *others* for *our* disturbances. When we ignore the causes, the conditions persist. Consequently, we chew on our grievances for days, weeks, and months on end. In effect, we practice animosity until ill-will becomes a habit of mind. This habit is called resentment. To make matters worse, resentment participates in future acts of perception, distorting our view of reality. The ghosts of our past haunt the present moment.

We resent some people before we meet them. They exhibit traits that once offended us, so they are lumped into adversarial categories that predate our initial encounter with them. A person raised by a controlling mother may, for example, become infuriated with bossy people, even if that person is their boss. The resentment does not see them as someone charged with managing the workplace. It sees a controlling mother, which causes problems in an adult world.

Perceptible anger does not always accompany resentment. Resentment can also manifest as a subtle aversion to certain types of people. Someone raised by a stepfather who was excessively attentive to details may later find that quality repulsive in others, fating them to suffer relationships with inattentive partners. These are admittedly manufactured examples meant to demonstrate resentment's versatility. It would take volumes to catalog resentment's many faces, which is beyond the scope of this book. For our purposes, it is enough to know that resentment is a shape-shifting apparition from our past that continues to spook us. With this working definition, we can begin to catalog our resentments.

The resentment inventory begins with a simple prayer, something to the effect of: "May whatever needs to be included on this inventory come to mind." Next, we grab a pen, a notebook, and start writing.

On the left side, make a vertical column under the heading "Who" (it may help to turn the notebook sideways). In this column, list everyone toward whom you hold a resentment. A good rule of thumb is to trust that if the name pops up, it deserves to be on the list. In retrospect grudges often seem frivolous, but hindsight is twenty-twenty, and resentments are never formed with clear vision. When the resentment was born, we were afraid and angry, which distorts our perception. Our account may sound ridiculous now, but at the time in question, we took it seriously. We are not here to retroactively judge our resentments. We are here to catalog them. If it rises to the surface, include it and its rationale, no matter how silly. Also, there is no statute of limitations on resentment. It may be five days old, five years old, or from when you were five years old. If it pops up, put it down. Write every name that comes to mind.

Who:
1) Mom
2) The Church
3) Any person, place, or institution you resent

The first column includes people, places, and institutions—basically, any resented noun. Resenting an institution, such as the Church, means carrying a perception based on the past, or our interpretation of the past, that bars us from impartially appraising the Church. Electing not to participate in Church life is not indicative of prejudice. An inability to acknowledge the Church's good works, on the other hand, does indicate resentment because it is a bias that prevents us from fairly calling balls and strikes.

Once the left column is completed, add another to the immediate right entitled, "The Cause." The second column is where we list the stated reasons for the resentments indexed in the first. We do not need a detailed account of what happened. The simpler, the better. This column is not asking for rationalizations, revisionist histories, or diary entries. A concise, honest, contemporaneous version of the grievance will suffice. Go down the list and for each resentment indexed in column one, briefly state the cause in column two.

Who:	The Cause:
1) Mom	Ran over my bike
2) The Church	Everyone was judgmental

Next, we list the effects of each. Resentment is a dead giveaway ego was involved. If ego was offended, it's because some need or desire went unfulfilled. There was an expectation—justified or not—that was not satisfied. For example, the desire to be recognized and accepted by our peers, when unmet, can leave personal and sexual relationships frustrated. In the third column, titled "Affects My," we record the impact of the events in column two; how they affected us at that time.

Who:	The Cause:	Affects My:
1) Mom	Ran over my bike	Self-esteem, security (fear)
2) The Church	Everyone was judgmental	Personal relations, ambitions (fear)

The first three columns reveal nothing new. We have long known the wrongs perpetrated against us, as well as their ill effects. We have been humming that tune for years, which is the problem. We are a broken record, singing the same ole' sad song. The power of the fourth Step resides in the next column.

"To conclude that others were wrong was as far as most of us ever got," and that isn't far enough. The wrongs of others, real or imagined, are beyond our reach. As long as we are focused on what we cannot change, we remain chained to our suffering, so "we turned back to the list, for it held the key to the future," says Wilson. "We were prepared to look at it from an entirely different angle."

We find liberation in the fourth column because it asks the all-important question: "Where am I to blame?" "Putting out of our minds the wrongs others had done, we resolutely looked for our own mistakes. Where had we been selfish, dishonest, self-seeking and frightened? Though a situation had not been entirely our fault, we tried to disregard the other person involved entirely. Where were we to blame?"[5] This is where we find freedom and power. Add this fourth and final column to the right under the heading, "Where am I to Blame?"

Who:	The Cause:	Affects My:	Where am I to blame?
1) Mom	Ran over my bike	Self-esteem, security (fear)	I left my bike behind her car. I relied on my bike to fit in, gain acceptance and approval from others.
2) The Church	Everyone was judgmental	Personal relations, ambitions (fear)	I only assumed they were judging me. I was judgmental of them. Eventually, I started gossiping and stirring the pot.

In the final column, we answer the question, "Where was I selfish, dishonest, self-seeking or frightened?" Freedom and happiness escape us because they are found where we refuse

---

[5] Bill Wilson, *Alcoholics Anonymous*, pgs 66-67, 1939

to look. When we identify and accept our shortcomings, they become workable. Insight transforms our suffering into potential, and if we follow through with the work ahead, suffering proves redemptive. The fourth Step initiates this phase change by bringing our attention back to ourselves.

The question "Where am I to blame?" works on two levels. It deals with the historical event and the mind-state. At the historical level, the question is answered, "I left my bike behind her car." I can't blame mom for running over my bike because I left it there. It's my fault. Simple enough. Similarly, we see that it is not the Church we resent, but judgmental people, and moreover, we resent them because we are subconsciously judgmental. These insights expose the blind spots that enable our resentments to persist.

Working Through Resentment

Resentments are mental states historically connected to events. The event is in the past, but the mental state is part of the mind's present configuration. We must see our faults at this level as well if we wish to live free of resentment. The question, "Where am I to blame?" must probe the mental state, not just the past event. In extreme cases, there is no other path to freedom.

Resentments live between our ears, and therefore can be laid at the feet of no one else. Others may have played a role in the historical event, but the mental state belongs entirely to us. Resentments are patterns of consciousness that outlive the circumstances that created them. Perhaps, they were justified at the time, but if they are listed here, it goes without saying that they've overstayed their welcome. They are a source of pain and suffering. Wilson alludes to this dimension of inventory work when he writes, "If somebody hurts us and we are sore, we are in the wrong also."[6] We have to remedy our soreness.

We delve into the mental state when we identify and examine the ongoing pattern. Take, for example, the "Mom" resentment above. The bike was not merely a means of transportation. It was an ego-prop, an accessory to some hypothetical ten-year-old's self-image. Consequently, the historical event negatively impacted "self-esteem, personal relations, and security." When the bike was run over, so too was the kid's ego. All this is typical of a ten-year-old. It is an innocuous example meant to demonstrate a deeper point. We see the essence of *re-sentment*, when we ask, "Do I still do that?" Obviously not with a bike, but with women, men, money, cars or clothes? "Do I improperly rely on external objects to finance self-esteem just as I relied upon the bike to gain acceptance and approval? If I fail to get what I want or later lose it, do I get upset? Does my ego get run over again?" If we answer "yes," then we have identified an immature pattern of consciousness—an area of our life where we failed to grow up. This is a resentment. Spirituality takes these shortcomings as the path. They are the potential spiritual practice cultivates.

In most cases, identifying our faults is good enough to make a beginning. We don't need to fret over the resentment's

---

[6] Bill Wilson, *Twelve Steps and Twelve Traditions,* pg 90, 1953

deeper layer. It is mentioned because there are extreme cases where distinguishing between mental states and physical events is critical on the first pass. When resentment is rooted in past trauma or abuse, it can be difficult to answer the question in the fourth column. For example, child abuse victims are not to blame. In fact, "Where am I to blame?" is an offensive question in the case of abuse. No child has ever caused an adult to abuse them. Ever. Therefore, we must rephrase the question. "Where am I to blame for the resentment itself—not the event but the enduring mind state?" Essentially we are asking ourselves, "Why do I continue to carry this around with me?"

It is easy to let go of unjustified resentments. When we see the foolishness of our grudges spelled out in black and white, they start melting away. On the other hand, when resentments are grounded in legitimate wrongdoing, they are difficult to dislodge. It is important to remember that resentment is toxic, whether it is legitimate or not. "Clinging to anger is like drinking poison and expecting the other person to die." Though often attributed to the Buddha, this little chestnut originated in Twelve Step circles, not Buddhist sutras.[7]

"No Scientific Christian ever considers hatred or execration to be 'justifiable' in any circumstances, but whatever your opinion about that might be, there is no question about its practical consequences to you. You might as well swallow a dose of Prussic acid in two gulps, and think

---

[7] Bodhipaksa, fakebuddhaquotes.com/holding-onto-anger-is-like-drinking-poison/, June 26, 2012

to protect yourself by saying, 'This one is for Robespierre; and this one for the Bristol murderer.' You will hardly have any doubt as to who will receive the benefit of the poison."[8] The pithier slogan, "anger is like drinking poison," comes from this mouthful, which is excerpted from *The Sermon on the Mount* by the renowned new-age preacher, Emmet Fox.

If there be any apocryphal text bordering on Twelve Step cannon, it is *The Sermon on the Mount*. This book still enjoys wide circulation in Twelve Step circles. Emmet Fox's teachings on God, love, and spiritual practice, particularly prayer, have curried favor with members of Alcoholics Anonymous ever since the founding generation. Many of the slogans commonplace in recovery culture, like "One Day at a Time," are distilled from his teachings. "Train yourself to be a man or woman who lives one day at a time," Fox says. "Live in today and do not allow yourself to live in the past under any pretense. Living in the past means thinking about the past, rehearsing past events, especially if you do this with feeling"—"rehearsing past events, especially with feeling" is essentially our definition of resentment, "re-sent information."[9]

Of all Fox's themes, Wilson was most interested in the notion that mind, when guided by spiritual principles, can heal the body. Though he did not take the mind-cure idea as far as Fox, Bill certainly thought it a useful metaphor for the relationship between alcoholism and spirituality, especially

---

[8] Emmet Fox, *The Sermon on the Mount*, pg 80, 1938

[9] Emmet Fox, *Stake Your Claim: Exploring the Gold Mine Within*, pgs 48-49, 1992

where resentment is concerned. The earlier quote from Wilson, "Resentment is the 'number one' offender," leads into AA's mind-cure theory: "It [resentment] destroys more alcoholics than anything else. From it stem all forms of spiritual disease, for we have been not only mentally and physically ill, we have been spiritually sick. When the spiritual malady is overcome, we straighten out mentally and physically."[10] Wilson thought resentment the pathogen that carries all manner of spiritual diseases. Justified or not, resentment infects and afflicts its host, not its target. This precept establishes the Twelve Step's uncompromising stance on resentment.

Everyone wants to be happy, and resentment obstructs happiness. It should, therefore, follow that victims of abuse want to be free of resentment. However, valid grievances are difficult to cast aside, even if they are known to cause suffering. Once again, pragmatism comes to our aid. "Are you right?" is a bad question. It misses the point, literally. Spirituality is not about being right. It's about happiness, contentment, well-being. "It is plain that a life which includes deep resentment leads only to futility and unhappiness," writes Wilson. "If we were to live, we had to be free of anger." The victim of abuse is right in their conviction, but they can be right in conviction and wrong in harboring resentment. The ensuing suffering verifies this claim. The question is, "How do we settle the grievance without justifying the misdeed?"

First, we have to see resentment's utility. We hold on to some resentments because they protect us against future

---

[10] Bill Wilson, *Alcoholics Anonymous,* pg 64, 1939

trespasses. Resentment creates a profile of the offense that includes the feeling of revulsion, which serves as a future deterrent. When the mind notices features peculiar to the original offense, revulsion is piqued. Disgust leads to aversion, thereby averting harm. Resentment is, first and foremost, a defense mechanism.

Next, we must see and accept that the resentment's usefulness has expired. Perhaps, as children, this response was helpful. A physically abused child, for example, learns to listen for slamming doors and raised voices because they are warnings to stay out of sight and out of mind. Though not ideal, the resentment was useful given the dire circumstances, but those circumstances have lapsed. We are no longer children. We are not helpless.

In an adult world, resentment breeds more conflict than it prevents. It drums up fear, anxiety, and animosity, which impair well-being and frustrate personal goals. Such fears moonlight as an aversion to conflict, which could be handicapping in a competitive workplace. It renders us overly agreeable, inhibiting our capacity to speak up and share our ideas. It silences us when we would rather offer a counterpoint, leaving us disheartened and bitter. Additionally, it sabotages our prospects of advancement. The resentment is no longer a means of self-defense. It is self-destructive.

Finally, we have to forgive the other person. This is where we typically run into a brick wall. Let me start by stating the obvious: Forgiveness is not an endorsement of the other person's behavior. Forgiveness does not reconstitute the merits of an action. Forgiveness is about healing.

Trauma leaves a psychological wound. Resentment is re-sent information. In the case of trauma, resentment is a pattern of thought and emotion rooted in the original wound. Every time the resentment is queued up, it resuscitates the offense it is intended to thwart, keeping the wound raw. Forgiveness isn't about redeeming the other person. It is about letting go of that aggravating train of thought. The other person is just a proxy, a symbol of the resentment. When we forgive them, we let go of the resentment and healing begins.

"Let go" is, perhaps, the most common bit of advice proffered, but scarcely is that counsel accompanied by instruction. When we are in distress, friends and therapists are quick to say, "You gotta let go of that," but seldom do they offer any practical guidance. This ambiguity leaves us with the impression that "letting go" is some kind of genie-like hocuspocus where, we close our eyes, nod our head, and abracadabra! We let go. Of course, this sort of magical thinking never works. So the question is how? How do we let go of resentment?

Bill Wilson is practical and succinct on this point: "This was our course: we realized that the people who wronged us were perhaps spiritually sick. We asked God to help us show them the same tolerance, pity, and patience that we would cheerfully grant a sick friend. When a person offended we said to ourselves, 'This is a sick man. How can I be helpful to him? God save me from being angry. Thy will be done.'"[11]

---

[11] Bill Wilson, *Alcoholics Anonymous,* pg 67, 1939

In the same vein, Buddhists employ a most helpful practice. They visualize the resented person and offer the following prayer: "May you be free of suffering and its causes; May you find the causes and conditions of happiness; I pray that you are never separated from peace and its causes." Don't let the simplicity of this practice fool you. It is simple but exceedingly difficult. It seems childishly unsophisticated, but visualizing an enemy and issuing well-wishes is harder than it sounds. The same applies to praying for those we resent. Healing is hard work.

Fear is the essence of resentment, and behind fear is suffering. The ego's knee-jerk reaction to suffering is always to pull away. Once again, this evacuation plan comes standard with resentment. It hardens us, making us guarded. Forgiveness is about dropping our guard. It is a practice of vulnerability, which is a strength building exercise. Forgiveness shows victims they are not broken; that they have not only survived, but can rise above their pain and suffering to find purpose in it.

These prayers are not magic spells. They need to be repeated for weeks, months, and maybe even years. A resentment rooted in the wrongdoing of others is deep-seated. It is difficult to rise above victimization, especially if you really are a victim. Justified or not, victimization is disempowering. It binds us to the causes of our suffering, endlessly rehearsing the offense. It takes time and effort to dislodge these entrenched mental and emotional habits. Some say, "I have forgiven them, but I refuse to pray for them or wish them happiness." A lack of willingness to pray for them or wish them well is proof against forgiveness. We can think and say what we will, but beneath that rhetoric is the complex of resentment: fear, anger, and aversion. These are the forces that diminish our willingness.

When we pray through the aversion, we unlearn the mind's fear-based reaction to adversaries. We simulate a selfless vantage point, cultivating a response characterized by courage, love, and tolerance. This effort carves out new pathways and installs real alternatives that we can practice in daily life. In this way, we embody a greater power and aspire to a higher point of view. When met by adversity, we can respond with patience, rather than anger. This is the promised transformation.

It is also worth mentioning that some of us may benefit from therapy. If we try in earnest the path above and find that the resentment persists, then perhaps we should enlist the services of a skillful and understanding professional. Seeking assistance is not a sign of weakness; nor is therapy a departure from the spiritual path. Our path is unique to us. It frequently includes individualized branches that meet our needs. When we come up against an intransigent resentment, the spiritual path seeks additional counsel. It does not double down on willfulness masquerading as spirituality.

Inventory Two: Fear

Having completed our inventory of resentments, we now turn our attention to fear. "This short word somehow touches about every aspect of our lives," says Wilson. "It was an evil and corroding thread; the fabric of our existence was shot through with it."[12]

In the third column of our resentment inventory, under the "affects my" heading, we see the word "fear" in brackets. Here is where our second inventory begins. We turn to a new sheet of paper, listing each of our fears in the left margin. We begin with those found on our first inventory, then add those fears with no apparent connection to resentment.

> **Fears:**
>
> 1) I am afraid that I am not enough: not smart enough, funny enough etc. I need a "cool bike," car, fashionable clothes, etc to complete me or help me "fit in."
>
> 2) I am afraid of failure

Self-centeredness is predicated upon insecurity. We are afraid that we are not enough. When we look deeper, we see this fear is intelligent. It is true. I am not enough, if "I" refers to the ego. The ego always falls short because it is incapable of encompassing the fullness of our person. And when ego falls short, it leaves us feeling inadequate, like we are missing something. As long as we identify with ego, insecurity will haunt us. This emptiness is at the heart of ego; it drives our pursuit of validation and approval. It turns our lives into a scavenger hunt.

We are constantly looking for our missing parts because we feel uncomfortable in our skin. Fear sends us into

---

[12] Ibid, pg. 67

relationships looking for our other half. It rummages through racks of clothes for the perfect outfit that enables us to fit in. It digs through books for that bit of esoteric wisdom that promises to solve all our problems. The ego feels broken and is obsessed with finding a fix. Unfortunately, the "fixes" it finds devolve into addictions.

Ego's fixes not only fail to fix us, the baggage they bring along increases our sense of inadequacy. Every time they fail, these self-reliant solutions reinforce the notion that we are fundamentally flawed, creating a vicious cycle of shame. The only appropriate response to this shame is a deep breath. We have to get out of our head. We have to let go of ego and relax into the silence of the body. There we hear the truth of shame: ego is insufficient; only a Higher Power will suffice.

These needy expeditions always end in disappointment because they search abroad for identity. Curiously, they look for self in other. The Steps turn within. We feel out of place because the image we have fashioned for ourselves is not true to our Self, not because we are out of touch with the latest fashions. Dressing our false-self up in the current trends—be they material, intellectual, or religious—is an attempt to camouflage our insecurity. Bill Wilson refers to this charade as "self-reliance."

The crux of the fear problem is self-reliance. When we identify with ego, we cling to what is not. Amidst the relentless onslaught of truth, maintaining a false-self is an exercise in futility. The ever-unfolding present moment inevitably rips our rickety self-image to shreds. And deep down, we know this is going to happen! In the back of our minds, we know reality is going to expose our dishonesty. The ego translates this foregone conclusion into a threat. It takes reality personally. Life appears to be something happening to us. As a result, we live in a defensive posture, which is what Wilson means when he says, *the fabric of our existence is shot through with fear.*

"Self-reliance was good as far as it went," writes Bill, "but it didn't go far enough." So, in the right-hand column, we ask ourselves why we had these fears: "Wasn't it because self-reliance failed us?" Simply stated, "Is my fear a symptom of trying to be something I am not?"

Fears:	Is this fear a result of self-reliance?
1) I am afraid that I am not enough: not smart enough, funny enough etc. I need a "cool bike," car, fashionable clothes, etc to complete me or help me "fit in."	Yes. I tried to construct a self-image around these objects, but I know it is false. I know it will eventually fail me, and as a result I am afraid and defensive.
2) I am afraid of failure	Yes. My fear of failure makes me afraid to exert myself, to put myself out there. So I rely upon an aloof image that pretends not to care.

Working Through Fear

What is the alternative to fear and self-reliance? "There is a better way," suggests Wilson, but what is it and more importantly, how do we steer that course? "We are now on a different basis," he answers, "the basis of trusting and relying upon God. We trust infinite God rather than our finite selves." Thus far, Wilson's alternative is ambiguous. It rolls off the tongue but appears to be little more than sentimentality. It is the next few lines that infuse his proposal with substance. "We are in the world to play the role He assigns. Just to the extent that we do as we think He would have us, and humbly rely on Him, does He enable us to match calamity with serenity."[13] This path rises above fear.

We are not what we think *about* ourselves. Our true nature belongs to the category of revealed truth. It is not self-authored but disclosed in self-examination, prayer, and meditation. These practices suspend ego, thereby revealing our True Self, the role we are assigned—and our capacity to match calamity with serenity is contingent upon our adherence to that role. When we are faithful to our Self in thought, speech, and deed, then, and only then, are we "trusting and relying upon God."

Ultimately, the effects of fear are calculated by the restrictions it places upon our actions. Fear is a problem when it suppresses authentic expression. It is not oppressive when we act in spite of its apprehensions. To the contrary, overcoming fear arouses self-worth and purpose. The spiritual journey is a meaningless, lackluster, self-absorbed stroll through the Shire without interior mountains like fear. They provide the resistance that turns the path into an ascent.

Summiting these mountains is not easy. It takes courage to walk the road less traveled when everything in us but the still-small voice clings to the easier, softer way. For this

---

[13] Bill Wilson, *Alcoholics Anonymous*, pg 68, 1939

reason, the spiritual path is traditionally referred to as the "Hero's Journey."[14]

Spirituality is not thrill-seeking. It turns into our fears because it accepts the world-as-it-is, and fear is a fact of our lives. It is part of the human condition. Therefore, spirituality does not posit a world free of fear, but a life characterized by freedom from fear. Spirituality does not wave angst away with wishful thinking or fluffy rhetoric. It uses spiritual practice to effect contact with a Power greater than fear, a power that enables life to triumph over fear.

We should pause here to address the collective sigh of every skeptic reading this God-laced antidote to fear. In the midst of angst, the skeptic is sure to find the notion of relying on God wanting. Is there a humanistic way to conceive of this dynamic, which is consistent with the principles outlined by Wilson but also compelling to the skeptic? There is, but at first glance, it appears to contradict everything said before. The alternative is Ralph Waldo Emerson's "Self-reliance."

In Emerson's transcendentalism, Self-reliance is a supreme virtue. It is important to note, however, that the word "Self" does not refer to the ego. Emerson maintains that the inauthentic man "deceives himself, and goes out of acquaintance with his own being," which is the higher Self he implores us to rely upon.[15]

---

[14] Joseph Campbell coined the term "Hero's Journey," which comes from the Buddhist tradition where it is referred to as the *Bodhisattvacaryāvatāra* or the Bodhisattva's [Great Being] Way of Life.

[15] Ralph Waldo Emerson, "Divinity School Address," 1838

Emerson defines "Self-reliance" as "the height and perfection of man," adding that it is effectively "reliance on God."[16] He is invoking the "larger and more godlike self" mentioned by William James in *Varieties of Religious Experience.* More religious people refer to this notion as "God within." It is our True Self. When Emerson speaks of Self-reliance, he means faithfulness to our authentic Self: "Insist on yourself; never imitate,"[17] he says, or as the oft-quoted version has it: "Be yourself; no base imitator of another, but your best self."

Like Wilson's God-reliance, Emerson's Self-reliance is willing, not willful. It consents to a self-existing order. Transcendental Self-reliance does not try to manufacture a persona; it adheres, instead, to our true nature: "Do that which is assigned you, and you cannot hope too much or dare too much," instructs the sage of Concord.[18] This Emersonian dictum is equal to Wilson's, "Do as we think He (God) would have us."

The difference between Wilson's God-reliance and Emerson's Self-reliance is another example of the skeptic and believer converging on the same center from two different starting points. "Every step so downward, is a step upward," observes Emerson. "The man who renounces himself, comes to himself."[19] The important point is not the language that

---

[16] Ralph Waldo Emerson, "Fugitive Slave Law," 1854

[17] Ralph Waldo Emerson, "Self-Reliance," 1841

[18] Ibid

[19] Ralph Waldo Emerson, "Divinity School Address," 1838

paves their respective ways, but that both the believer and skeptic converge on a point above and beyond fear. Twelve Step pragmatics measure both God-reliance and Self-reliance by the same standard: Does it overcome fear?

Bill Wilson instructs us to ask God "to remove our fear and direct our attention to what He would have us be." The question is "What would God have us be?" We must answer this question with humility because we do not know. We do not know who we are until we become it. Those alienated slivers of our Self that make us whole are the groans, the yearnings, the aspirations we must follow into every moment, but "no man yet knows what it is, nor can," notes Emerson, "till that person has exhibited it."[20] The best we can do is put ourselves out there in good faith. We are going to make assumptions that prove absurd, but we are also going to make gains, and with each gain we draw closer to the vital power that nudged us in that direction.

The Catholic monk, Thomas Merton, weaves together these dueling themes of faith and uncertainty in his famous prayer: "My Lord God, I have no idea where I am going. I do not see the road ahead of me. I cannot know for certain where it will end; nor do I really know myself, and the fact that I think I am following your will does not mean that I am actually doing so." These words portray a humble faith that swats away certainty, but the prayer does not end in spiritual gridlock. Merton concludes by showing us the way out of this predicament: "But I believe that the desire to please you does

---

[20] To couch it in Emerson's God-son's pragmatics, one might say, *we must become true.*

in fact please you. And I hope I have that desire in all that I am doing."

Spirituality isn't about getting the answer right. It's not about having the right theology or philosophy. It has nothing to do with certainty. Spirituality is about living a life sacrificed to higher principles. Thus, spiritual longing is satisfied by the expressed desire to take the high road, to do the next right thing. When we aim to do the next right thing, with no regard for fear's protestations, then—and only then—do we outgrow fear. Angst recedes not because we got it right, but because we dared to act, to go beyond ego's boundaries into the arena of the unknown where we encounter a Higher Power. God triumphs in the ascendancy of principles, and principles rise by way of action.

Failure is inevitable—nay, necessary—on the spiritual path. We are going to miss the mark many times and be forced to adjust. These adjustments lead to precision both in understanding and execution. Our actions are a bow that shoots the contents of our character at targets spread across the field of daily life. We will not hit the bullseye every time: some will sail over, others will fall short, and a few will strike the target. If, however, we keep our sights honest, the average increasingly trends toward the center. As long as our actions follow the promptings of our heart, our life will, over time, more and more faithfully adhere to the dictates of a Higher Power.

Sexual Inventory

"Now about sex." No three words amidst a moral inventory could be more unsettling, yet this is Wilson's abrupt segue into the most guarded realm of human behavior. The rationale behind a sexual inventory is pretty straightforward: Behavior is behavior, and since selfishness indiscriminately exploits behavior, we need to inventory every class of behavior. The fourth Step singles out sex only because it is too often classified "confidential" by the reticent mind. It is easy for ego to hide resentment, fear, and selfishness behind the partition of sex. Thus, the fourth Step targets sex to ensure there are no nooks and crannies left unexamined.

Sex is essentially like every other behavior, so there is no need to restate the above material about fear, resentment, and self-centeredness. All of it applies equally to sex. It is worth mentioning, however, that sexuality, like religion, falls within the dominion of conscience, and that the Twelve Steps do not intrude on this sacred space. They recognize the individual's right to determine the nature of their intimate affairs. "We do not want to be the arbiter of anyone's sex conduct," Wilson states. The Steps are not concerned with our sexual orientation. They have no opinion on monogamy or polyamory. They are disinterested in our choice of partner and the number of partners we take. They focus entirely on the ethics that characterize these relationships.

"We all have sex problems. We'd hardly be human if we didn't. What can we do about them?" This straightforward attitude is the approach the Steps take toward sex. Nothing about the theory has changed. Self-centeredness, fear, and resentment subvert a life of meaning and purpose. This axiom is no less true where sex and intimate relationships are concerned, so Step Four combs through our sex life, looking for manifestations of ego. It subjects "each relation to this test: was it selfish or not?"

Since sex is no different than any other form of behavior, the inventory process is the same. To begin, we write the names of those we hurt in the left-hand column. Next, we look at our behavior. We ask ourselves, "Did we unjustifiably arouse jealousy, suspicion or bitterness?" Then, we, ask, "Where were we at fault? Where had we been selfish, dishonest, or inconsiderate?" We conclude with, "What should we have done instead?"[21]

Who:	Did I arouse jealousy, suspicion or bitterness?	Where was I selfish, dishonest, or inconsiderate?	What should I have done instead?
1) Casey	Yes. I often ignored Casey's calls and talked about ex-lovers.	I did not take Casey's feelings into consideration. I led Casey on.	I should have been honest with Casey.
2) Charlie	I constantly brought up Charlie's past partners as a way of getting assurances about us.		I should have addressed my fears and been more trusting of Charlie.

The final column—"What should we have done instead?"—enables us "to shape a sane and sound ideal for our future sex life." This question gives us leeway to shape our sexual ideals, rather than forcing us to adopt external customs. It is sexuality *as we understand it.*

---

[21] Bill Wilson, *Alcoholics Anonymous,* pg 69, 1939

Identifying the point at which we depart from our principles enables us to envision other possibilities. Using our shortcomings to outline healthy alternatives, we sketch a map for future relationships. This alternative becomes the ideal to which our conduct adheres. This ideal is not set in stone. It is a rough draft, but a good beginning. We revise and refine it as conscience dictates. In this way, sanity is resurrected in our intimate affairs. This model applies to single persons and married couples alike; the latter may even find a joint effort useful.

Before closing the book on sex, it is worth mentioning that sexuality and spirituality are not at odds. Puritanical religion suppresses sexuality. However, this is not true of all religion, and certainly not Twelve Step spirituality. The Steps are about becoming fully human, and sexuality is deeply human, so the Steps embrace sexuality as a part of our journey. Wilson reminds us that "our sex powers were God-given and therefore good, neither to be used lightly or selfishly nor to be despised and loathed." Sexuality is not taboo in Twelve Step spirituality. It is sacred.

Storytelling

What are we to do with Step Four's catalog of resentments, fears, and sexual conduct? The fifth Step reads, "Admitted to God, to ourselves, and to another human being the exact nature of our wrongs," which amounts to sharing our story with another human being.

Storytelling is a vital part of Twelve Step spirituality, and arguably the most recognizable feature of recovery communities. We've all seen people sharing their struggles in silver screen A.A. meetings. However, this book deals with the Steps themselves, not the fellowship. Therefore, it doesn't cover this facet of Twelve Step culture in great detail. That said, storytelling was the first means of transmitting the Steps, and it continues to play a critical role in their dissemination. Therefore, any serious exploration of the Steps is forced to touch upon it. Since storytelling gives us a window into Step Five, now is a good time to explore this practice.

Storytelling has always been the Steps' main mode of transmission. *Alcoholics Anonymous* may be one of the best-selling books of all time, but A.A.'s message is predominantly passed from one generation to the next via an oral tradition. A.A. meetings and private mentoring (sponsorship) facilitate this oral tradition.

In "speaker meetings," the keynoter shares their "experience, strength, and hope" with the group. This is also the standard format for speaking in discussion meetings, which encourage members to share their experience on the day's topic. Similarly, sponsors are not qualified clinicians or spiritual gurus. They are mentors that use their experience to guide those still suffering into recovery. In every facet of A.A. culture, "experience, strength, and hope" are the guiding principles. This blueprint is extracted from the personal stories in the back of the *Big Book*. These stories account for more than half of the text's girth, so storytelling is central even in A.A.'s written tradition.

The Twelve Steps have a talent for promulgating themselves among men and women alike, regardless of race, class, politics, or religion. The Steps also have a knack for navigating generational waters, and these talents stem from their method of transmission. The oral tradition keeps the Steps fresh and resonant. The text is still relevant, but the language is seen by many as archaic, especially younger generations. Meetings and sponsorship update the language. They provide modern commentary. The oral tradition serves more than a thesauric purpose, however. Storytelling is a Twelve Step sacrament, so to speak. It brings the Steps to life by casting living members of the fellowship as representatives of Twelve Step principles and inviting others into the recovery mythos.

In Twelve Step mythology, real people from all walks personify the heroic tale of transformation—not ancient accounts of mythical cave dwellers and miracle workers who feel far removed from the plight of us mere mortals. It is the "experience, strength, and hope" offered by these ordinary people that welcomes prospects onto the Twelve Step path. They are the tangible, imperfect, proof-positive evidence that hope lies in wait for those who follow. Old-timers are, in this sense, the shamans of the Twelve Step world, using their personal stories to dramatize the spiritual journey.

The genius of Twelve Step storytelling is that it aims to establish not only a bond of mutual suffering but an identification with someone who has suffered and since recovered. "Our stories disclose in a general way what we used to be like, what happened, and what we are like now," says Wilson. The "what we used to be like" angle invites the audience to identify with the speaker through the medium of shared suffering; whereas "what we are like now" enables the still suffering listener to see the speaker as hope incarnate. This piece of the formula makes real the possibility of transformation. These two shores are bridged by "what happened," which is the instructive link. It outlines the steps taken by the speaker from "what it used to be like" to "what it is like now." Wilson then adds, "If you have decided you want what we have and are willing to go to any length to get it, then you are ready to take certain steps." Of course, these steps are "The Steps." In other words, storytelling sets the stage for the A.A.'s cardinal sacrament, the Twelve Steps.

The story begins with powerlessness and unmanageability, but that is just half the equation. "The feeling of having shared in a common peril is one element in the powerful cement which binds us," the *Big Book* says. "But that in itself would never have held us together as we are now joined. The tremendous fact for every one of us is that we have discovered a common solution."[22]

The element of "common peril" brings the narrator down to the newcomer's level, enabling them to identify. The narrator's recovery and transformation invites the still suffering onto a higher path. When the newcomer identifies with the recovered, the solution becomes common. This is the magic of Twelve Step storytelling. It recasts the lives of ordinary folk in the format of a hero's journey, making the spiritual path more accessible.

---

[22] Bill Wilson, *Alcoholics Anonymous,* pg 17, 1939

Finding a Guide

The fourth Step has both feet firmly planted in the past but fixes its gaze on the future. In the fifth Step, we leave the past behind and begin down the path of transformation. Here, our "what it was like" begins to turn into the joy of "what it is like now." This is the transformative power of telling our story.

Sharing the intimate details of our past with another person is scary. For this reason, Wilson says we must be "willing to go to any length." This willingness is brokered by despair and hope.

We long to be free and to claim for ourselves a more meaningful life, but despair of ever throwing off our old ways. This is the echo of Step One. Second, the hope personified in those who have gone before us issues the call to adventure. For this reason, the person we choose to hear our fifth Step is important. We are looking for someone who embodies the gains we hope to make. Unfortunately, this is not always easy to find.

Most of us would, for obvious reasons, like to avoid this hair-raising Step. There are checks built into Twelve Step fellowships that hold individuals accountable to Step Five, most notably sponsorship. Those of us who haven't the benefit of such accountability may see an opportunity to excuse ourselves from this practice. Without the benefit of a ready-made support group, there is no immediate candidate to hear our life story. The ego might use this as a convenient justification to bypass Step Five. We should think twice before taking this detour. It is a trap.

Efforts to circumvent this leg of the journey belong to the ego. We should exhaust every option in our search for an honest, understanding person who is willing to hear our fifth Step and respect our confidentiality. We have to search our contacts for a friend or insightful acquaintance—perhaps a priest, minister, spiritual mentor, or therapist. They may have little or no experience with the Twelve Steps, but so long as they are tight-lipped and respectful of our objectives, this is not a problem.

Experience with spiritual practice is more important than familiarity with the Steps. We are looking for a fellow traveler. If our search turns up empty-handed, we should seek a referral. If we ask around, we are sure to find a therapist, counselor, priest, minister, or rabbi willing to hear our inventory. Once we find someone who fits the bill, "We pocket our pride and go to it, illuminating every twist of character, every dark cranny of the past."[23]

Instructions for the fifth Step are quite simple. We sit with the person who has agreed to hear our inventory and read it to them. We do not provide additional commentary, and they do not psychoanalyze us. If they have experience, insight, or feedback to offer, we hear it. We do not rationalize or justify our story. We share it. We simply read each line from left to right, and they listen.

---

[23] Bill Wilson, *Alcoholics Anonymous,* pg 75, 1939

Admit One

The fears of those approaching Step Four are often misplaced. The fourth Step is a dossier of confidential information. Step Five opens that dossier, inviting another into the private recesses of our soul where our past specters lurk. For this reason, Step Five is the more foreboding side of the ego-deflating duo.

Each of the Twelve Steps aims to deflate our ego, but obviously, some are more deflating than others. "When it comes to ego deflation," Wilson says, "few Steps are harder to take than Five."[24] In other words, deflation at depth is how we ascend to our highest Self. This is the meaning of Emerson's "Every step so downward, is a step upward." Step Five brings us closer to our True Self by exposing our false-self—and in doing so, brings us closer to God.

In Step Four, we catalog our demons. In Five, we invoke them. We do not merely call forth the exact nature of our wrongs; we present them to someone else. We manifest our shortcomings. Sharing our secrets makes them common knowledge and as such, real. Injecting our deepest secrets into reality forces us to accept them, which is the gist of "admit."

Much like "belief" and "decision," the word "admit" has popular connotations that do not comport with its usage in the Steps. The word "admit" usually means "to confess or disclose," but this is only half of the fifth Step. Step Five

---

[24] Bill Wilson, *Twelve Steps and Twelve Traditions,* pgs 55 and 70, 1953

certainly involves confession. However, confession is a ritual that facilitates acceptance, which is the deeper meaning of the word "admit." Confession without acceptance is deception.

When we purchase a movie ticket, it reads, "Admit One." Our ticket gets us in the theater; "to admit" means "to let in." We are admitting the truth of who we are and where we are at in Step Five. We are conceding the contents of our inventory. This act of acceptance is crucial to the development of humility. "The attainment of greater humility is the foundation principle of each of A.A.'s Twelve Steps," writes Wilson. He defines humility as "a clear recognition of what and who we really are, followed by a sincere attempt to become what we could be."[25] The second half of his definition, "become what we could be," pertains to Steps Six and Seven, which the next chapter addresses. The fourth and fifth Steps deal with the front end of his definition: "A clear recognition of what and who we really are."

Steps Four and Five are not an appraisal of our whole being. They are a snapshot of where we stand right now; that is why they are so intimidating. They hone in on the details we want to ignore, magnifying our shortcomings that breed powerlessness and discontentment. Unfortunately, there is no other entry point. We must enter our path where it is darkest.

Many find solace in the rationalization that an admission to only ourselves and God is adequate. This is just a churched-up version of the earlier rationalization that sought to avoid sharing our inventory with another person—and again, this

---

[25] Bill Wilson, *Twelve Steps and Twelve Traditions*, pg 58, 1953

loophole belongs to ego. The Twelve Steps reject any attempt to privatize the path. Another person with whom we can be entirely honest is an indispensable part of Step Five. Sharing with another facilitates acceptance. "Until we actually sit down and talk aloud about what we have so long hidden, our willingness to clean house is still largely theoretical. When we are honest with another person," Wilson writes, "it confirms that we have been honest with ourselves and with God." Conversely, we are not being honest with ourselves, if we cannot be honest with another. This is the measure of progress in Step Five.

Humility is self-honesty. It is not only truthfulness with ourselves and others, but being true to our Self when no one is looking. Ego makes us prone to self-deception, which threatens the attainment of greater humility and makes self-disclosure a risky endeavor. The feedback of others, though imperfect, is not tangled in our self-spun web of delusion. The other person may be caught up in their web, but where we are concerned, they have no stake, which is precisely why their assistance is needed.

Most of us lead double lives. There is who we are when no one is looking and our "stage character," as Wilson puts it. "This is the one he likes his fellows to see. He wants to enjoy a certain reputation, but knows in his heart he doesn't deserve it." There is no room on our fourth Step for the stage character. Therefore, the person hearing our fifth Step sees past our ego, and because their mind is unstained by our delusions, they function as a clear mirror, reflecting back only what is real.

The confessor also shows us how to accept our shortcomings with grace. We expect them to run for the hills when we share our deepest secrets. When they do not flinch, we are surprised. They demonstrate what we thought impossible. They don't judge, cringe, or reprimand us; nor do they try to smooth it over. They are unmoved. Undisturbed. This grace proves the unacceptable within ourselves is indeed acceptable; that we do not have to turn away from our suffering; that we can work with it. It shows us that shortcomings define ego's limitations, not our true potential. Suddenly, dead ends have outlets. We are not stuck.

Acceptance is not a passive state that apathetically tolerates imperfection. It unapologetically acknowledges our shortcomings and takes responsibility for our imperfections. It does not hide them; nor does it medicate them with affirmational melodrama. It takes them onto the path, which is why Wilson says, "More realism and therefore more honesty about ourselves are the great gains we make under the influence of Step Five."[26]

We make our shortcomings real by being honest about them. Once accepted, they cease to handicap us. They become pockets of potential waiting to be tapped by further practice. This realization of our shortcomings does not happen unless we share them with another person. Sharing is what makes them real.

---

[26] Bill Wilson, *Twelve Steps and Twelve Traditions*, pg 58, 1953

Conclusion

In Steps Six and Seven, we are asked to give up our character defects, but we cannot give up what we do not possess. In Four, we identify those shortcomings. In Five, we take possession of them. It is by admitting them that we take hold of them, which the ritual act of sharing facilitates. "No defect can be corrected unless we clearly see what it is. But we shall have to do more than see." Now that we have taken possession of our shortcomings, it is time to give them up. Onward to Steps Six and Seven.

11 THE PERFECT OBJECTIVE

"Finally I am coming to the conclusion that my highest ambition is to be what I already am. That I will never fulfill my obligation to surpass myself unless I first accept myself, and if I accept myself fully in the right way, I will already have surpassed myself." ~ Thomas Merton

1940 was a difficult year for Bill and Lois Wilson. Their Brooklyn home was foreclosed. They moved into a tiny loft on 24th St. in Manhattan, which doubled as A.A.'s first clubhouse. Eighteen months after the publication of *Alcoholics Anonymous* but four months before the *Post* article that sparked A.A.'s success, Bill's efforts appeared to be in vain.

It was a cold, stormy November night. Bill's internal conditions mirrored those without. He was in the midst of a crippling depression. Bill's slide into despair was interrupted by a knock at the door. Tom, the clubhouse janitor, poked his head into the Wilson's loft and said, "There's some damn bum from St. Louis down there. Do you want to see him?" "No, Tom... Not tonight," Bill replied. Tom turned to walk away, but before he pulled the door shut Bill reluctantly blurted out, "Yeah, Tom, send him up."

Naturally, Wilson assumed his unannounced visitor was a drunk in need of help. His acquiescence was owed more to the force of habit than eagerness. Wilson's depression made the visit most unwelcomed. Little did he know, this meeting would forever alter the trajectory of both his life and Alcoholics Anonymous.

The slow, labored steps ascending the staircase portended an exceptionally desperate case. "Finally a figure appeared in my doorway," Wilson recalled. "His coat was drawn about him. It was covered with sleet. He wore a hat which looked something like a cabbage leaf—also covered in snow. It was eleven o'clock at night. When he threw back his coat, I saw he was a clergyman."[1]

Fr. Ed Patrick Dowling was ordained a Catholic priest in 1931. Soon thereafter, he became associate editor of *The Queen's Work*, a Catholic publication founded by the Jesuits of the Missouri Province. He held this position until his death in 1960. Dowling was also a genealogist, spiritual director, social justice advocate, and a great friend to Alcoholics Anonymous.

---

[1] Bill Wilson, speech "Father Ed Dowling, Rev Sam Shoemaker 1955," YouTube

Fr. Dowling was a loving and compassionate man, more contemplative than intellectual, more attune to service than parish ministry. The Jesuit mainstream judged him a fringe figure in their academic order. When Dowling passed, they did not think he merited a funeral at St. Francis Xavier, the illustrious "College Church" built by the Jesuits on the campus of St. Louis University. The Provincial Superior intervened, however, and Dowling was buried at the College Church.

"The grounds were packed with cars and people who came from all over the country" to pay their final respects to the unorthodox Jesuit.[2] This sweet man left an indelible mark on those close to him. Most of all, Bill Wilson. The A.A. co-founder considered Dowling his sponsor for two decades. While Dowling's fellow Jesuits discounted his life, members of Alcoholics Anonymous poured into St. Louis to celebrate it. They came to bid farewell to the man Wilson called, "One of the greatest spiritual figures that we (of A.A.) may ever know."[3]

The Mark of Ed Dowling

"Fr. Dowling's shock of tousled white hair and his bulky figure gave him an added air of authority as he expounded his views at meetings," one of his Catholic colleagues remembered. "His opinions and ideas were often unconventional." Perhaps his unusual perspective enabled

---

[2] Robert Fitzgerald, S.J., *Soul of Sponsorship,* pg 103, 1995

[3] Bill Wilson, "This Matter of Fear," *Grapevine,* January 1962

him to see the similarities between A.A.'s Twelve Steps and the spiritual practices of his Jesuit order. These similarities piqued his curiosity. He alluded to the budding fellowship of recovering alcoholics in *The Queen's Work,* but the journalist and seeker in him wanted to learn more. His curiosity took him to New York to meet the architect of A.A.'s spiritual path.

Fr. Dowling was an intensely spiritual man. In the Twelve Steps, he saw a profound, yet practical approach to spirituality. Dowling's ringing endorsement of A.A.'s program is recorded in the *Big Book's* fifth appendix: "Alcoholics Anonymous is natural; it is natural at the point where nature comes closest to the supernatural, namely in humiliations and in consequent humility. There is something spiritual about an art museum or a symphony, and the Catholic Church approves of our use of them. There is something spiritual about A.A. too, and Catholic participation in it almost invariably results in poor Catholics becoming better Catholics."[4] Dowling did more than endorse the Steps, however. He enhanced them. His influence on Wilson's life is reflected in the co-founder's later commentary on the Steps, especially Six and Seven.

Twelve Steps and Twelve Traditions was published in 1953. On balance, the *Twelve and Twelve* is a deeper tract than the *Big Book*, which is why historian Ernest Kurtz calls it "the New Testament" of Alcoholics Anonymous. Even if one disagrees with this assessment, they must admit the companion piece's superior handling of Steps Six and Seven.

---

[4] Ed Dowling, "Religious Views on AA," *Alcoholics Anonymous*, pg 574, 1976

In 1939, Wilson offered only two paragraphs of instruction on these Steps. Fourteen years later he fleshed out two chapters, totaling nearly four thousand words. These thirteen pages are widely considered Bill's best writings, and they are unquestionably evidence of Dowling's enriching effect upon their author.

In the *Twelve and Twelve*, Wilson approaches Steps Six and Seven from an angle entirely missing in the *Big Book*. This perspective is omitted in his first effort because he took it from Fr. Dowling, whom he met in November of 1940, a year-and-a-half after the publication of *Alcoholics Anonymous*. While Dowling's influence is noticeable throughout the *Twelve and Twelve*, it is unmistakable in Steps Six and Seven. Wilson all but credits him with the insights therein, using a quotation from Fr. Ed to frame Step Six: "This is the Step that separates the men from the boys." Sticking with this expression, Bill W. was a spiritual boy when the great Jesuit found him.

Dowling went to New York expecting to meet a spiritual giant. Instead, the snow-clad clergyman found the shell of a man. Bill felt as if the walls were closing in on him, literally and metaphorically. He had little to show for five years of hard work and personal sacrifice. He saw his large home on Clinton St. downgraded to a measly studio apartment, and his financial woes were not receding. The silver lining was his physical sobriety, but when Fr. Dowling entered Wilson's claustrophobic loft and life, the A.A. co-founder had none of the emotional sobriety his text promised.

When the forty-two-year-old priest's labored ascent finally ended, he removed his hat and overcoat, and eased his arthritic body into the room's lone chair. Next, Dowling revealed the reason for his visit. He explained the parallels between A.A.'s Twelve Steps and the Exercises of St. Ignatius, a well-known path of spiritual practice outlined by the Jesuit order's founder, Ignatius of Loyola. Bill never rose from his bed. Wilson confessed he'd never heard of Ignatius or his Exercises—an admission Dowling welcomed with a hearty laugh. This honesty immediately endeared him to Bill. Suddenly, Wilson "realized with great joy that he was the clergyman who had put that wonderful plug for A.A. into *The Queen's Work.*"[5] Thus began the lifelong partnership between Bill W. and Fr. Ed Dowling.

Fr. Dowling was more than a friend. Recounting their initial meeting, Bill said, "In A.A., practically all of us know someone with whom we especially identify." In Twelve Step communities, this person is called a "sponsor." On that cold night, Bill W. met the man with whom he especially identified, his sponsor. As they talked, the icy emotional block embalming Wilson's spiritual life thawed. Perhaps it was the saintly priest's warm, trusting demeanor. Maybe it was Wilson's backlog of burdensome thoughts and feelings pining for release. Whatever the cause, Bill worked a fifth Step with the St. Louis clergyman that evening.

"He told Dowling not only what he had done and had left undone—he went on to share with his new sponsor the thoughts and feelings behind those actions and omissions,"

---

[5] Bill Wilson, talk to the A.A. Manhattan Group, 1955

writes Kurtz. "He told of his high hopes and plans, and spoke about his anger, despair, and mounting frustrations. The Jesuit listened and quoted Matthew: 'Blessed are they who hunger and thirst.' God's chosen, he pointed out, were always distinguished by their yearnings, their restlessness, their thirst." Given his lifelong obsession with being "number one," Bill assuredly took comfort in being counted among "God's chosen." If Wilson's depression was flattered into retreat, the consolation was only fleeting. When he asked if there was ever satisfaction of this divine restlessness, the priest bluntly responded, "Never. Never any."

Fr. Dowling "continued in a gentler tone, describing 'divine dissatisfaction' as that which would keep Wilson going, always reaching for unattainable goals, for only by so reaching would he attain what—hidden from him—were God's goals."[6] This concept of "divine dissatisfaction" later found its way into the *Twelve Steps and Twelve Traditions*.

At the close of Step Six in the *Twelve and Twelve*, Wilson returns to the quote from Dowling: "So the difference between 'the boys and the men' is the difference between striving for a self-determined objective and for the perfect objective which is of God."[7] Steps Six and Seven were conceived in 1939, but they blossomed the following year, when Dowling revealed their secrets to Wilson.

---

[6] Ernest Kurtz, *Not-God: A History of Alcoholics Anonymous,* pgs 98-99, 1979

[7] Bill Wilson, *Twelve Steps and Twelve Traditions,* pg 68, 1953

The tension between progress and perfection is palpable in the life of Bill Wilson. He always set his sights high—often achieving, but falling painfully short on more than one occasion. This tension is also one of the historical fault lines that split Alcoholics Anonymous from the Oxford Groups.

The Oxford Group professed moral absolutes. They didn't just aim for perfection, they expected it—or at least the pretense of it. Perfect honesty, unselfishness, charity, and love were not ideals used to measure progress in the Oxford Group. They were unyielding codes of piety. Such an environment breeds resentment and duplicity.

When people feel perfection is a precondition of acceptance, they labor to create and maintain its facade. In time, they resent the effort and those who demand it. Alcoholics struggled in vain to navigate this minefield. "We saw people going broke on this sort of perfection," Wilson remembers, "trying to get too good by Thursday."

The bunch that broke away to form Alcoholics Anonymous rejected spiritual and moral perfectionism. They preferred the more relaxed and realistic standard of progress. The oft-quoted line from *Alcoholics Anonymous*, "We claim spiritual progress rather than spiritual perfection," stands as a monument to this preference. That said, progress does not replace perfection in the Steps. A.A.'s practice "progress *by way of* perfection," rather than "perfection or bust," which sets them apart from the Oxford Group. This standard facilitates progress without setting aspirants up for failure. It keeps them going, reaching, and in reaching, attaining those goals hidden from them. In brief, Twelve Step spirituality is idealism perpetually on its way.

The opposing forces of progress and perfection sat at the heart of A.A.'s program for fourteen years, like a Twelve Step koan waiting to be solved. Bill squares the paradox in his 1953 sequel. His resolution bears the mark of Fr. Ed Dowling.

Instincts and Character Defects

Step Six reads, "Were entirely ready to have God remove all these defects of character." At first glance, this Step is indistinguishable from a moral absolute. The words "entirely" and "all," when paired with the removal of character defects, reeks of the perfectionism A.A.s repudiated in the Oxford Group. *Alcoholics Anonymous* does not address this seeming contradiction, but then again, much about Steps Six and Seven are left unexplained in the original text. Concise definitions of key terms like "defects of characters" and "shortcomings" are glaringly omitted, as well as detailed instructions for renouncing them. In the companion text, however, these concepts are unpacked. Strangely, the whole conversation is rooted in a word never mentioned in the *Big Book*, "instincts." Our exploration of Step Six begins with these "innate impulses and behaviors."

Wilson grounds his theory of "character defects" and "shortcomings" in human nature. In the *Twelve and Twelve,* he writes: "Every normal person wants, for example, to eat, to reproduce, to be somebody in the society of his fellows. And he wishes to be reasonably safe and secure as he tries to attain these things." These drives are not wicked, sinful, immoral, corrupt, unnatural, or abnormal. They are not to be repressed or condemned. Bill sees them as innate or God-given, calling them our "our great natural assets." Thus, the Steps do not propose an austere program of asceticism. "So far as we know," writes Wilson, "it is nowhere on the record that God has completely removed from any human being all his natural drives."[8] The instincts are part and parcel of human nature, and the Twelve Steps do not deny human nature. They restore it.

Step Three names selfishness and self-centeredness as the principal causes of insanity. Self-centeredness bends and twists reality, rating the contents of consciousness on a sliding scale of self-interest. Ego sees what it wants to see, which is shaped by its immediate desires. Selfishness publishes this nearsightedness in the field of action. It tries to arrange the external world according to ego's hierarchy of instant gratification. The sixth Step essentially applies this egoic model to our inner life.

Reality does not begin where our skin ends. It includes our interior life. Our thoughts, feelings, intuitions, and instincts participate in reality—even when they fail to accord with actuality. In short, delusions have standing in reality; they exist as delusions.

Delusion stems from ego using the logic it is evaluating to conduct the evaluation. The Steps refer to this inbred delusion as insanity, which is more than a mental state. In

---

[8] Bill Wilson, *Twelve Steps and Twelve Traditions,* pgs 64-65, 1953

Twelve Step spirituality, insanity applies to both mind and body. It is not merely a point of view disconnected from reality; insanity also refers to actions that are alienated from our true nature.

The ego sees both inner and outer phenomena through the same lens, self-centeredness. It grades our thoughts, feelings, intuitions, and impulses on their fidelity to instant self-gratification. For example, the ego elevates dishonest motives to the rank of action when they avoid unpleasant consequences or elicit rewards. Similarly, it prefers flattering thoughts to critical insights, resulting in delusions of grandeur. When this self-serving standard usurps the higher aim of our instincts, Wilson says, they "exceed their proper functions."[9] At this point, our natural drives go off the rails, and our inner life is a train wreck.

Undoubtedly, there is gratification found in the fulfillment of natural drives, but we deviate from the principles of a meaningful life when gratification itself becomes the driving force. These deviations are costly. They refuse to endure hardship or forego personal gain for the benefit of others. They are not willing to sacrifice immediate pleasure for long-term progress. These deviations purchase cheap indulgences at the inflated price of personal maturation, departing from the path preordained by our highest Self in order to either avoid pain or pursue pleasure.

This easier, softer way is often well-worn before we realize the damage done to our soul. Without higher order

---

[9] Bill Wilson, *Twelve Steps and Twelve Traditions,* pg 42, 1953

principles as our guide, the ego runs up and down this trail, carving the pleasure principle into our character. It maims and disfigures our true nature, fabricating a second nature. When we refer to something as our second nature, we mean it is a habit. Defects of character are habits of selfishness and self-centeredness, and ego personifies these habits.

Bill Wilson defines character defects as "instincts gone astray."[10] The first truth from which self-centeredness parts is the truth of our Self. Ego institutionalizes second order perceptions and behaviors. They are "second order" because they bypass their primary objective to satisfy the expectations of a secondary self. For example, sex is obviously gratifying, but the gratification is an enticement, not the aim. There is nothing wrong with enjoying sex, but when the means and ends are confused, we mistake pleasure for love. This confusion builds a relationship on the unstable foundation of fleeting pleasure, instead of compatibility and character, which are more pertinent to the ultimate aim of sex: creating and maintaining a healthy family. A more modern strand of this second order agenda veers even further off the path, choosing pixelated partners over real companions.

Character defects are the patterns of thought and behavior that constitute *our* ego. They serve a false-self but they are phenomena, and are therefore observable. When we connect the inventoried dots on our fourth Step, a portrait of *our* ego begins to emerge. The fourth Step catches our character defects because they belong to ego and inevitably lead to disappointment and resentment.

---

[10] Bill Wilson, *Twelve Steps and Twelve Traditions,* pg 50, 1953

Defects of character misappropriate natural drives and therefore, fail to satisfy our deepest longings. The ego doesn't endlessly want because it is greedy. It never stops wanting because *it is the wanting*. Ego is constitutionally discontented because its methods are unfulfilling. Lust, for instance, always falls short of love's mandate. As a result, character defects are also called shortcomings. The path of practice ahead aims to outgrow these shortcomings, restoring our original nature.

Clearly, not all habits are unhealthy. Habit is a form of learning; itself, a neutral mechanism. In the employ of our true nature, habits are vital. In fact, spiritual practice habituates principles that accord with our higher nature and unlearns those that don't. Steps Four, Five, Six, and Seven focus on the process of unlearning, seeking to "remove" our character defects; whereas Eight, Nine, Ten, Eleven, and Twelve upload new, meaningful habits. The issue is not with habit, but ego. Self-centeredness subordinates our instincts to base impulses, principally fear.

Fear is "the chief activator of our defects," says Wilson. But Bill isn't talking about a healthy fear of snakes. He specifically says "self-centered fear," by which he means, "fear that we would lose something we already possessed or would fail to get something we demanded."[11] Expectation is also part of the fear complex. Bill alludes to expectation with the word "demand."

---

[11] Bill Wilson, *Twelve Steps and Twelve Traditions,* pg 76, 1953

Expectation is the inverse of fear. We demand "this" because we are afraid of "that." Self-centered fear and expectation are opposite sides of the same coin, the fight or flight response. In other words, self-centered fear is psychological stress.

Stress is not a defect. It is an organism's instinctual response to a threat or stressor. More precisely, stress mobilizes that response. When a grazing wildebeest senses a stalking lion, stress suppresses the vulnerable wildebeest's non-essential functions and increases blood pressure and glucose levels, sending a jolt of energy through the prospective entree's veins. Stress is the fight or flight response. This response finances the next thirty seconds of high-stakes competition. Obviously, this is not what Bill had in mind. He is referring to psychological stress.

People do not google "how to deal with stress" because they're tired of fending off hungry lions. Those searches are owed to malfunctioning stress responses. People react to a rival's promotion or a snarky online post as if a predator is lurking because these stressors threaten the status of their psychological self. They challenge certain egoic premises, triggering an identity crisis. In defense, ego commandeers our built-in fight or flight response. This glitch is called psychological stress.

Self-centeredness installs a psychological self at the center of the world. This homunculus thinks life is happening to it. Self-centeredness makes ego the common measure of all things, and from that vantage point, everything is personal. It is *our* world. Does the chatty clerk shooting the breeze with the customer ahead of me not know I have somewhere to be? Is the underperforming player on my fantasy football team trying to make me look like an idiot? Does the person sitting at this green light want me to be late? In each case, the answer is "No!" They probably don't even know we exist, and we know this on an intellectual level. Nevertheless, it *feels* personal. We experience it as a threat because it challenges our ego.

When the fight or flight response is triggered, the ego doesn't usually start biting, kicking, punching, or running to neutralize the threat. Psychological or self-centered stress recasts "fight" as "gossip barbed with our anger," which Bill calls, "a polite form of murder by character assassination."[12] It may also take a more direct approach, verbally lashing out at the perceived threat. "Flight" might manifest as a literal retreat to solitude; or it may take the form of a psychological retreat, suppressing ideas and emotions.

We settle on the fight or flight strategies that reliably capture and secure our interests. Ego discards those that do not work, and adds the most successful strategies to its arsenal of character defects, fashioning a thoroughly superficial personality driven by fear.

The ego cannot create. It isn't real. It's a false-self, so it co-opts and repurposes our existing infrastructure. It confiscates our instincts, weaponizing them in its bid to secure pleasure and avoid discomfort. This is particularly problematic when it comes to fear or the stress response.

---

[12] Bill Wilson, *Twelve Steps and Twelve Traditions,* pg 67, 1953

The false-self is fragile, triggered by the flimsiest of circumstances. When someone one-ups a know-it-all with a bit of trivia, it feels threatened; constructive criticism seems like an inquisition to the perfectionist; when we identify with outward appearances, aging is a vicious assault on our personhood. Think about that for a second: aging or *living* is threatening from ego's viewpoint. Even worse, ego cannot escape this insecurity. Truth besieges the false-self from every side, making stress (or fear, as Bill would say) a chronic fact of life.

Self-centered fear diminishes our well-being in every imaginable way. It "drives us to covet the possessions of others, to lust for sex and power, to become angry when our instinctive demands are threatened, to be envious when the ambitions of others seem to be realized while ours are not," writes Wilson. "We eat, drink, and grab for more of everything than we need, fearing we shall never have enough."[13] Stress weakens physical health, prevents peace of mind, staves off happiness, and anxiously forbids meaningful exploration.

A Humanism, Not an Asceticism

Twelve Step spirituality is about being fully human, not inhumanly perfect. Instincts are vehicles of our humanity. "Without them," Bill says, "we wouldn't be complete human beings." They push the agenda of our inmost nature into the

---

[13] Bill Wilson, *Twelve Steps and Twelve Traditions,* pg 49, 1953

world of action and responsibility. Thus, the Twelve Steps do not aim to remove our instinctual drives. They do not deny the instincts. The Steps seek to embody them in their highest form; to follow the true course of our natural drives.

In the fulfillment of our instincts, we find meaning. When, in the course of events, the thrust of an instinct is actualized, that moment is said to be meaningful. In that instance, a piece of our inmost nature is realized or made real. For this reason, Emerson says, instinct is "the essence of genius, virtue, and of life." It voices our original nature. That said, we must overhaul the attitudes that steer these instincts.

The Steps are not naïve about our instincts. They are aware of their "power," as well as their tendency to "overreach themselves." Steps Six and Seven aim to drastically revise "our old attitudes toward our instincts," tempering and redirecting "our desires for emotional security and wealth, for personal prestige and power, for romance, and for family satisfactions."

Character defects are points at which we depart from our true nature. When the instincts "drive us blindly," writes Wilson, "or we willfully demand that they supply us with more satisfactions or pleasures than are possible or due us, that is the point at which we depart from the degree of perfection that God wishes for us here on earth."[14] Steps Six and Seven are not moral absolutes that appraise our essential worth. They promote an earthly perfection—not an inhuman

---

[14] Bill Wilson, *Twelve Steps and Twelve Traditions,* pg 65, 1953

ideal, but an equilibrium—that balances progress and perfection.

The words "entirely" and "all" are concerning to some. They appear to represent a degree of perfection that is unattainable and therefore, a source of great frustration. Upon closer examination, both "entirely" and "all" are softened by the word "ready." Twelve Step spirituality endeavors to cultivate an honest, heartfelt *desire* to live in accord with higher principles. It is this desire that pleases the divine longing, not its flawless execution. Step Six is all about willingness.

Willingness isn't a platitude used to conceal indifference. "Any person capable of enough willingness and honesty to try repeatedly Step Six on all his faults," says Fr. Dowling, "has indeed come a long way spiritually." It is hard to let go of greed when it produces the desired outcome. Gluttony is tempting when it promises instant comfort. When angry, it is difficult to pause and examine our faults—yet that is precisely what Step Six requires. It calls for a perfect willingness, a sincere desire to rise above selfishness and self-centeredness, which is measured by effort, not rhetoric. It states "the best possible attitude one can take in order to make a beginning on this lifetime job."[15]

Principled living is not a "lifetime job" because it is an impossible task. It takes a lifetime because the duty entailed is coextensive with our lifespan. It is a responsibility embedded in the structure of our being. Principled living is a

---

[15] Bill Wilson, *Twelve Steps and Twelve Traditions,* pg 65, 1953

marathon, not a sprint. The journey of a thousand miles begins with a single step, but it requires countless more, so better to focus on the process rather than the destination. That's the difference between progress and perfection.

At first glance, cultivating the willingness required to part with our shortcomings seems easy. "Practically everybody wishes to be rid of his most glaring and destructive handicaps," Wilson concedes. "No one wants to be so proud that he is scorned as a braggart, nor so greedy that he is labeled a thief. No one wants to be angry enough to murder, lustful enough to rape, gluttonous enough to ruin his health. No one wants to be agonized by the chronic pain of envy or to be paralyzed by sloth."[16] However, these extremes do not span the expanse of our shortcomings. Our willingness must go further.

The Ugly Truth About Our Shortcomings

Seldom do we lack willingness where our most egregious and ruinous defects are concerned. We run deficits where our more moderate vices are concerned. For example, the alcoholic can hardly congratulate themselves for wanting to shrug off an addiction that threatens their life and breeds misery for their loved ones. Just as the equestrian plagued by hemorrhoids abstains from horseback riding out of necessity, we part with our most flagrant and crippling defects out of self-interest. Willingness must transcend self-interest if it hopes to rise above ego.

---

[16] Bill Wilson, *Twelve Steps and Twelve Traditions,* pg 66, 1953

In his treatment of Step Six, Bill Wilson makes use of the "Seven Deadly Sins." The Seven Deadly Sins is a list of shortcomings originally compiled by Evagrius Ponticus, an influential Christian theologian and contemplative.[17] The list was intended to serve a diagnostic function, which is how Wilson uses it. Still, if you prefer another system, then by all means. The list is helpful only in that it provides us with characteristics that enable us to chart our patterns. There are plenty of other categorical systems, such as Buddhism's "ten non-virtuous actions." Identifying the points at which we depart from our True Life matters more than the names attributed to those points of departure. For our purposes, we'll proceed with the Seven Deadly Sins: pride, gluttony, anger, lust, greed, sloth, and envy.

The compass of each category stretches from the extreme to the moderate. If we were to chart our willingness to part ways with our shortcomings, we would likely notice a decline as we move from the severe into the socially acceptable range. And it is this sharp decline that is largely responsible for our seeming inability to part with many of our character defects. The uncomfortable truth is that we like them.

On the surface, physical violence is separated from verbal ridicule by several degrees but beneath the surface—which is to say, in the spiritual realm—both are both anger. Separating the two is haggling over magnitude. Most readily admit that when anger escalates to physical violence, it has

---

[17] Also one of the Desert Fathers, a group of contemplative monks that lived in the deserts of Lebanon, Egypt, and Syria in the 4th century.

gone too far, but who among us does not occasionally feel justified in weaponizing anger with libelous gossip? Does it not provide us with a comfortable air of superiority? And in this false sense of superiority is the ego not gratified?

The Steps do not claim perfection, but they do force us to struggle against perfect ideals in the name of progress. We may never fully realize these ideals, but that's not the point. The struggle is the point. These ideals choke off selfishness and self-centeredness wherever they are found.

The Steps operate on the spiritual plane and at that level, force and slander are of one taste. Anger is anger, as far as the Twelve Steps are concerned. Clinging to socially acceptable anger is clinging to anger, plain and simple. It goes without saying that if we hold onto something, we can't let go of it. Clinging to gossip keeps alive the possibility of violence because it gives sanctuary to anger.

We can say the same of all our defects. Unchecked envy that leads to theft or fraud is intolerable to most everyone, but how much time and energy is wasted wanting what we do not have or resenting those who have it? Jesus says of lust, "You have heard that it was said, 'You shall not commit adultery.' But I say to you that everyone who looks on another with lust has already committed adultery in their heart."[18] Who among us is not guilty of such "imaginary sex excursions?"

Wilson offers similar critiques of greed, gluttony, and sloth: "Isn't it true that we like to let greed masquerade as

---

[18] Matthew 5:27-28, NRSV

ambition? When gluttony is less than ruinous, we have a milder word for that, too; we call it 'taking our comfort.' Consider, too, our talents for procrastination, which is really sloth in five syllables."[19] In every case, we are quick to dismiss the extreme, while holding tight to its subtler cousin, even though both fall short of our true nature, making them shortcomings. Step Six states that little progress can be made unless we are *willing* to "entirely" part ways with "all" our defects of character.

Many ask, "How can we accept the entire implication of Step Six? Why—that is perfection!" Bill unapologetically responds, "We shall need to raise our eyes toward perfection, and be ready to walk in that direction," tapering at the end: "It will seldom matter how haltingly we walk. The only question will be, *Are we ready?*" Steps Six and Seven state perfect ideals but emphasize readiness, rather than the unerring execution. An essential part of readiness is preparation.

Humility

Just as Steps Four and Five capitalize on the willingness cultivated in Three, Step Seven realizes the readiness harnessed by Six. It is where our honest desire becomes a humble effort. Step Seven reads, "Humbly asked Him to remove our shortcomings."

The seventh Step is anchored by the word "humbly," which, for some, is a scare word. It conjures off-putting

---

[19] Bill Wilson, *Twelve Steps and Twelve Traditions,* pg 67, 1953

images of piety that do not comport with modern sensibilities. Therefore, let's pause to consider the meaning of humility before proceeding.

The Steps do not indulge cheap substitutes. Beliefs that bear no fruit are immaterial opinions, as far as the Steps are concerned. Likewise, contrived piety is no substitute for genuine humility. False piety is the behavioral equivalent of empty spiritual rhetoric; the latter is plagiarism, the former imitation, and as Emerson says, "Imitation is suicide."[20] There is no life in either. Plagiarism and imitation omit something vital, even when they mouth the right words and mime the right behaviors. The missing ingredient is humility.

"The basic ingredient of all humility," writes Wilson, is "a desire to seek and do God's will." God's will is revealed by the percolations of our inmost nature. If deviating from our true nature is a defect of character, then we seek the will of God by earnestly aspiring to that nature. *This aspiration is humility.*

The soul is always uncharted territory. Who we are is forever expanding into the present moment. When we fall in love for the first time, certain aspects of our character, hitherto unknown, are called forth; still more surfaces when we suffer our first heartbreak. When our first child is born, more is revealed; and so it is with loss. This unfolding carries on until our last breath.

---

[20] Ralph Waldo Emerson, "Self-Reliance," 1841

Humility doesn't say that we are broken. It reminds us that we are never complete. We may be whole, full, or content, but finished we are not. Our true self is not an outcome achieved but a center of experience in which we abide. This center is comprised of mirror-like awareness, which alone is empty enough to reflect the ever-unfolding present. This awareness is the principal source of truth, and humility designates conscience as its spokesperson.

Humility is not groveling, but it is subservient. It serves the provocations of our inmost being. Emerson says it best, when we writes, "No law can be sacred to me but my nature. The only right is what is after my constitution. The only wrong what is against it."[21] This standard wrests command from ego, providing us with a navigational compass. This compass is conscience, which intuits and holds fast to the promptings of our heart, keeping us true to our path. This is what Wilson means when he writes, "The seventh Step is where we make the change in our attitude which permits us, with humility as our guide, to move out from ourselves toward others and toward God."[22]

Humility is, in essence, an honest desire to seek and do the will of our Higher Power, which in practice, is an adherence to our highest Self. This requires a renunciation of those shortcomings deemed socially taboo, as well as those eliciting no complaint from others. Humility is no more concerned with public conduct than it is with how we conduct

---

[21] Ralph Waldo Emerson, "Self-Reliance," 1841

[22] Bill Wilson, *Twelve Steps and Twelve Traditions,* pg 76, 1953

ourselves when no one is looking. It peers even into our private thoughts.

Envious enough to steal blots out the light of our Higher Power, no less than masquerading as someone we are not to win the affections of others. Envy is a mental state before it is an action, and both produce pain and discontentment. For this reason, humility maintains a healthy awareness of our imperfections. However, its efforts never go the way of morbid reflection. Instead, humility sees hope in our imperfections. It points out our shortcomings because humility finds room to grow in them.

Since humility binds us to the sacred law written on our heart, it also demands we study that law. Humility insists that we plumb our depths because we cannot adhere to a law of which we are ignorant. This probe begins with Step Four and continues with Five, Six, and Seven, but we must persist in searching our minds and hearts, for humility is a lifelong commission.

Practicing Step Seven

The formal practice of Step Seven is carried out by saying the following prayer: "My Creator, I am now willing that you should have all of me, good and bad. I pray that you now remove from me every single defect of character which stands in the way of my usefulness to you and my fellows. Grant me strength, as I go out from here, to do your bidding. Amen."[23] The wording is, once again, optional.

We say every word slowly, allowing the meaning of each to fall on us. However, the seventh Step is not merely an event that separates Six and Eight. This prayer, and more importantly, its spirit must join us in daily living. This involves mindfully saying the prayer throughout the day, allowing the weight of "I am now willing that you should have all of me" to rest on our heart. But it also means learning to pray unceasingly; that is the prayerful language of intentional action.

It's naïve to believe that some prayerful formula can magically overcome our deeply rooted character defects. We cannot wish them away. The Twelve Steps demand more. If our inventory suggests that we are predisposed to fits of rage, for example, it is not enough to hope that we will respond to our next provocation with tolerance. We must work in the interim to prepare ourselves. We have to pray for those we resent on a daily basis. Praying for those we disdain simulates resentment, giving us a chance to install the circuitry needed to return love and compassion the next time, instead of hate, the next time we are angered. In this way, we train or prepare ourselves to respond differently in the real world. As the great theologian, Meister Eckhart said, "What we plant in the soil of contemplation, we shall reap in the harvest of action."

Humility scoffs at the entitled arrogance that awaits an effortless triumph over our defects. Instead, it prepares. It does

---

[23] Bill Wilson, *Alcoholics Anonymous*, pg 76, 1939

the footwork. "If we ask, God will certainly forgive our derelictions," writes Wilson. "But in no case does He render us white as snow and keep us that way without our cooperation."[24]

We are co-operators in this process, and our cooperation comes in the form of preparation. We have to be proactive, laying the groundwork for change *before* temptation arises. If lust is a weakness of ours, we might find it helpful to preemptively derail those libidinous trains of thought. Prayer is useful to this end, but in the run of life, we can't expect to deflate excited thoughts, unless we are aware of them. Thus, a daily routine that includes meditation must be part of our regimen.

Not all preparation involves overt spiritual practices, like prayer and meditation. If we struggle with gluttony, it may prove wise to eat a healthy snack in advance of a sugar craving. If jealousy besets us, we might benefit from a grateful account of our blessings, in lieu of another envious report of our debts. The main point is that we cooperate; that we proactively engage the process, instead of reactively redressing our defects.

Step Seven is not wishing to have all of our shortcomings removed, nor is it a "full frontal assault" on them. When "letting go" consists only of abstaining, we are white-knuckling it. Humility is willing, not iron-willed. It first appeals to a Higher Power, but then it takes action. Humility is participation in something bigger than self.

---

[24] Bill Wilson, *Twelve Steps and Twelve Traditions,* pg 65, 1953

We often wait for suffering to force us to change, but it need not be that way. In the beginning, suffering brings us to spirituality. However, this coercion isn't required. "We saw we needn't always be bludgeoned and beaten into humility," writes Wilson. "It could come quite as much from our voluntary reaching for it as it could from unremitting suffering. A great turning point in our lives came when we sought for humility as something we really wanted, rather than as something we must have. It marked the time when we could commence to see the full implication of Step Seven: 'Humbly asked Him to remove our shortcomings.'"[25]

Step Seven is a turning point in our spirituality. It inaugurates a life of principled living, which is the highest order of freedom, freedom from ego.

---

[25] Bill Wilson, *Twelve Steps and Twelve Traditions,* pg 75, 1953

12 MAKING AMENDS

"Do the right thing. It will gratify some people and astonish the rest." ~ Mark Twain

Novices skimming the Twelve Steps often glad-hand with the first three proposals, dismiss the next six, and pay lip-service to Steps Ten and Eleven in route to Twelve where they see themselves exalted in selfless service. Of course, the Steps bluntly reject this wishful thinking, saying, "You can't give away what you do not have." They test our concern for the suffering multitudes by checking our willingness to amend the suffering we caused others. Steps Eight and Nine are the gauntlet.

Altruistic intentions worn on the sleeve are phony when our closet is full of skeletons. Disingenuous motives are ulterior motives, and hiding behind these motives is the usual suspect, ego. This is ego's latest attempt to circumvent the uncomfortable, deflating stages of the journey. Step Nine does more to dislodge ego than any other Step. It is where transformation takes physical form.

Any spiritual path worth its weight in salt encourages adherents to devote their life to service. Purposeful living is selfless living. Therefore, all authentic paths empty into love and charity. The Twelve Steps are no different. They fit us to be of maximum service to our fellow man, but they do so responsibly. They instruct us to set right our wrongs before they send us to help others.

Useful Alterations

The ninth Step reads, "Made direct amends to such people wherever possible, except when to do so would injure them or others." Contrary to popular belief, an amends is not an apology. An apology is a defense, as in Plato's *Apology*, which records Socrates' defense against trumped up charges of corruption. Another example is *apologetics*, the discipline of defending an ideological position.

Apologies tend to strike a defensive tone: "I'm sorry, but…." The first half is disarming; whereas, the second act is self-defense. "I'm sorry" sets the stage for everything after "but," which cites the faults of others or extenuating circumstances to annul personal responsibility: "I'm sorry I lost my temper, but I didn't get enough sleep last night." The ninth Step is about changing direction, not defending the present course.

Steps Four through Nine are the nucleus of A.A.'s path structure. They come from the "sharing of sins" and "restitution" in the Oxford Group. However, these practices do not belong to A.A.'s forerunners, or to A.A. for that matter. They are rooted in the centuries-old traditions of confession, interior penance, and restitution, which are common to all spiritual traditions. A.A.'s pluralism recast these universal practices in the irreligious language of inventory, admission, letting go, and amends. While the Steps do not use the terms "sin" and "restitution," examining these terms will shed light on the path ahead.

Sin and repentance go hand in hand. "Sin" means to be "misguided" or "to miss the mark."[1] Repentance is the *adjustment*, the course correction. It comes from the Greek word "metanoia," meaning "to look back, regret mistakes, and change direction." In other words, to repent is to amend our ways. Repentance is the renewal of our minds and hearts. It restores our "will and life" to sanity.

In contrast to an apology and consistent with the character of the Steps, an amends demands action. The word "amendment" is perhaps most often associated with the U.S. Constitution. James Madison, one of the architects of that document, defines an amendment, in *Federalist* 43, as a "useful alteration." In other words, to "amend" is to change something for the better.

When we make a direct amends, we produce a change in behavior that sets right the wrong in question. For example, if

---

[1] Greek, *hamartia* /Hebrew, *hatta'h*

we stole money or borrowed without repaying, the amends is a reimbursement, not remorseful mumblings. An indirect amends is a change of behavior designed to correct misguided patterns of behavior that harms others. It can also be used to right a wrong committed against someone who is unavailable for a direct amends.

The central refrain of Step Nine is "What can I do to make it right?" The amends brings us face-to-face with the aggrieved party. We acknowledge our wrongdoing, then ask, "What can I do to make it right?" This all-important question puts the ball in the other person's court.

The ninth Step is indifferent to what we want and don't want. It makes no account of our inconveniences and is impervious to our fears and expectations. It is single-pointedly focused on righting the wrongs we committed. "What can I do to make it right?" ensures that the amends is "other-centered." It concentrates us on what we can do for them, which takes ego out of the equation.

Amends are selfless acts, and since selfless action is the essence of spiritual transformation, each amends sows seeds of awakening. Of course, these acts must be sustained to bring about lasting change, but with each amends a bit of our potential is realized. For this reason, Bill Wilson concludes his ninth Step commentary in the *Big Book* with a description of life on the other side of the spiritual experience, commonly referred to as "The Promises."

The Promises claim that "we will lose interest in selfish things and gain interest in our fellows. Self-seeking will slip away. Our whole attitude and outlook upon life will change."[2] Why do we suddenly "lose interest in selfish things and gain interest in our fellows?" The amends process realigns our consciousness. It establishes higher order principles as our polestar, instead of self-interest.

Step Nine initiates a tectonic shift in our orientation toward life. This shift is not instantaneous, however. It begins with the fourth and fifth Steps, which focus on our faults, instead of the wrongdoing of others. It continues with Steps Six and Seven, converting the inventoried material into a healthy awareness of our shortcomings. Step Eight goes further, translating that material into an action plan. The ninth Step returns to the scene of the crime to do what is right, not what is expedient, thereby ushering in an ecstatic experience.

The word "ecstatic" comes from the Greek *ekstasis*, which means "standing outside oneself." It is an "out of ego" experience. When we execute a proper amends, we step out of self-interest—and therefore, outside of ego—resulting in a spiritual awakening. This is the gradual *metanoia* promised by the Twelve Steps.[3]

Define Harm

We can break Step Eight into two parts: "Made a list of all persons we had harmed" and "became willing to make

---

[2] Bill Wilson, *Alcoholics Anonymous,* pg 84, 1939

[3] Bill Wilson and William James refer to it as the "educational variety" of spiritual experience.

amends to them all." We will begin with the first part, which requires a definition of "harm." What does it mean to harm someone in the context of Step Eight?

Restricting "harm" to those excesses wherein most of us do not traffic is impractical and too convenient. Harm certainly includes physical abuse, theft, and infidelity but it is not limited to such extremes. "What happens when we wallow in depression, self-pity oozing from every pore, and inflict that upon those about us?" Wilson asks. "What happens when we try to dominate the whole family, either by a rule of iron or by a constant outpouring of minute directions for just how their lives should be lived from hour to hour?"[4] These subtler examples widen the scope of harm, forcing us to scrutinize our behavior more intensely.

Step Eight assesses harm on multiple levels. "To define the word 'harm' in a practical way," writes Wilson, "we might call it the result of instincts in collision, which cause physical, mental, emotional, or spiritual damage to people." Our definition of harm must span all four levels: physical, mental, emotional, and spiritual. When we steal money from someone or lash out at them physically, the harm done is obvious. When we steal peace of mind from them or rob them of their emotional security, the harm is not so clear. "It neither picks their pocket nor breaks their leg." Nevertheless, they lose something of value, and our definition of harm must account for those losses.

---

[4] Bill Wilson, *Twelve Steps and Twelve Traditions,* pg 81, 1953

The eighth Step also rejects the cold, unfeeling standard that tallies only offenses motivated by ill-will. Wrongdoings are frequently born of ignorance and insensitivity; still, the effects are no less stinging. Our definition of harm must reckon with these thoughtless transgressions as well.

Every relationship comes with obligations. We owe our children affection, direction, and patience. Yet, they are deprived of these needs when business monopolizes our time and energy. Of course, our intent is not to withhold love; rather, ego hijacks the instinctual drive toward meaning, purpose, and fulfillment to pursue our interests irrespective of other's rights and needs. Is this inattentiveness not a product of self-absorption? The eighth Step does not write this damage off. It logs it as a dereliction of duty.

We arouse jealousy and angst when we behave without regard for those with whom we are intimately involved. The harm is not necessarily deliberate, but it is nevertheless a misdeed. Similarly, the space surrounding us is inhospitable when our patience is thin, and our temper is chronically flared. As a result, family and coworkers suffer our poor spiritual hygiene, even though we are unmindful of it. Self-care is our responsibility, not theirs. When we fail to meet this responsibility, the eighth Step holds us accountable.

Selfishness doesn't just pick pockets and breaks legs, it also breaks hearts and strips people of their autonomy. Self-centeredness doesn't just ignore the rights of others, it denies them the right to be "an other." It casts them as supporting characters in ego's drama. "On that basis we are almost always in collision with something or somebody, even though our motives are good."[5] When we act selfishly, we do so at the expense of others, and this expense is what Step Eight means by "harm."

Now that we have a working definition of harm, we can begin compiling our eighth Step list. Most of these offenses are on our personal inventory, but we should also search our memory for those not included on our fourth Step. The list itself is simple. We write down every instance in which our instincts collided with the needs or rights of another resulting in spiritual, emotional, mental, or physical damage— regardless of whether your motives were good or not. Include the name and the harm done. Having completed our list, we can proceed to part two of Step Eight, "became willing to make amends to them all."

Personal Relations

"Steps Eight and Nine are concerned with personal relations." According to Wilson, the goal is to "develop the best possible relations with every human being we know." He describes this endeavor as "a moving and fascinating adventure," wherein we aspire to "live in the greatest peace, partnership, and brotherhood with all men and women."[6] This high-minded ideal lifts our gaze toward perfection. It is not a moral absolute by which we calculate our worth. It is a perfect ideal that facilitates progress, like the objectives stated in Six and Seven.

---

[5] Bill Wilson, *Alcoholics Anonymous,* pg 60, 1939

[6] Bill Wilson, *Twelve Steps and Twelve Traditions*, pg 77, 1953

Direct amends is the charge of Step Nine. An amends is a change in behavior. This adjustment proceeds from self-reflection. We see where we are off target, then correct course. Therefore, an examination of our interpersonal conduct is a prerequisite of Step Nine. This examination is a critical piece of Step Eight. "The purpose of making restitution to others is paramount," but as Bill states, "it is equally necessary that we extricate from an examination of our personal relations every bit of information about ourselves and our fundamental difficulties that we can."[7] Our eighth Step is a guidebook to better relations before it is a list of amends.

"Since defective relations with other human beings have nearly always been the immediate cause of our woes," Wilson says that "no field of investigation could yield more satisfying and valuable rewards than this one."[8] This investigation reveals the miscalculations that pave the way for our misdeeds. "Calm, thoughtful reflection upon personal relations can deepen our insight." Simply put, patience becomes a more practicable objective when we see and appreciate the consequences of our impatience. Acknowledging the price others pay for our indifference makes us more mindful of their thoughts and feelings; a sincere desire to be more loving and affectionate is aroused when we walk a mile in the shoes of those who suffer our preoccupations.

---

[7] Bill Wilson, *Twelve Steps and Twelve Traditions*, pg 80, 1953
[8] Ibid, pg. 80

Interior Restitution

Seldom do we pause to feel the collateral impact of our conduct upon others. Even rarer is a just appraisal of the long-term consequences we dole out to bystanders. If we wish to change directions, such considerations are in order. We must not only see with the mind's eye but empathize, feeling the hidden—and often, long-lasting effects—of our attitudes and actions. Cultivating compassion for friend and enemy alike is an indispensable part of learning to "live in the greatest peace, partnership, and brotherhood with all men and women." This is easier said than done, which is why Step Eight says we have to "become willing."

Willingness is easy to come by where loved ones are concerned. We are tender toward those closest to us, and merely recounting our trespasses inspires us to do better. It is easy to empathize with our spouse, children, and friends because we see their humanity. We see them as vulnerable, well-intentioned people trying to be happy and avoid suffering. As a result, we readily take their thoughts and feelings into account. We are not as quick to feel the pain of those we resent.

Empathy is more elusive with enemies. The forces of resentment dehumanize them. Self-centeredness depicts them as inherently antagonistic, deserving of the misdeeds our selfishness deals them. We cannot right a wrong if the animosity that underlies the wrongdoing is still active.

We have to work harder to see foes as vulnerable, well-intentioned people. While the path forward is more difficult, it is, in essence, the same. With few exceptions, foes are no different than friends. They are people trying to be happy and avoid suffering; only their efforts collided with ours. We glean this truth when we move past our hardened thoughts and feelings about them, which takes work. Once again, prayer is our vehicle. It applies a higher theory of mind and opens the pathways of compassion.

We go through the names on our eighth Step list, praying for each, friend and enemy alike. The wording is optional, but it should convey an attitude of kindness and tolerance, as well as the aspiration to embody that attitude. For example:

> Picture their face; allow that image to become vivid. Then, offer a prayer: "[Name of the aggrieved], I want you to be free of suffering, especially the harm I caused you by [insert wrongdoing here]; I hope you find true happiness and all its causes; [God], grant me the willingness to do whatever is within my power to aid them on their journey."

When resistance persists, remember that our enemies are not "enemies" from their side. There are those who love and care for them, just as there are those who despise our loved ones. "Friend" and "enemy" are equalized in the realization that both are self-centered categories of thought. The resistance is within us. It does not emanate from them. This resistance is a symptom of resentment, which is a trapping of ego. It is the hemlock we are trying to purge from our system. Sustained prayer and meditation is the treatment. Continue to pray for them until the resistance falls away.

Making Direct Amends

In Step Nine, we go out of ourselves into the world of action and responsibility intent on contributing to the lives of others. This is where transformation takes place. The ninth Step is where the tight, self-centered rotation of ego reverses course and begins pouring into the stream of life.

This change in direction requires a great deal of momentum. The amends process actualizes the momentum generated in the previous Steps. The ninth Step uses action to incarnate this potential, which constitutes the "personality change" that Wilson called a "spiritual awakening." Our journey is near the summit; much is at stake. Therefore, it is critical that we quickly complete the process, lest our momentum fizzle out.

Once our eighth Step list is complete, and we have studied it and reconciled ourselves to the task ahead, it is time to act. While we are careful not to attempt any amends without first preparing ourselves, we are just as careful not to hide behind over preparation. "Let's not talk prudence while practicing evasion," Wilson cautions. Once we "feel confident in our new way of life" and begin "by our behavior and example, to convince those about us that we are indeed changing for the better," Wilson says it is "safe to talk in complete frankness with those who have been seriously affected." The only caveat being, "except when to do so would injure them or others."

Since a disregard for the well-being of others is the crux of our wrongdoings, a proper amends takes the well-being of others into account. "We may be quite willing to reveal the very worst," but as Wilson notes, "we cannot buy our own peace of mind at the expense of others."[9]

For instance, if we were unfaithful and our partner knows nothing of it, we do not drop that in their lap to clear our conscience. First, we unburden our conscience with a confessor. Then, we determine whether or not to salvage the marriage. Saving the marriage begins with discontinuing our dishonest behavior, but does not stop there. The amends goes further. It includes reinvesting in our partner, healing the wounds we inflicted. We have to live the amends. The living amends may still require a full confession, but we make that determination in consultation with a dispassionate advisor, such as a therapist or priest—never on a whim. Irresponsible disclosures threaten to hurt spouses and children. We cannot save ourselves at their expense because doing so is self-centered and therefore not a change in direction. It is counterproductive.

Similarly, disclosing misdeeds to an employer that could result in termination affects our dependents. Since our children did not commit the offense, they should not pay for the disclosure. The burden rests with us to find an indirect but honest way to rectify the wrongdoing. "When to do so would

---

[9] Bill Wilson, *Twelve Steps and Twelve Traditions*, pgs 84-85, 1953

injure them or others" is a restriction, not an exemption. It does not preclude an amends but charts an alternative course that honestly and thoughtfully steers toward the welfare of others.

The bar for this provision is clear: Does it harm others? If so, we can't remedy harms done by harming still more, so we look for an indirect route, pursuing creative countermeasures that actively address the harm done while avoiding reckless pronouncements. If the amends threatens the comfort of no one but ourselves, then we proceed with direct action.

Direct amends brings us face-to-face with the aggrieved party, unless an in-person meeting is impossible, in which case we phone or write. We may proceed first with friends and family, or elect to get the more difficult ones out of the way first. That is a matter of personal preference, but getting your feet wet with the easier amends may prove prudent. The commentary that follows starts with friends and family, then proceeds to more contentious relationships.

Friends and loved ones generally welcome our efforts. It is easy to contact them, explain our objectives, and make right the wrongs done. When we ask, "What can I do to make it right?" the most common response is likely to be, "Keep doing what you're doing. I want you to be happy." It's easy to gloss over this reply. However, we should be more diligent. Those two sentences may be intended to put the matter to rest, but there is more than meets the eye. These people do care about us. They really do want us to be happy, and we should take their wishes seriously.

"Keep doing what you're doing" does not mean "It's water under the bridge." It literally means, "Keep doing these things. Continue on this path of honest, principled living." When we take seriously "I just want you to be happy," it is an injunction to live a meaningful life. Flesh out what they're saying, and you hear, "I want you to commit yourself to the causes of happiness. I want you to make time for prayer, meditation, personal inventory, study, and exercise." This interpretation turns a threadbare response into a living amends.

Undoubtedly, there will be others more skeptical of our efforts. Perhaps they still love us and care about us, but have long suffered our behavior or been gravely wounded by it. Naturally, they are guarded against us. It is important not to reach for a tragic apology that aims to instantaneously repair the trust it took years to break. Such detours are taken by needy egos that cannot endure the suspicion or disdain of others. The question "What can I do to make it right?" safeguards against such insecurities. Ask the question and listen to their response. *Listen.* Don't talk. Rather than working on their skepticism with words, take their response to heart. Let action do the talking over the weeks, months, and years ahead.

Remember, an amends is not an apology. Of course, we may say, "I am sorry" but this must be followed by "What can I do to make it right?" Silence must punctuate this question, and in turn, this silence must morph into action. We ask, listen, and act. Otherwise, it is a personal defense posing as an amends. If we owe money, for example, then "I am sorry" must be followed with a check. Demonstrations of good will do more to reconcile broken relationships than proclamations. As the old saying goes, "Actions speak louder than words."

There may be still others who mock our efforts. When we put the question to them, they respond, "What can you do?! You can go to hell. That's what you can do!" We do not retaliate or try to persuade them of our cause. They have told us what to do, and we do it. We get lost. We leave them alone, focusing on the indirect amends. We see where our past behavior created this most unfortunate situation, and vow to never again treat a person like that. This vow isn't self-assuaging lip service. If action does not accompany the vow, it is an empty promise. Making good on this promise means committing ourselves to a regular diet of prayer, meditation, and self-reflection. Ultimately, it is about changing our behavior, not their mind. The ninth Step focuses on our attitudes and behaviors, not theirs.

In some cases, the amends can take an hour. In others, ten years. Appropriate compensation for a heated exchange may be a heartfelt admission of wrongdoing coupled with a sincere, ongoing effort to be more considerate in the future. On the other hand, making amends to our parents for a decade of deceit and freeloading, may require a proportionate period of volunteer lawn service. Whatever the case, we commit ourselves to the work entailed in living this amends.

Conclusion

At the outset, Step Nine appears daunting, but like Four and Five, it is liberating in hindsight. The ninth Step is where transformation becomes tangible. In the aforementioned "Promises," Bill Wilson says, "We will not regret the past nor wish to shut the door on it. We will comprehend the word serenity and we will know peace. No matter how far down the scale we have gone, we will see how our experience can benefit others."[10]

The promise that we cease regretting the past is striking, the claim that we will wish to leave that door open because it stands to increase the well-being of others is downright astonishing. It implies that our past wounds become a source of strength; that the vulnerabilities we desperately tried to conceal overthrow ego in a selfless revolution that sacrifices our pain for the benefit of others. This is the epitome of transformation, and it is a testament to the redemptive power of Twelve Step spirituality.

Redemption recasts yesterday's traumas as present-day assets. Those chapters of our life we once closed are left open so the still-suffering can read their words of hope and purpose. Our pain becomes the inner source whence our contribution to the world pours forth. When we find ourselves opposite someone in pain, the hope we offer them comes from our past—from the one place we refused to look, our suffering.

---

[10] Bill Wilson, *Alcoholics Anonymous,* pgs 83-84, 1939

13 SPIRITUAL MAINTENANCE

"A man's true greatness lies in the consciousness of an honest purpose in life, founded on a just estimate of himself and everything else, on frequent self-examinations, and a steady obedience to the rule which he knows to be right, without troubling himself about what others may think or say, or whether they do or do not that which he thinks and says and does." ~ Marcus Aurelius

The recognition of powerlessness in Step One opens the door to the search for Power in Two, just as the willingness found in Three finances our efforts in Four, and the catharsis of Step Five gives way to renunciation in Six and Seven, which leads to a course change in Eight and Nine. This rhythmic structure constitutes a systematic approach to spiritual practice.

One of this format's flaws is that it creates the illusion of a flat path, where the Steps are presumably taken One, Two,

Three, Four, Five, all the way through Twelve, at which point they are either abandoned or repeated. Those belonging to recovery communities are inclined toward the latter. They commonly work the Steps from beginning to end, *ad infinitum*. Those not belonging to recovery communities are more likely to view the Steps as a novel exercise: completed, then discarded. Neither conforms to the intentions of the Twelve Steps.

The problem with discarding the Steps is obvious: Unless they (or an equal path) are continually engaged, the gains made recede. The Steps promote spiritual fitness, which, like physical fitness, requires maintenance. Spiritual practice no more renders one permanently fit than a year of running guarantees a lifetime of optimal health. As practice waxes and wanes, so too does fitness.

Episodically working the Steps is a more complicated problem than simply discarding them. "Powerlessness" and "unmanageability" are key features of Step One. The goal of the Steps is to establish conscious contact with a Power by which we can live; that is, install higher order principles that restore sanity, freedom, and purpose. In a word, the Steps are "empowering," and once we are empowered, Step One no longer resonates. The remaining Steps remedy powerlessness and therefore, render Step One obsolete.

The Twelve Steps begin with powerlessness and unmanageability, so reworking them makes sense only if we are powerless and life is unmanageable. If Step One still resonates, there are two possibilities. First, the Twelve Steps failed to accomplish their objective in the first place. In this case, they are ineffective and repeating them doesn't make sense. This is a possibility. The Steps do not work for everyone. Common sense dictates that we drop them if they do not work for us. Since we take up what resonates and return to what works, repeating the process makes sense only if we revert to powerlessness and unmanageability after the Steps sent those afflictions into remission.

For the rinse-and-repeat theory to be sensible, the Steps must first establish conscious contact and remedy hopelessness; then, following a period of inaction, conscious contact has to atrophy and hopelessness has to return, requiring a second run through the Steps. While this rationale is intelligible, it is not the rationale of the Steps. It is predicated upon a "period of inaction," an error Wilson calls "resting on our laurels." The antidote he proposes is Step Ten.

Resting on Our Laurels

Laurels are ceremonious wreaths that signify accomplishment, like those placed on the heads of Olympians. The laurels to which Wilson refers are the spiritual benefits reaped from the Steps. We bask in our glory, so to speak, when we take for granted the peace and stability acquired through spiritual practice. These benefits are not self-sustaining. They are results. When the precipitating actions are discontinued, so too are the benefits.

"It is easy to let up on the spiritual program of action and rest on our laurels," Wilson says.[1] When we are not compelled

---

[1] Bill Wilson, *Alcoholics Anonymous,* pg 85, 1939

by suffering, complacency easily sets in, tempting us with laziness and cheap comforts. This tendency sells us short. It fails to plumb our depths, turning spirituality into a roundabout that merely skims the surface. Moreover, it conditions us to believe that rock bottom precedes every phase of spiritual growth; that suffering is the only available launching pad. This idea forestalls emotional and spiritual maturation. It excludes the possibility of frontiers beyond immediate relief, shackling us to square one: powerlessness and unmanageability.

We abridge the path when we settle "for only as much perfection as will get us by in life."[2] This approach redacts Steps Six and Seven, which stated that we needn't "be bludgeoned and beaten" into character building; that spiritual growth can come from "voluntary reaching" rather than "unremitting suffering."[3] This omission makes us prone to backsliding. It leaves us spiritually disengaged until suffering demands action and then, we exert ourselves no more than is required to pacify our pain. Thus, for every mile we advance, we retreat another, reducing the path to a Pong-like oscillation between unbearable suffering and periods of remission.

This recidivistic model schedules regular landings at the port of unmanageability. There our efforts are renewed, once more reviving the conscious contact atrophied by inaction. Again, this is not by design. The notion that rock bottom is the universal starting point for spiritual growth is antithetical to the Twelve Steps. They are designed to avoid the inaction that

---

[2] Bill Wilson, *Twelve Steps and Twelve Traditions*, pg 68, 1953

[3] Bill Wilson, *Twelve Steps and Twelve Traditions*, pg 75, 1953

recalls suffering. If the Steps were a flat-path punctuated by repose, they'd end at Step Nine before Ten instructs us to *continue*.

Maintenance

The tenth Step reads, "Continued to take personal inventory and when we were wrong promptly admitted it." The key word here is "continue." It guards against resting on our laurels by turning the path into a spiraling ascent that uses past accomplishments as a launching pad for future discoveries. The Twelve Steps are not intended to be repeated or discarded, but continued—that is, adopted as a way of life.

This level of perseverance is attainable only by those who see "character building as something desirable in itself."[4] This higher motivation is cultivated in Steps Six and Seven but in the tenth Step, growth for its own sake overtakes the evasion of suffering as our principal motivation. It becomes the thread of continuity that ties the Steps together, turning Twelve Step spirituality into a continuum of practice.

"As we work the first nine Steps we prepare ourselves for the adventure of a new life. But when we approach Step Ten we commence to put our A.A. way of living to practical use," Wilson says.[5] The tenth Step distills the previous nine proposals into a user-friendly format that enables the practitioner to continue sharpening the principles of surrender, self-analysis, humility, and restitution. In the spirit

---

[4] Bill Wilson, *Twelve Steps and Twelve Traditions,* pg. 72, 1953

[5] Bill Wilson, *Twelve Steps and Twelve Traditions,* pg. 88, 1953

of continuity, Step Ten also insists that we keep up the fight even when there is no struggle. "Day by day, in fair weather or foul," we are expected to chisel time into our day for prayer, meditation, and self-examination.

Steps Four through Nine disperse the clouds of self-centeredness, allowing the light of truth to break through. This "breakthrough" is called a "moment of clarity." In this moment, the curtains are drawn back and our life is illuminated. Step Ten keeps our conscience clear by continually checking our thoughts, words, and deeds against higher principles.

Step Ten is often described as a maintenance step. It is important to note, however, that Ten does not seek to maintain gains already made. "Holding ground" is the definition of "resting on our laurels." Step Ten aims to maintain conditions favorable for spiritual growth. It sustains the rate of growth by tending to the process, not by defending previous advancements. Progress demands the forfeiture of territories gained.

As we progress, the path narrows. We become conscious of God's presence in increasingly subtle ways, requiring diverse methods of self-examination that differ in precision and scope. We need methods capable of penetrating the deepest recesses of our soul and still others suited for daily life.

Retiring At Night

The tenth Step makes a habit of self-examination, humility, and restitution by fixing them into our daily routine. It is repetition that transmutes these practices into a way of life. Repetition demands a more expedient format than the one found in Steps Four through Nine, which is too bulky for daily use. Step Ten is more compact.

"Although all inventories are alike in principle, the time factor does distinguish one from another."[6] The encyclopedic inventory conducted in Four is not only too time-consuming for daily implementation, it also successfully removed the mounds of psychological debris that necessitated such an exhaustive effort in the first place. This sweeping process is still used for annual or perhaps bi-annual house cleanings, but our present objective demands a more concise model.

The tenth Step is a pithy technique that keeps our house in order and further develops our moral faculty. The development of this faculty is essential because a healthy, outspoken conscience is the only moral check petite enough to enter the stream of life. Step Ten aims to make self-examination a "working part of the mind."

The layout proposed by Bill Wilson is a simple ledger of the day's good and bad deeds. We end each day with a review of its proceedings. "We cast up a balance sheet, crediting ourselves with things well done, and chalking up debits where

---

[6] Bill Wilson, *Twelve Steps and Twelve Traditions,* pg 89, 1953

due."[7] In short, we list on one side all our successes and our failures on the other side.

Outcomes do not necessarily define "success." We may have failed to achieve the desired result but worked hard on the project, so we can celebrate our efforts. Conversely, we may reach a profitable result but by less than savory means—which deserves scrutiny, rather than praise. Moreover, following the dictates of conscience does not preclude the possibility of offense. When altruistic motives provoke objections, we evaluate our methods.

Where there are misdeeds, we carefully examine our motives. "Were we resentful, selfish, dishonest or afraid?" Wilson asks. "Do we owe an apology? Have we kept something to ourselves which should be discussed with another person at once?" And then, the all-important question, "What could we have done better?"[8] We conclude each day with such reflections. This practice keeps our conscience clear and in due time, makes self-inquiry habitual.

The balance sheet can take innumerable forms, but whatever form it takes, it needs to be brief. Persistence accomplishes the ultimate aim. The more complicated and time-consuming the practice, the less likely we are to persist. It makes self-examination a habit. Since simple methods prevent lapses, simplicity best serves the end goal. It aids in disciplining the mind.

---

[7] Bill Wilson, *Twelve Steps and Twelve Traditions,* pg 89, 1953

[8] Bill Wilson, *Alcoholics Anonymous,* pg 86, 1939

We can supplement Wilson's format with Benjamin Franklin's practice of virtue journaling (mentioned in Chapter Ten).[9] Franklin utilized inquiries akin to those prescribed by Wilson, but charted his progress in the practice of thirteen virtues, intending to "acquire the habitude" of each. Like the Seven Deadly Sins in Step Six, the list is amenable to our beliefs and aspirations. The value of Franklin's method is in its format. It simply measures the distance between our behavior and our professed values. Franklin's inventory is included here because it so neatly fits into the tenth Step that it hardly feels like an addendum. His pragmatic approach to spirituality and character building, in many ways, foreshadows Twelve Step spirituality.

The thirteen virtues Franklin charts are temperance, silence, order, resolution, frugality, industry, sincerity, justice, moderation, cleanliness, tranquility, chastity, and humility. "I made a little book, in which I allotted a page for each of the virtues," Franklin explains. "I ruled each page with red ink, so as to have seven columns, one for each day of the week, marking each column with a letter for the day. I crossed these columns with thirteen red lines, marking the beginning of each line with the first letter of one of the virtues, on which line, and in its proper column, I might mark, by a little black spot, every fault I found upon examination to have been committed respecting that virtue upon that day."[10] The virtue Franklin

---

[9] The author has also compiled a revised virtue journal available for purchase online, entitled: *Benjamin Franklin's Virtue Journal: A Diary of Self-Improvement by Benjamin Riggs*

[10] Benjamin Franklin, *The Autobiography of Benjamin Franklin,* pg 105, 1888 (For more information on Franklin's virtue journaling see Chapter 9 in his autobiography, "Plan for Attaining Moral Perfection")

focuses on rotates every week so that each is given special attention once in a thirteen-week cycle, which he repeats four times a year. The example below is the first seven-day cycle, "Temperance."

Temperance	Sun.	Mon.	Tues.	Wed.	Thur.	Fri.	Sat.
Temperance	❖			❖			❖
Silence			❖			❖	
Order	❖				❖		
Resolution		❖			❖		
Frugality			❖			❖	
Industry				❖			❖
Sincerity	❖	❖			❖		
Justice			❖			❖	
Moderation				❖			❖
Cleanliness	❖	❖			❖		
Tranquility			❖			❖	
Chastity				❖			❖
Humility		❖			❖	❖	

We can map the misdeeds revealed by Wilson's inquiries on to Franklin's graph. This combination effectively detects shortcomings and charts their frequency, and it does all of this in short order. Of course, we can choose to use only Wilson's or Franklin's method, or elect for an entirely different means of self-examination. The method is a matter of personal preference. Brevity and accountability are the only indispensables.

Journaling

Some might be turned off by the businesslike approach of charts and ledgers. They may instead prefer the practice of journaling. Journaling has a host of benefits, but it can also become time-consuming and wander off the rails of objectivity. These are two pitfalls we must avoid.

Avoiding lengthy methods is crucial. They endanger the daily routine. We can sidestep this snag by keeping the obligation to no more than ten minutes, perhaps extending it on occasion for pleasure or necessity.

Preserving objectivity is also critical. When journaling is venting in written form, it fails to provide personal accountability. Venting may be helpful and cathartic, but it is not an inventory practice. We avoid this rabbit hole by using writing prompts that tether the exercise to the principles of self-examination.

Using a stream of consciousness technique is also helpful. The charts and ledgers above provide little space for ego to rationalize and pontificate. Journaling is susceptible to both. Stream of consciousness uses tempo to shield the page from ego's contrivances. The hurried pace affords no time to prepare a statement and in this way, promotes rigorous honesty.

To begin the practice, write the prompt at the top of the page, "What good did I do with this day?" Write for five minutes on this prompt. Do not lift the pen from the page. In stream of consciousness journaling, you are a stenographer. Do not censor yourself. Write whatever comes to mind. If you get stuck, rewrite the topic where your pen sits. Do not stop writing until the time expires. When the five minutes has passed, write "Where did I fall short?" at the top of the page, and repeat the same instructions using this prompt. When you identify a shortcoming, investigate your motives.

The Spiritual Axiom

It does not matter whether we choose Wilson's or Franklin's method, journaling, or some combination of all three. If we commit ourselves to a daily inventory practice, then self-reflection will, in due time, become a working part of our mind. One could say it becomes "second nature," but in point of fact, self-examination belongs to the first order.

Self-examination promotes sanity and ethical behavior. Therefore, self-examination is a moral obligation. This work falls to "conscience," which probes mind and body for thoughts, words, and deeds that depart from our highest Self.

The conscience is designed for introspection; that's why we are better off finding a single fault in ourselves than a thousand in someone else. We have no jurisdiction over the lives of others. Identifying their faults brings us no closer to happiness. We do, however, make progress when the fault-finding mind turns inward. The intellect is in its natural posture when it is attuned to our thoughts and actions—to what we can control. This insight serves as the basis of Bill Wilson's spiritual axiom.

Initially, self-examination is a formal exercise, but persisting in this practice awakens our conscience. It habituates self-reflection and amplifies our moral voice, bringing self-examination into the world of action and responsibility. At this point, conscience begins to audit our thoughts, words, and deeds in real-time, rather than waiting until the day's end. Wilson calls this a "spot check" inventory.

A single line of code serves as the basis for self-analysis. This line reads, "It is a spiritual axiom that every time we are disturbed, no matter what the cause, there is something wrong with us."[11] An axiom is a self-evident truth. What about this statement is axiomatic or self-evident? Are there not instances in which others wrong us? Yes, and the above statement does not suggest otherwise. Wilson's axiom does not say others can do no wrong. It says the disturbance belongs to us, even if the other person is in the wrong. The other person is responsible for their actions, but not our state of mind. Fear, anger, jealousy, stress, and all the rest arise within the envelope of our skin, and are therefore our responsibility; that is the self-evident truth.

Wilson's spiritual axiom interprets emotional disturbances as warning signs. It sees them as alarms that sound when self-will supplants sanity and truth. We shouldn't confuse emotions and disturbances, however. They are not the same thing. Emotions become disturbances when the ego projects them onto others. Blame alienates emotion. When we put our feelings on others, we can't do anything with them because "others" lie outside our jurisdiction. Disempowered, the emotional energy mounts until it reaches the level of a disturbance.

---

[11] Bill Wilson, *Twelve Steps and Twelve Traditions,* pg 90, 1953

Emotions are experiences that arise within us. When we blame others, we cut ourselves from the truth of that experience. This is the source of insanity. The spiritual axiom sounds the alarm, triggering an internal audit that reintegrates our mind, body, and emotions. This investigation is, in essence, no different than the formal reviews discussed above. It differs only in application. The spot check inventory instantly combs through the preceding moments looking for the point we departed from God's will.

Since the disturbance belongs to us, it is incumbent upon us to pacify them before responding to our counterpart, lest we commit an offense deserving of an amends later. Therefore, self-restraint is a key component of the spot check inventory. Real-time reviews attempt to calm disturbances amidst the storm, requiring restraint not only of tongue and deed but the mind as well. We have to "pause when agitated or doubtful," Wilson says. Pausing "when agitated or doubtful" is easier said than done. This talent is acquired through practice. The training includes examining our successes and failures, as well as daily prayer and meditation.

Conclusion

The spiritual axiom transforms all obstacles into the path, adding a new dimension to our spirituality. The formal methods of self-analysis are too cumbersome to penetrate the present moment. Only conscience is slender enough to go with us into all of our affairs.

The awakening of conscience transforms daily life into the spiritual path. However, this is just the beginning. We need to grow in that awakening. We have to improve upon conscious contact, which requires prayer and meditation.

14 THE TWELVE STEP GOD

"The unconsciousness of man is the consciousness of God." ~ Henry David Thoreau

Bill Wilson was besieged by competing camps when he set to work on *Alcoholics Anonymous*. He was charged with the seemingly impossible task of designing a spiritual program that steered clear of both religiosity and materialism. This meant a path that included God, faith, and belief but not obligatory faith or belief in a particular God. The path had to be all-inclusive, while simultaneously having "depth and weight." Meaningless fluff wouldn't suffice. This is a difficult line to toe.

The only way to arrange an effective path that satisfies religious, spiritual, and skeptical seekers is to chart an interior course. In *Alcoholics Anonymous*, Wilson does precisely that. He paves the way with practices inherited largely from the Oxford Group, but the Twelve Steps are not a replica of the Oxford Group's program. They possess a unique character, a tone foreign to the Oxford Group. In a word, this characteristic might be called "mysticism."

The word mysticism has dreamy, occult-like connotations not endorsed by the Steps. Pragmatism tempers the Step's inward tendencies, fashioning a blue-collar mysticism that unites contemplative practice with action and carves out a path that connects our inmost being with daily life.

The Oxford Group was practical but lacked this air of mysticism, which the Steps take from Carl Jung and Emmet Fox. Jung furnishes inceptive observations that fix the Steps on an inward course; whereas, Fox supplies the crowning principle of that course. Jung and Fox join Silkworth, James, and Dowling, capping the list of Wilson's muses. These people, along with A.A.s pioneers, set the Steps apart from their more heavy-handed predecessors.

God or Belly?

In January of 1961, Bill Wilson wrote to Carl Jung, "To you, to Dr. Shoemaker of the Oxford Groups, to William James, and to my own physician, Dr. Silkworth we of A.A. owe this tremendous benefaction." Bill goes on to say, "Very many thoughtful A.A.s are students of your writings. Because of your conviction that man is something more than intellect, emotion, and two dollars' worth of chemicals, you have especially endeared yourself to us." Undoubtedly, Bill W. was one of those "thoughtful A.A.'s" who found the Swiss doctor endearing.

Bill greatly admired Carl Jung. He came by this admiration honestly. Wilson witnessed stunning demonstrations by men and women of science that nourished his insatiable curiosity, fired his imagination, and stirred his ambitious spirit. But Wilson was not alone. The scientific discoveries made in the late 18th and early 19th centuries were cashed in for shares of the public's trust. The invention of the telephone, the light bulb, and the automobile, coupled with the Wright Brother's flight at Kitty Hawk, medical advancements, Einstein's theories of relativity, and the publication of Freud's *Interpretation of Dreams,* all contributed to science's increasing prestige.

At the turn of the 20th century, Psychology was trending in America's intellectual marketplace. In 1909, the world's foremost psychiatrist, Sigmund Freud, was invited to deliver five lectures at Clark University in Worcester, Massachusetts. This was his first and only trip to the United States. His principal protégé, Carl Jung, accompanied him on this journey.

Both Freud and Jung were received in the lecture hall at Clark University by the "Father of American Psychology," William James. Jung and James used the occasion to pick each other's brains. "I spent two delightful evenings with James alone, and I was tremendously impressed by the clearness of his mind and the complete absence of intellectual prejudices," Jung recalled. The two great thinkers primarily discussed parapsychology and the psychology of religious experience.[1]

---

[1] Letter from Carl Jung to Virginia Payne, July 23, 1949

The work of William James and Carl Jung neatly overlapped with Bill Wilson's needs. As philosophers and psychologists with a keen interest in religion and spirituality, James and Jung had one foot in the distinguished world of science and the other in the great beyond. Consequently, they were perfectly positioned to bridge the hemorrhaging gap between the religious and atheistic factions that threatened Alcoholics Anonymous in its infancy.

In these intellectual giants, Wilson discovered a psychological interpretation of spiritual experience that reconciled religionists and skeptics with A.A.'s spiritual but not religious center. This psychological view replaced religious conversion with interior reformation. Furthermore, James and Jung were internationally renowned. Since Wilson was an anonymous drunk, citing these great minds amplified his voice and legitimized his work.

When William James met Sigmund Freud in 1909, he told the founder of psychoanalysis, "The future of psychology belongs to your work." William James passed away one year later. Freud died six months after the *Big Book* was published. When the *Post* article that launched *Alcoholics Anonymous* hit newsstands in 1941, Carl Jung was the most prominent psychiatrist in the world. Of particular interest, were his ideas about religion and spirituality. Jung returned to America in 1937, delivering a series of lectures at Yale University. These lectures were published the following year under the title, *Psychology and Religion*.

When the *Big Book* went to print, Jung was not only the world's leading expert on the psychology of religion, but he also had a loose affiliation with the emerging Twelve Step movement—a fact Bill was prepared to advertise. According to Wilson, the "astonishing chain of events" that begot Alcoholics Anonymous started in Jung's "consulting room."[2] Of course, he is referring to the doctor's analysis of Roland Hazard—the alcoholic businessman who, upon his return to the States, introduced Bill's childhood friend, Ebby Thacher, to Sam Shoemaker and the Oxford Group. This connection enabled Wilson to claim association with the famed psychoanalyst without awkwardly overreaching, which conferred still more legitimacy on the tenderfoot fellowship.

Bill invokes the Swiss psychiatrist's considerable prestige in the second chapter of *Alcoholics Anonymous*, "There is a Solution." He summarizes Jung's counsel to Hazard, placing special emphasis on their parting exchange. The renowned doctor underscored the hopelessness of Roland's alcoholic condition and encouraged him to seek a spiritual solution. However, he was careful to differentiate between religion and spirituality. Jung told Hazard that "while his religious convictions were very good, in his case they did not spell the necessary vital spiritual experience." Inserting this remark enabled Wilson to stress the differences between spirituality and religion with supreme authority.

Wilson also included Jung's definition of spiritual experience. "Exceptions to cases such as yours have been occurring since early times," Jung told Hazard. "Here and

---

[2] Letter from Bill Wilson to Carl Jung, January 23, 1961

there, once in a while, alcoholics have had what are called *vital spiritual experiences*." He defines these experiences as "huge emotional displacements and rearrangements," wherein "ideas, emotions, and attitudes" that were "once the guiding forces of the lives of these men are suddenly cast to one side, and a completely new set of conceptions and motives begin to dominate them."[3] This psychological interpretation of the spiritual experience is the inceptive idea that turns the Steps within.

Readers of *Alcoholics Anonymous* find a footnote at the bottom of page twenty-seven that refers them to an appendix entitled, "Spiritual Experience." This footnote is pinned to Jung's description of spiritual experience. The postscript did not appear in the book's first printing. It was added two years later. Wilson wanted to clarify the terms "spiritual awakening" and "spiritual experience," which readers initially confused with "sudden and spectacular upheavals." To clarify, he turned once more to William James. He stressed that spiritual awakenings vary in nature and that the most common class is slow developing. Wilson labeled this gradual class, "the educational variety," a phrase borrowed from James. In this brief postscript, Wilson also redeployed Jung's psychological interpretation of spiritual experience.

The appendix defines "spiritual awakening" as a "personality change sufficient to bring about recovery from alcoholism." Wilson's "personality change" is synonymous with Jung's "rearrangement of ideas, emotions, and attitudes." Both point to an interior or psychological transformation. The

---

[3] Bill Wilson, *Alcoholics Anonymous,* pg 27, 1939

postscript does offer one new insight. It suggests that the Steps functionally favor an inner Higher Power.

There are numerous references to an immanent God in the original text. At times, it even categorically endorses an indwelling conception of God. For instance, "We found the Great Reality deep down within us. In the last analysis it is only there that He may be found."[4] The appendix goes further. It quantifies this claim. "With few exceptions," Wilson indicates, "our members find that they have tapped an unsuspected inner resource which they presently identify with their own conception of a Power greater than themselves."[5]

"Few exceptions" means "nearly everyone." Bill's rationale for the appendix was to elucidate points that were vague in the original text and to add new insights. Therefore, he added this estimate for one of two reasons: Either the main text did not sufficiently stress the value of an indwelling God, or an indwelling conception of God proved most useful among the membership following the book's first printing. Whatever the reason, the message is clear: The majority of Twelve Step practitioners find a Higher Power within themselves.

The Steps make no requirement of this inlying Higher Power. They afford everyone the right to fashion a God-idea that best suits them, which includes an extrinsic Divine Being. That said, Wilson's "inner resource" is not inconsistent with religion. He goes on to say, "Our more religious members call

---

[4] Bill Wilson, *Alcoholics Anonymous,* pg 55, 1939

[5] Bill Wilson, *Alcoholics Anonymous,* "Spiritual Experience," 1941

it God-consciousness," which amounts to "the Christian concept of the Holy Ghost or Holy Spirit which resides in us all," as Scott Peck notes in the *Road Less Travelled*. However, the idea is compatible with any spiritual viewpoint, not just Christianity. For example, the concept of "Buddha-nature" easily maps onto the notion of an inner-resource. Furthermore, it greases the wheels of skeptics who want to couch their experience in humanistic terms. In point of fact, it greases most everyone's wheels, which is the larger point: An indwelling conception of God is better suited for Twelve Step spirituality.

This introspective angle plays well with most belief systems. This point of view is particularly useful on the Twelve Step path because the Steps aim to rearrange our ideas, emotions, and attitudes. Twelve Step spirituality is an inside job, and as a result, the Steps functionally favor an indwelling Higher Power.

Since the Steps look within, they often lead practitioners to conclude that their Higher Power emanates from an "unsuspected inner resource." This inner resource is reminiscent of Jung's archetypal God, which he defines as a "pattern in the individual" that "has at its disposal the greatest transforming energies of which life is capable." Paraphrasing Jung, "God" is a "superior power" in the "psyche," an inner resource. Jung's theory of archetypes is central to his work in religious psychology. When Wilson accepted Jung's definition of spiritual experience, he accepted an inceptive idea that fated the Steps to lean toward an indwelling God, giving them a mystical character.

It seems unlikely that Wilson unwittingly accepted this fate. To the contrary, he advertises it in the spiritual appendix. He also makes archetypal references to God in the original text, notably: "Deep down in every man, woman, and child, is the fundamental idea of God."[6] Strictly speaking, an "archetype" is a "fundamental idea." In another letter to Jung, Wilson writes, "Years ago some of us read with great benefit your book *Modern Man in Search of a Soul,"* adding that the views therein "had an immense impact upon some of the early members of our A.A. fellowship." Bill tells the aging doctor that *Modern Man in Search of a Soul* was yet "another example of your great helpfulness to us of A.A. in our formative period." That book came out in 1933, six years before the *Big Book.* Perhaps Wilson was impressed with Jung's psycho-spiritual views, and intentionally fashioned a path with the great doctor's ideas in mind. It is impossible to say for sure, but Jung's impact on the Steps is unquestionable.

"There is in the psyche some superior power, and if it is not consciously a god, it is the 'belly' at least," Jung opines with his trademark *Gnostic* flare.[7] Ultimately, this idea is his gift to Alcoholics Anonymous. It is subliminally present in his counsel to Hazard. Jung fleshes this idea out in a 1961 letter to Bill Wilson.

"There are many reason I could not give a full and sufficient explanation to Roland,"[8] Jung confesses to Wilson,

---

[6] Bill Wilson, *Alcoholics Anonymous,* pg 55, 1939

[7] Philippians 3:19 NRSV (verse Jung is interpreting)

[8] Jung's ideas are often multidimensional and inceptive. This is evidence that the ideas Wilson adopted were both.

"but I am risking it with you, because I conclude from your very decent and honest letter, that you have acquired a point of view above the misleading platitudes one usually hears about alcoholism." He goes on to explain that Hazard's "craving for alcohol was the equivalent on a low level to the spiritual thirst of our being for wholeness." Jung then tells Bill that the wholeness for which we thirst is "union with God."

If the thirst for God is not quenched consciously, Jung believes it becomes "a devil"—by which he means, a "belly" or an "addiction." In Roland's case, it became alcoholism, and his doctor prescribed spirituality. "You see, alcohol in Latin is *'spiritus,'* and you use the same word for the highest religious experience," Jung notes. "The helpful formula, therefore is: *spiritus contra spiritum.*" Jung's greatest contribution to Twelve Step spirituality is the insight that *spiritual principles triumph over addiction.*

Carl Jung was a student of Gnosticism with a particular affection for the Gospel of Thomas. Undoubtedly, he plucked much of the wisdom shared with Wilson from this text, which includes the following aphorism: "If you bring forth what is within you, what you bring forth will save you. If you do not bring forth what is within you, what you do not bring forth will destroy you." Jung responds, "I therefore consider it wiser to acknowledge the idea of God consciously. For, if we do not, something else is made God, usually something quite inappropriate and stupid such as only an 'enlightened' intellect could hatch forth."[9]

---

[9] Carl Jung, Two Essays on Analytical Psychology, pg 71, 1966

Wilson wasn't an avowed Gnostic like Jung, but he was as a recovering alcoholic. He knew just how stupid and inappropriate the sick mind's hatchlings could be, so the Steps acknowledge God consciously. However, the concept of "conscious contact" comes not from Jung, but Emmet Fox.

The Sum and Substance of the Path

Emmet Fox was an Irish-born preacher who, in 1931, immigrated to the United States where he ordained in the Divine Science Church, and became a leading figure in the New Thought movement. Fox laced his teachings with a distrust of organized religion, prosperity theology, a dash of Catholic mysticism, and a heavy dose of "mind-cure" pop psychology. This recipe was well-received by the suffering masses during the Great Depression, which included Bill W. and his troop of recovering drunks.

Emmet Fox's sermons were wildly popular. He regularly filled grand venues like New York's Hippodrome, Carnegie Hall, and Madison Square Garden. Among those in attendance was Bill Wilson. A friend of Wilson's, Melvin Barger, later said Bill and "other pioneer A.A.'s attended Emmet Fox's lectures in New York in the late 1930s and benefited from them." This is corroborated by a 1966 article in A.A.'s *Grapevine:* "When the early groups were meeting in New York, members would frequently adjourn after a meeting and go to Steinway Hall to listen to Fox's lecture."[10] This same article mentions a man named Al Steckman, who

---

[10] Igor Sikorsky, "Emmet Fox and Alcoholics Anonymous," Grapevine, February 1966

worked closely with Bill for years. Steckman eventually became *The Grapevine's* first editor. He also authored A.A.'s preamble. His mother, interestingly enough, was the personal secretary to none other than Emmet Fox.

Fox is not listed among those who contributed to the development of Alcoholics Anonymous, yet his impact on A.A. culture is undeniable. Some A.A. groups still make his pamphlets available to newcomers. His book, *Sermon on the Mount,* though apocryphal, is more widely read by Twelve Steppers than some official literature. Jim Burwell, the agnostic who vigorously lobbied to qualify "God" with "as we understood him," once said that Bill got a "basic insight of spirituality from Fox's *Sermon on the Mount.*"[11] Moreover, certain turns of phrase in the Twelve Step lexicon originate with Fox. Chief among them, "conscious contact."

"Strange as it may seem to you, there exists a mystic power that is able to transform your life so thoroughly, so radically, so completely," promises Fox, "that when the process is completed your own friends would hardly recognize you, and, in fact, you would scarcely be able to recognize yourself." The preacher goes on to say, "But where, it will naturally be asked, is this wonderful, mystic Power to be contacted? Where may we find it? And how is it brought into action? The answer is perfectly simple," Fox answers. "This Power is to be found within your own consciousness, the last place that most people would look for it." Then, he introduces the all-important concept: "You only need to make

---

[11] Jim Burwell, *Memoirs of Jimmy: The Evolution of Alcoholics Anonymous*

conscious contact with this Power to set it working in your affairs."[12]

The book quoted above, *Power Through Constructive Thinking,* was published in 1932, three years before Bill's trip to Akron. Wilson never includes Fox on A.A.'s list of contributors, but the New Age thinker obviously influenced the rhythm of the Twelve Steps.

Wilson inserts "conscious contact" in the eleventh Step, and the directive to "practice these principles in all our affairs" in Step Twelve. He not only borrows the expression; he utilizes Fox's idea. Wilson bases the division of labor in Steps Eleven and Twelve on the principle that conscious contact sets God to work in our lives—just as Fox suggested.

We cannot practice these principles in all our affairs unless we are aware of the principal source. God is the first principle of our spirituality. It is the point upon which all beliefs converge; the foothold wherefrom action thrusts; the ground of meaning and being that centers our will and life. Our Higher Power is our highest concern, and Step Twelve aims to raise that concern in all that we do. This requires a point of contact that pervades every facet of our lives. Only consciousness witnesses our every thought, word, and deed. Consciousness alone goes with us into everything we do. Therefore, consciousness must be the point of contact with God.

---

[12] Emmet Fox, *Power Through Constructive Thinking*, pgs 1-3, 1932

The goal of the Steps is a spiritual awakening. According to Wilson, an "awareness of a Power greater than ourselves is the essence of spiritual experience." This awareness is "conscious contact." Thus, the path aims to effect a consciousness of God's indwelling presence, which enables us to carry out the charge of Step Twelve, "practice these principles in all our affairs."

Conscious contact makes our Higher Power real. It realizes God by raising our ultimate concern in the affairs of daily life. However, conscious contact is not self-sustaining. If we rest on this laurel, the connection withers. The tenth Step maintains this connection by persisting in the practices that established it. The eleventh Step goes further.

Step Eleven utilizes prayer and meditation to deepen our awareness of God's presence. Wilson also lifted this insight from Fox, who, in the same book, wrote, "The more you pray, the more time you spend in meditation and spiritual treatment, the more sensitive you become."[13] Step Eleven seeks through prayer and meditation to improve conscious contact by heightening our sensitivity.

This chapter explored the contributions of Carl Jung and Emmet Fox to Steps Eleven and Twelve. It explained how their ideas turned the Steps within, adding a mystical or contemplative dimension to the path. Now that the stage is set, we turn our attention to Step Eleven, the practice of prayer and meditation.

---

[13] Emmet Fox, *Power Through Constructive Thinking*, pgs 40, 1932

15 SOUGHT THROUGH PRAYER AND MEDITATION

"Let us be silent, that we may hear the whispers of the gods."~ Ralph Waldo Emerson

The Twelve Steps do not prepare us for a life of solitude. We are not training to become hermits; rather husbands, wives, mothers, fathers, friends, sisters, brothers, and coworkers. That said, the Steps have a contemplative component that seeks an interior solitude amidst daily life.

Twelve Step spirituality aims not to withdraw from the world, but to immerse ourselves in the details of it. Included among these details is our inner life. There is a point of stillness that resides deep within us that does not fluctuate with good fortune or bad; instead, it is an equilibrium amidst the changing tides. It is the rock upon which our spiritual structure rests. This point of stillness is "conscious contact," and it is "sought through prayer and meditation," which is the concern of Step Eleven.

The Origins of Step Eleven

Alcoholics Anonymous derives Step Eleven from the Oxford Group practice of "quiet time." Frank Buchman received this practice from F.B. Meyer, who wrote, "The Spirit of God within thee and the presence of God without thee cannot be discerned whilst the senses are occupied with pleasure, or the pulse beats quickly, or the brain is filled with the tread of many hurrying thoughts."[1] Meyer offered Buchman similar counsel when the two met at Penn State. This advice became "quiet time" in the Oxford Group program.

In the Oxford Group, quiet time was a practice of sitting and waiting in silence for God's guidance. It was observed not only in private but at public meetings as well. Those who fled the Oxford Group to form Alcoholics Anonymous preferred to use meetings for discussion.

A sleuth of irritants accompany early sobriety: acute withdrawals, the constant threat of relapse, familial troubles, and economic woes. These gadflies make prolonged periods of silence most unwelcome. Lulls in the meeting invite discomfort and worry into the mind of a newly sober alcoholic. It is, therefore, not surprising that the alcoholic faction of the Oxford Group preferred discussion to silence. In discussion, the still-suffering alcoholic finds consolation, inspiration, clarity, and support.

---

[1] F.B. Meyer, *The Secret of Guidance,* pg 105, 1896

When the alcoholics lobbied to reduce or eliminate quiet time, Oxford Group mainstays understandably refused. Relenting would have fundamentally altered their gatherings, resulting in a format more akin to the forthcoming A.A. meeting. Their refusals quickly turned spiteful, however.

As the number of alcoholic Oxford Groupers increased, tragic tales of alcoholism began to dominate discussion periods. Non-alcoholics did not identify with these struggles. As a result, they felt alienated and marginalized. In response, they weaponized quiet time, lengthening the periods of silence to check the alcoholics' habit of sharing "views, not news of what God had done."[2] This reprisal only escalated the tension between the two camps.

The split between the Oxford Group and what came to be known as Alcoholics Anonymous was preordained. Quiet time was one of several disputes guaranteeing this outcome. When the alcoholics did break away, they implemented a meeting format that enabled them to share their experience, strength, and hope with the still suffering alcoholic. Today, Alcoholics Anonymous conducts a variety of meetings. They include single speaker and group discussion formats, as well as *Big Book* and Step studies, but not quiet time. Apart from the moment of silence heralding in the meeting, A.A. settled on formats bereft of silence.

The public practice of quiet time presented unique challenges for A.A.'s pioneers. In addition to those mentioned above, religion was a divisive subject. Drunks were attracted

---

[2] Ernest Kurtz, *Not-God: A History of Alcoholics Anonymous*, pg 44, 1991

to the "booze cure" proffered by Bill W. and Dr. Bob, not religion—which was the main purpose of Oxford Group gatherings. They were a Christian group that (obviously) welcomed religious testimony. The alcoholics, on the other hand, were anything but uniform. They adhered to all manner of spiritual and religious beliefs, and preferred a fellowship devoid of outside affiliation. Therefore, coupling the revelatory exercise of quiet time with group discussion led to testimonies that sowed discord, rather than harmony; yet, another reason Alcoholics Anonymous banished quiet time from their meetings.

A.A.'s founding generation was not opposed to the practice of quiet time. They were just opposed to practicing it publicly. A.A.'s early members knew from personal experience that it was indispensable to sober living. The vast majority thought a daily regimen of prayer and meditation the cornerstone of their *personal* spirituality. However, they all agreed that it was a personal affair and better suited for private practice. So they placed it in the program, instead of the meeting format. Quiet Time became Step Eleven.

The Underlying Intent of Step Eleven

One aim of Step Eleven is to pacify the self-centered, idle chatter of the thinking mind. In this sense, it is in keeping with F.B. Meyer's original guidance. Once again, we cannot discern "the Spirit of God within" or "the presence of God without," if our "brain is filled with the tread of many hurrying thoughts." Using an analogy remindful of Buddhist meditation instruction, Meyer adds, "It is when the water stands that it becomes pellucid, and reveals the pebbly beach below." Meyer then counsels the reader to "Be still, and know that God is within thee and around!"[3]

Meyer's pellucid state is commonly referred to as "serenity" in Twelve Step literature. Serenity is only one attribute of conscious contact. Step Eleven is more than a stress reduction exercise. Yes, it cultivates peace and clarity, but it also awakens a selfless conscience that advocates for principled action. This is why prayer and meditation precede Step Twelve's call to practice these principles in all of our affairs.

We cannot practice spiritual principles in all our affairs unless the first principle of our spirituality is connected to the faculty that apprehends our affairs, namely consciousness. Thus, the Twelve Steps turn within before going out into the world. Step Eleven shines the light of consciousness on our Higher Power, enabling that Power to become incarnate in Twelve.

Prayer and meditation supply us with the vital spiritual nutrient of silence. Silence fosters direct contact with our Higher Power because it abandons what we think about God, ourselves, and the world in which we live. Silence creates the space God needs to reveal Itself.

The eleventh Step is often skimmed over in Twelve Step groups. Standing in its stead is a diet of diffusive prayers and daily readings from calendared books. Bill Wilson once

---

[3] F.B. Meyer, *The Secret of Guidance,* pg 105, 1896

remarked that "something was lost from A.A. when we stopped emphasizing the morning meditation."[4] That something is silence. It is the ingredient missing from this unbalanced diet.

To be clear, there is nothing wrong with reading these daily inspirations. It is a fine practice. They inform, inspire, and make one think, but they do not settle the mind. They are food for thought, not a vehicle for transcending thought. Lacking silence, they nourish the thinking mind, rather than conscious contact. Therefore, they are not a substitute for eleventh Step meditation.

Similarly, windy prayers that swirl around self-interest are not in keeping with Step Eleven, which instructs us to pray "only for knowledge of His will for us and the power to carry that out." Selfless prayer patiently waits and listens, raising the consciousness of our Higher Power. Selfish prayer pleads its case. It tries to compensate for ego's inadequacies by chasing acclaim and prosperity. The former emanates from an interior resource; whereas, in the latter, "something else is made God, usually something quite inappropriate and stupid."

In recovery communities, inadequate eleventh Step practice is frequently offset by excessive service work, which includes everything from helping others to volunteer positions at one's home meeting. Bill Wilson was aware of this imbalance, and in 1958, penned an article entitled "Take Step Eleven," wherein he says, "If we expend even five percent of

---

[4] *Dr. Bob and the Good Oldtimers*, pg 178, 1980 (AA World Services)

the time on Step Eleven that we habitually (and rightly) lavish on Step Twelve, the results can be wonderfully far-reaching."[5] This imbalance is not limited to Twelve Step circles. It is common in all spiritual traditions.

In the following chapter, we will address this imbalance in greater detail. For now, suffice it to say that charity is not a Power greater than ourselves; it is the expression of a Higher Power. Service work is no more a substitute for the practice of prayer and meditation than those practices are for service work. Confusing the two contaminates our spirituality. When we derive self-esteem from helping others, the "other" becomes a commodity in our self-centered economy. We must first find meaning within ourselves (contemplation), then lovingly gift it to others via relationship (service).

One last thought on the diminished role of prayer and meditation in Twelve Step culture: the fruits of contemplative practice are slow ripening. "Sudden and spectacular upheavals" may come to pass, but real understanding and spiritual maturity takes time to develop. These fruits belong to the educational class of spiritual experience. Bill Wilson's eleventh Step writings are a case in point. His later works are demonstrably more insightful than his earlier efforts. Step Eleven in the *Twelve and Twelve* and his *Grapevine* articles on prayer and meditation far surpass his commentary on the subject in *Alcoholics Anonymous*. This disparity is unsurprising. When he wrote the *Big Book,* he had little experience with prayer and meditation. The fellowship was

---

[5] Bill Wilson, "Take Step Eleven," *The Grapevine,* June 1958

also inexperienced at that time. They had little institutional knowledge about prayer or meditation to draw upon.

Alcoholics Anonymous was the fellowship's declaration of independence from the Oxford Group. In the movement's early days, Wilson had to prioritize growth for A.A. to survive. Service work was simply more valuable than prayer and meditation at the time. The pages of *Alcoholics Anonymous* devote an entire chapter to "Working with Others," and only a few paragraphs to prayer and meditation. This trend is reversed in *Twelve Steps and Twelve Traditions*, a volume that reflects the spiritual maturation of both its author and the fellowship, as well as A.A.'s viability. Nevertheless, *Alcoholics Anonymous* is the fellowship's primary text, and as such, the dominant force in Twelve Step culture.

A.A.'s primary purpose is "to stay sober and help other alcoholics to achieve sobriety." Undoubtedly, the original text better serves this objective, but it hamstrings the fellowship with regards to more profound Steps. The *Big Book's* grip on Twelve Step culture omits the profundity of Steps Six, Seven, Eleven, and even Twelve, forestalling the "next major development in A.A."

Wilson addresses this stagnation in a 1958 article entitled, "The Next Frontier: Emotional Sobriety." In this article, Wilson says that many old-timers who have put the "A.A. 'booze cure' to severe but successful tests still find they often lack emotional sobriety." Bill admits that he has been there, stuck between physical sobriety and emotional immaturity. He sympathetically assures the reader that "it's a hell of a spot," entirely devoid of "peace and joy." Then, Wilson throws a lifeline to the still-suffering inhabitants of this A.A. purgatory. It is also a dominant theme in the *Twelve and Twelve.*

Bill says that "emotional sobriety" is the "next major development in A.A." It consists of cultivating "maturity and balance." According to Wilson, this leg of the journey brings us to a "quiet place in bright sunshine," where the mind "no longer races compulsively in either elation, grandiosity or depression."[6] Emotional sobriety is a byproduct of conscious contact, which is enhanced by regular prayer and meditation. Therefore, the next frontier is deeper engagement with Step Eleven.

Be Quick to See Where Religious People Are Right

Twelve Step culture runs along two parallel tracks. There is the body of literature and the oral tradition passed down by the fellowship. The oral tradition began with Ebby and Wilson but blossomed into a fellowship when Bill W. met Dr. Bob. The written tradition started four years later with the publication of *Alcoholics Anonymous.* Both the book and the fellowship were born into a world of enormous demand.

In the wake of Prohibition's failure, America yearned for a solution to the drink problem. Bill and Bob were confident

---

[6] Bill Wilson, "The Next Frontier: Emotional Sobriety," *The Grapevine*, January 1958

in their booze cure and did everything they could to proliferate it. Each man possessed talents that fit them to serve their emerging movement in distinct ways.

Today, millions of people the world over gather in meetings of Alcoholics Anonymous. Often hanging on the walls are portraits of their founders. Dr. Bob and Bill W. worked well together, in part, because they were very different. Wilson was ambitious, charismatic, insatiably curious, and mystically inclined. Dr. Bob was industrious, conservative, patient, and unassuming. The long-term plan to disseminate their solution was the publication of a book. This assignment fell to Wilson. The immediate strategy was passing the message on from one suffering alcoholic to another, "twelfth Step work." This was a collective effort, more or less, spearheaded by Dr. Bob.

Aptly nicknamed "The Prince of Twelve-Steppers," Bob Smith, along with Sister Mary Ignatia, ministered to throngs of drunks at St. Thomas Hospital in Akron. According to *Alcoholics Anonymous*, Dr. Bob mentored "more than 5,000 alcoholic men and women."[7] In his fifteen years of sobriety, Smith worked with, on average, one alcoholic a day—a feat that requires tremendous dedication. This dedication to service is Dr. Bob's legacy. His name and face may be less recognizable, but seared in the fellowship's collective mind is his passion for twelfth Step work. In modern times, the demand is less urgent than in Bob's time due to the advent of

---

[7] *Alcoholics Anonymous*, pg 171, 2001, "Dr. Bob's Nightmare," Bob Smith

treatment centers, but service work remains the watchword of recovery culture.

The body of literature and the oral tradition typically run parallel, but they do part from time to time, and these divergences generally mirror the contrasting personalities of Bill Wilson and Bob Smith. The forward-thinking Wilson was always willing to follow the next big idea through to its conclusion, and he certainly believed Step Eleven was the launching pad for A.A.'s next phase of growth.

Bill Wilson continually sought further instruction in prayer and meditation, consulting with everyone from Fr. Dowling to the Christian mystic, Gerald Heard. As a result, his views on the subject were ever-evolving. Dr. Bob, on the other hand, was more traditional, maintaining the Oxford Group practice of quiet time, which included prayer and reflection upon the scriptures. His legendary "keep it simple" attitude served him well in the field of sponsorship, but made him suspicious of mystical pursuits like contemplative prayer and silent meditation.

In a meeting with Fr. Dowling, Dr. Bob expressed "a sincere respect for the Jesuit order because of its social activities," but said he was "a bit scandalized at the thought of the Trappist order"—a contemplative sect of Christian monastics. He disapproved of them passing "life in silence and prayer." Fr. Dowling was taken back by Dr. Bob's criticism. Wilson's mentor defended contemplative practice, telling Bob that "trafficking with God in prayer is a pretty high society and a very influential social activity."[8]

Fr. Dowling was a student of silent meditation and interior prayer. This interest is partly what attracted him to the Twelve Steps. He immediately intuited their contemplative dimension. Then again, Dowling always saw depth in the Steps that their purveyors overlooked.

Bill didn't appreciate the full breadth of Steps Six and Seven until Fr. Ed enlightened him. Similarly, Dr. Bob was oblivious to the bounties of Step Eleven. He didn't realize that "trafficking" in silent meditation and prayer was the thrust of A.A.'s eleventh Step. This much was obvious to the priest, which is why Bob's remarks caught him off-guard.

Dowling promptly wrote Bill following his conversation with Dr. Bob, divulging the contents of their disagreement. The *Twelve and Twelve* was published three years after Bob's death. The chapter on Step Eleven begins with a possible reference to that conversation and a certain repudiation of the sentiment. In his prelude to Step Eleven, Bill joins his Jesuit mentor in defending "serious meditation and prayer" as the "principal means of conscious contact."

"We A.A.'s are active folk," Wilson writes, "enjoying the satisfactions of dealing with the realities of life, usually for the first time in our lives, and strenuously trying to help the next alcoholic who comes along. So it isn't surprising that we often tend to slight serious meditation and prayer as

---

[8] Robert Fitzgerald, *Soul of Sponsorship*, pg 28, 1995

something not really necessary." He goes onto to say that the fellowship tends to regard prayer and meditation as the "mysterious skill of clergymen," an esoteric tandem that "might help us to meet an occasional emergency," but is otherwise superfluous to daily living. Bill emphatically responds, "Prayer and meditation are our principal means of conscious contact with God."[9] Here, the oral tradition parts ways with the literature, and since the written tradition serves as the basis of this book, it follows Bill W.'s lead, not Dr. Bob's.

Bill's conservative treatment of prayer and meditation in the *Big Book* has nothing to do with disinterest in the subject matter. Rather, he had little to say on the subject because, at the time, he was wet behind the ears. Some attribute his meager offering to A.A. etiquette, suggesting that he refused to instruct people in the private areas of spirituality. This explanation is flatly rebuffed by his later willingness to do just that in the *Twelve and Twelve*.

Whether we dress prayer and meditation with religious, spiritual, or secular skins is a matter of personal preference, but prayer and meditation, as such, are non-negotiable practices within the Twelve Steps. And as obligatory practices, they require instruction. There can be no imperative without guidance. When, in due time, Wilson had tested guidance and insight to offer, he did. Earlier in his career, however, he deferred to those with more experience.

---

[9] Bill Wilson, *Twelve Steps and Twelve Traditions,* pg 96, 1953

In *Alcoholics Anonymous*, Wilson augments his scant eleventh Step commentary with two lines: "Be quick to see where religious people are right. Make use of what they offer."[10] These two sentences not only compensate for the author's inexperience but also state the obvious: Prayer and meditation have been the exclusive domain of religious seekers for millennia, and we should listen to what they have to say.

The world's religions incubate contemplative traditions equipped with exercises that facilitate transcendence and enhance conscious contact with a Higher Power. These traditions have produced men and women of remarkable wisdom who have much to offer on the topic of prayer and meditation. Wilson, a neophyte, initially yielded to the experts, and so does this book.

What follows is a comprehensive exploration of prayer and meditation that mirrors Wilson's writings on Step Eleven in two important ways. It is open-minded and relies on insights culled from the world's great spiritual traditions.

Obviously, there is no obligation to adopt the theology, the metaphysics, or the mythos of any contemplative cited, however realized they might be. It is their insight into the human condition and their practical instruction that is of importance, not the vernacular adorning these gems. Whether they describe their experience as the coming of God-consciousness, the revelation of Christ-consciousness, the realization of Buddha-nature, or the dawn of basic awareness

---

[10] Bill Wilson, *Alcoholics Anonymous*, pg 87, 1939

is a trivial matter compared to the treasure of practical experience contained in the millennia of committed exploration. Moving forward, the reader should abide by the exegetical maxim of Twelve Step spirituality, "Keep what works and leave the rest."

The Underlying Principle of Prayer and Meditation

Talking about prayer and meditation in a vacuum is difficult. Prayer and meditation play off indwelling principles, and these practices do not make sense until we establish those principles. This is true for believer and skeptic alike.

Believers tend to tacitly accept the principles that establish prayer but ignore the underlying rationale for silent meditation. Conversely, skeptics more readily accept meditation than prayer, writing the latter off as superstitious nonsense. Therefore, we need to establish a first principle that makes sense of both prayer and meditation. The previous chapter went a long way toward this end, but we must go further. We need to unpack the concept of spiritual experience.

This chapter uses William James' verdict in *Varieties of Religious Experience* to frame prayer and meditation.[11] In a nutshell, James asserts that the Higher Power we feel ourselves connected to is a "subconscious continuation of our conscious life." This view dovetails with Wilson's "inner

---

[11] Unless stated otherwise

resource." It differs only in that it implies our ordinary state of mind is just one hue on the spectrum of consciousness. "Our normal waking consciousness, rational consciousness as we call it, is but one special type of consciousness," writes James, "whilst all about it, parted from it by the filmiest of screens, there lie potential forms of consciousness entirely different." Step Eleven aims to explore these possibilities.

The backdrop provided by James maps onto the Twelve Step path. It is introspective, and it appeals to a broader audience. Believer and skeptic alike can cast their personal views on to James' backdrop because he bases it on a fundamental truth. He rests his theory on a "recognized psychological fact," namely that consciousness is the center of experience.

Consciousness is the essence of experience; to experience something is to be conscious of it. This indefectible truth envelopes everything from mundane affairs to spiritual experiences. Basing his theory on this fact enables James "to preserve a contact with 'science' which the ordinary theologian lacks." This welcomes skeptics into the fold. Furthermore, it permits him to put forth a practicable explanation of spiritual experience.

Wilson says that an "awareness of a Power greater than ourselves is the essence of spiritual experience." What exactly are we aware of? What are we experiencing? James submits that we are experiencing psychic changes; that we are transitioning from the default mode of consciousness into deeper, richer, clearer states of mind. This insight is crucial. It suggests that prayer and meditation facilitate these changes, thereby supplying us with one of Step Eleven's two operational principles.

Believers are likely to judge this theory too materialistic for their taste. They should reconsider. James argues that this idea actually vindicates "the theologian's contention that the religious man is moved by an external power." How? Because "one of the peculiarities of invasions from the subconscious region" is that they "take on objective appearances," suggesting "to the subject an external control." James' theory only explains the hither side of spiritual experience. It does not touch the farther side, leaving it to the individual to decide what, if anything, initiated the shift in consciousness. This feature makes his theory even more compatible with Twelve Step spirituality.

One final takeaway from James' conclusion: When he says that "invasions from the subconscious" are "objective appearances" that suggest "to the subject an external control," he is effectively saying that spiritual experiences are ecstatic events. They get us out of self. Of course, this is one of our objectives, but the eleventh Step is not satisfied with ecstatic episodes. It isn't content with intervals of conscious contact. Step Eleven aims to improve upon conscious contact, increasing the frequency and duration of these invasions, as well as our talent for inviting them.

Prayer and meditation do not merely initiate conscious contact; they also habituate it. They practice *inviting* and *abiding* in these progressively selfless states of awareness, transforming episodes of conscious contact into a "working part of our mind."[12] This principle underlies Step Eleven's daily dose of prayer and meditation.

The Vital Act of Prayer

Quoting Auguste Sabatier, a "liberal French theologian," James writes in *Varieties*:

> "Religion is nothing if it be not the vital act by which the entire mind seeks to save itself by clinging to the principle from which it draws its life. This act is prayer, by which term I understand no vain exercise of words, no mere repetition of certain sacred formula, but the very movement itself of the soul, putting itself in a personal relation of contact with the mysterious power of which it feels the presence—it may be even before it has a name by which to call it."

Sabatier goes on to say, "Wherever this interior prayer is lacking, there is no religion; wherever, on the other hand, this prayer rises and stirs the soul, even in the absence of forms or of doctrines, we have living religion."[13] This "living religion" is akin to Twelve Step spirituality and its principal means, "interior prayer," conforms to the objectives of Step Eleven.

Interior prayer is synonymous with contemplative prayer, and you hardly need to quote a liberal French theologian to justify its use. From the Desert Fathers to

---

[12] Bill Wilson, *Alcoholics Anonymous*, pg. 87, 1939

[13] William James, *VRE,* "Lecture XIX" / Auguste Sabatier, *Esquisse d'une Philosophie de la Religion*, 1897, pgs 24-26

Meister Eckhart, John of the Cross, and the Quakers, Western spirituality has a long history of contemplative practice.

In antiquity, God was thought to dwell in the temple; that is why only the high priests entered the Holy of Holies. "Do you not know that your body is a temple?" St. Paul asks the Corinthians. Paul is saying God dwells in the body, not a building. The word "contemplation" comes from the Latin *com·templum*, meaning "that which is done in the temple." Contemplative prayer brings us into the temple or the body where we contact God's indwelling presence.

God dwells within us, but not as a nut inside a shell. The presence of God pervades our being. It is ever-present, yet we are screened from it by a veil of thoughts. Interior prayer lifts this screen. It sifts through the endless stream of self-referencing thoughts that overlay God-consciousness. When these scales fall from our mind's eye, consciousness receives a God's-eye view. This transparent eyeball sees the world and its people as they are, not as ego would have them be. This is the vital principle from which the mind draws life, sanity—and prayer restores us to sanity.

Prayer and Personal Relations

Meditation works to heighten sensitivity and deepen contact with our Higher Power; whereas prayer renders that contact "conscious." It makes an otherwise mysterious experience intelligible, bringing us into "personal relation" with a Higher Power.

The phrase "personal relationship with God" can complicate matters, particularly prayer. Often, it is thought to mean "God is a person." This impression can sabotage prayer. It can turn the practice into a faith-based form of arbitration for believers, and altogether derail the efforts of skeptics.

There is nothing about an anthropomorphic God that disqualifies it from the Twelve Steps. It isn't even inconsistent with our working hypothesis. It is an over-belief the theist can hold above their spiritual experience by attributing divine causality to the psychic change. Still, this is a theistic mode of belief, which non-theists are not obliged to endorse in thought or deed. Therefore, it is not built into Step Eleven. "Personal relations" does not mean "God is a person" in Twelve Step spirituality.

"Personal relations" does not attribute human attributes to our Higher Power. The phrase qualifies our "relationship," not God. Personal relations refers to the way in which we relate to God, rather than the nature of God. In a personal relationship, we relate to our Higher Power in a personal way.

Prayer establishes personal relations by communing with God *like a person.* It communicates or uses our words to consciously connect with a Higher Power. In prayer, we talk to God *like* a person, which helps make that mysterious power intelligible or personable.

Believers readily relate to God in a personal way. The non-theistic person, on the other hand, struggles with prayer, even when they admit a Higher Power. Why? Because their Higher Power possesses no personal attributes. It is thoroughly impersonal. As a result, conversing with it ties their mind in knots. If there is nothing out there, who am I talking to? The above explanation of "personal relations" does not answer this question. It renders the question obsolete.

God is not an entity, as far as non-theists, mystics, and skeptical seekers are concerned. It is an impersonal presence. Their reasons are pretty sound: Our Higher Power is, by definition, our ultimate concern. Simply put, God is either everything or it is nothing. Conceiving of God as *a* person or *a* being, even if supreme, implies that God is "this" but not "that." It confines God to the realm of finitude, depriving it of ultimacy, as the theologian Paul Tillich noted. Thus, God must be everything—not *a* being, but Being-itself. From this standpoint, God does not exist. It is Existence-itself, which is deserving of impersonal labels like "The Absolute." Prayer uses our words to bring this impersonal presence into personal relation.

Human beings are social creatures. We crave community. Communication is the standard mode of communion. Language has the power to transform an "I" and a "you" into a "we." Prayer repurposes this skillset, relating to our Higher Power as a person would. This transforms the "I" and "Thou" into a single consciousness, famously captured by Meister Eckhart: "The eye with which I see God is the same with which God sees me. My eye and God's eye is one eye, and one sight, and one knowledge, and one love."[14] Prayer communes with The Absolute.

---

[14] Johannes "Meister" Eckhart, *Sermons*, "True Hearing: Sermon IV"

"The Absolute" is a valuable philosophical term. It even pairs well with meditation, casting the practice as a silent descent into our being where we make contact with Being-Itself. In prayer, however, this term is too impersonal. It relates to our Higher power like a robot or a textbook, not like a person.

Prayer aims to involve a Higher Power in our lives. It is difficult to *feel* involved when we are invoking sterile abstractions like "The Absolute." Such prayers lack feeling because they address our head, not our heart. Our Higher Power may be an impersonal presence, but to embody that presence, we must pray with our whole body, not just our intellect. We have to suspend doubt and personally relate to our Higher Power to involve it in our personal affairs.

"The Absolute" is not inconsistent with Twelve Step spirituality. The term just isn't fit for prayer. It is too literal, too rational. "Mystical states are more like states of feeling than like states of intellect," says James.[15] Prayer enters these states only when it addresses the experience directly. The words have to point past their literal and obvious meaning to the inlying point of contact, which necessitates figures of speech that convey feeling, meaning, and value—not facts. It requires metaphor.

Metaphor captures what common speech cannot. It does this by departing from the literal use of language. Metaphor figuratively says that one thing *is* another. For example, a sports fan may refer to a dominant athlete as "a beast."

---

[15] William James, *Varieties of Religious Experience,* "Lecture XVI"

Clearly, they do not mean to say, "They are a lower-level animal." Rather, "beast" means "exceptional athlete," there is more to this figure of speech. The fan isn't merely assessing talent. They are expressing how witnessing that talent makes them feel. "They are a beast!" conveys excitement and astonishment in a way that exceeds common language. The words point past their literal and obvious meaning to the experience that commissioned them, publishing the fan's feelings. For our purposes, the metaphor is "God."

"God" differs from the "beast" metaphor because it points to an incomparable reality, "The Absolute." There is no adequate counterweight. The only way to formulate the metaphor is to say "God," "God Is," or "God is God"—the final arrangement essentially being equal to Moses' rendition on Sinai: "I am that I am." That said, "God" is similar to the "beast" metaphor in that it captures qualities that escape common speech: awe, reverence, and ineffability. "The Absolute" cerebrally admits these qualities, but it does not contact them, and therefore, does not bring an experience of The Absolute into personal relation. It keeps the ineffable at an analytical distance. "God" is a more personable term.[16] It involves us in The Absolute. This involvement is called praying.

---

[16] The same can be said of Brahma, Shiva, Vishnu, Allah, Jesus, and Mary, as well as numerous Buddhas and Bodhisattvas. God is used because it is the most common term—not to mention, the one employed throughout the Steps.

In prayer, we practice suspending doubt. We drop our rationale façade and relate to "The Absolute" like a person, instead of a Vulcan. That said, prayer doesn't make our Higher Power a person. Any reading to the contrary mistakes the metaphor for a fact and fails to engage the principle of prayer. The principle in play is relatively common. It is the premise of literature and film. For example, we readily identify with fictional wand-wielding wizards and superhuman vigilantes on the silver screen. We happily look past obvious implausibilities to the moral of the story, which involves us. This transforms the hero's adventure into our adventure. We exercise this principle in daily life as well, and we do it without a second thought.

For instance, many pet owners enjoy personal relationships with their dogs and cats. They talk to them like people. This relationship does not hurl pet owners into a existential crisis. They do not waste away, anxiously pondering the nature of their dog or cat. Instead, they find the relationship enriching. They feel closer to their pet when they communicate their love and excitement in a personal manner. Their pet does not understand the words, but they do pick up on the feeling expressed and they respond like a dog or cat with welcomed tail wagging or affectionate nudges. Prayer need not be more complicated than enjoying a meaningful work of fiction or talking to our pet.

This intuitive skill becomes complicated when we wander into the labyrinthine dominion of spirituality because we overlook the metaphor. We do not realize that "God" points past itself to an experience of *The Absolute*. As a result, we do not pray. We spin our wheels in thought. There is no involvement, no contact. It is a one-sided conversation: The rational mind asking and answering its own questions. One-sided conversations do not change minds. Similarly, cerebral prayer does not change our mind. It fails to affect a psychic change.

Selfish prayers are no less effective than cerebral ones, but they can be more dangerous. The believer is more likely to happen upon this pitfall than non-theists, mystics, and skeptics since the latter is reluctant to believe in a supernatural Power. In any case, prayer is not a negotiation. Haggling over points of self-interest commandeers prayer for ego's purposes, which reinforces self-centeredness.

When we fixate on what we lack, what we want, and how to get it, our mind is self-centered—even if religious jargon cloaks our thoughts, and this drama unfolds under auspices of prayer. Selfish demands do not improve conscious contact or restore sanity. Instead, they promote the worst kind of insanity, marooning us on an unaccountable island of self-delusion. "The A.A., or indeed any man, who tries to run his life rigidly by this kind of prayer, by this self-serving demand of God for replies, is a particularly disconcerting individual," Wilson writes. "To any questioning or criticism of his actions he instantly proffers his reliance upon prayer for guidance in all matters great or small. He may have forgotten the possibility that his own wishful thinking and the human tendency to rationalize have distorted his so-called guidance."[17]

---

[17] Bill Wilson, *Twelve Steps and Twelve Traditions*, pgs 103-104, 1953

Selfish prayers do not listen but clamor on, mistaking self-will for God's will. They relate to God like an ego, rather than a person. They try to shake God down, forgetting that Gods do not respond like people. The dog barks and wags its tail; the cat purrs and nuzzles; God returns vitality, patience, love, compassion, courage, and meaning—not convenient rationalizations. When prayer mollycoddles, vindicates, justifies, or panders, it is safe to assume that ego has asked and answered its own question.

How to Pray

Prayer is a private language. It is an inner-dialect that we have to learn how to speak. Traditional prayers help us achieve fluency. They teach us how to pray. For this reason, Bill Wilson starts us with the prayer of St. Francis:[18]

> "Lord, make me a channel of thy peace—that where there is hatred, I may bring love; that where there is injury, I may bring forgiveness; where there is discord, I may bring harmony; where there is error, I may bring truth; where there is doubt, I may bring faith; that where there is despair, I may bring hope; where there is darkness, I may bring light; and where there is sadness, I may bring joy.
> Lord, grant that I may seek to comfort rather than to be comforted—to understand, than to be understood—to love, than to be loved. For it is by

---

[18] This prayer is commonly attributed to St. Francis of Assisi but is found nowhere in his writings. The author is anonymous.

giving that we receive. It is in pardoning that we are pardoned. It is by dying that one awakens to Eternal Life. Amen."

This prayer is not a magical incantation. Don't merely recite it. Experience the prayer's "inner essence." Read it "several times very slowly," Wilson says, "savoring every word and trying to take in the deep meaning of each phrase and idea."[19]

Words are powerless when estranged from truth. According to Jung, it is the "real occurrence," those "visible things" or their "echo in the human soul" that infuse words and ideas with meaning. Similarly, prayer is meaningful when it maps onto our soul. Disembodied prayers ring hollow because they fail to point past themselves to the real occurrences within. These occurrences are objectively true even if the subjective ideas that elicited them are not. So let us return to our prayer, but with our ear turned toward these inner truths.

The meaning of this prayer resides within us. When "Lord" is said with intention, humility resounds and the mind prostrates itself before "The Absolute," placing consciousness in the service of a Power greater than self. Ego deflation converts the mind into an instrument, a "channel" that facilitates the flow of "peace," "love," "truth," "forgiveness," "harmony," "faith," "hope," and "joy." These are the inner resources this prayer taps.

---

[19] Bill Wilson, *Twelve Steps and Twelve Traditions*, pgs 99 & 101, 1953

The Prayer of St. Francis focuses on what we can contribute to life, not what we stand to gain. It comes from a place of abundance. The source of abundance is our Higher Power. It is the interior fountain brimming with spiritual principles. This prayer flows from the source to the surface, irrigating our most barren affairs with spiritual principles. It aspires to embody God's presence amidst "hatred," "deceit," "injury," "discord," "uncertainty," "despair," "darkness," and "sadness." Mere recitation does not fulfill this aspiration. We have to look past "love," for example, to the truth it signifies. Every virtue in this prayer corresponds to an indwelling potential that must be actualized. Initially, we make contact with forgiveness by visualizing ourselves pardoning an injury. This simulation arouses real forgiveness, which then pours forth in daily life.

Even the final word of this prayer, "Amen," conveys a deep spiritual truth. "Amen" means "so be it." The world is indifferent toward our demands. We remain on life's sidelines if compliance with our expectations is the cost of our participation. "Amen" embraces the present moment, however imperfect. It works with the world-as-it-is, muting the "shoulds," "coulds," and "what ifs." In Twelve Step culture, this principle goes by the name "acceptance."

And Acceptance is the Essence of Meditation

No spiritual principle gets more airtime in recovery communities than acceptance. Acceptance owes its popularity to the catchy passage that extols its virtues:

> "And acceptance is the answer to all my problems today. When I am disturbed, it is because I find some person, place, thing, or situation—some fact of my life—unacceptable to me, and I can find no serenity until I accept that person, place, thing, or situation as being exactly the way it is supposed to be at this moment. Nothing, absolutely nothing, happens in God's world by mistake. Until I could accept my alcoholism, I could not stay sober; unless I accept life completely on life's terms, I cannot be happy. I need to concentrate not so much on what needs to be changed in the world as on what needs to be changed in me and in my attitudes."[20]

This passage comes from a personal story in the third and fourth editions of *Alcoholics Anonymous* entitled, "Doctor, Alcoholic, Addict." Dr. Paul O. is the story's author. Strangely, this reading has its detractors. They are mostly A.A. purists or *"Big Book* thumpers" who resent the ascendancy of a non-canonical maxim, as well as the story's enfranchisement of drug addicts. The latter is not our concern. Our interest lies with the maxim, which is the paragraph's first sentence: "Acceptance is the answer to all my problems today."

Let's begin with what acceptance isn't. For starters, it is not spiritual duct tape. We can't use it to jerry-rig character defects. "Acceptance" is not interchangeable with "Well,

---

[20] Paul O., *Alcoholics Anonymous*, "Dr. Alcoholic-Addict," pg 417 4th ed. (often called "449," a title derived from the 3rd edition page number where the passage first appeared)

whatcha gonna do?" It is not apathetic, and it does not justify inaction. When we accept a problem, we admit the need for a solution. If the problem is personal, then the onus is on us to implement the solution. Acceptance does not relieve us of personal responsibility.

Finally, acceptance shouldn't be confused with approval. Critics frequently say, "I don't have to like something to accept it." This is true, but it is neither here nor there. Reality isn't asking for approval, and acceptance isn't offering it. Like "admit," "to accept" means to "let in." Acceptance admits reality.[21] If we don't like reality, that is our problem.

Dr. Paul's adage is, essentially, a variation of Wilson's spiritual axiom, which states that "every time we are disturbed, no matter what the cause, there is something wrong with us." Paul goes further, identifying the unnamed cause. He says, "When I am disturbed, it is because I find some person, place, thing, or situation—some fact of my life—unacceptable to me." When we discard, suppress, ignore, or otherwise manipulate reality because we find some fact therein disagreeable, a disturbance arises. This disturbance is the impact of our immovable, stubborn mind colliding with the unstoppable force of reality. From this point of view, serenity and insanity hang in the balance of every moment. Acceptance is the adjudicating faculty.

---

[21] Acceptance is virtually synonymous with admission. Thus, it is a fundamental element of Twelve Step spirituality, making the protestations of its critics strange indeed.

Next, Paul proposes a solution: "I can find no serenity until I accept that person, place, thing, or situation as being exactly the way it is supposed to be at this moment." Reality is not going to conform to our expectations. We either need to resign ourselves to a life of helpless discontentment, or learn to live in a messy world—which begins with acceptance. We cannot work with the present moment unless we first admit its contents. We have to drop what we think and let reality in. This practice is traditionally called meditation.

Acceptance is the essence of meditation. In meditation, we practice affirming the present moment. We watch as the mind chases after the past and future. We do not reject these strivings. We acknowledge them. They belong to the order of reality. It's a fact that we are reminiscing and anticipating in the present moment. Even if the accompanying narrations are delusional, they are psychic events. Meditation accepts this fact. It accepts thought as thought and because it does, meditation returns us to the present moment. We reconnect with reality when we notice we have departed from it. The simple act of noticing restores sanity.

Meditation as a New Pair of Glasses

Meditation improves conscious contact in four important ways. First, it establishes direct contact with the present moment, grounding our awareness in reality. Second, meditation reestablishes our connection with present moment over and over again, habituating sanity. This effort makes us more sensitive to departures from reality and more capable of returning to reality. Third, meditation deepens our awareness.

As we become more adept at abiding in the present, we spend less of our allotted practice time working back to reality and more time plumbing the depths of consciousness. Clarity increases as our awareness deepens because ego does not stir up impediments. This clarifying effect is the fourth way meditation improves upon conscious contact. It transcends the haze of self-centeredness, permitting us to see the world anew. Meditation does not create a new world; rather, it gives us "a new pair of glasses."

New Pair of Glasses is a popular book in recovery circles. It explores Twelve Step spirituality through the lens of its title concept. The author, Chuck Chamberlain, takes the book's namesake phrase from Fr. Ed Dowling, whom he met at A.A.'s second annual World Convention. The convention was held in St. Louis that year—Dowling's hometown—and he was the Sunday morning keynote speaker. Following his address to the 17,000 in attendance, Fr. Ed joined Chuck C. and his wife for coffee.

"He never drank much coffee. He asked me questions for an hour and a half! He wouldn't quit," Chamberlain jokingly recalled. He told the persistent priest, "I'd love to hear ya talk. Talk!" Dowling immediately asked another question. He loved talking to alcoholics. When the stream of questions finally dried up, Chamberlain pressed him for some spiritual insight. Dowling softly replied, "Sometimes I got to believe that heaven is a new pair of glasses." Chuck turned to his wife and said, "What's the difference? I sit in the same chair I sat in for fifty years in hell," referring to his drinking, "and now thirty-six years and ten months in heaven," referencing his sobriety. "The same chair! Nothing happened to the chair.

Nothing happened to the living room. Nothing happened to the wife or kids. Something happened to me."[22]

Heaven is not out there or later on. "They will not say, 'See here!' or 'See there!' For indeed," Jesus observes, "the kingdom of God is within you."[23] The kingdom is a new pair of glasses, a new "attitude and outlook upon life," to quote Wilson. This is an attitude of simplicity, which meditation fosters.

The ordinary appears extra-ordinary through the lens of simplicity. Every chirping bird sings as it ought, every tree stands where it should, ornamented with not a leaf too many, until the moment one is discharged, falling to a spot seemingly chosen for it. We are one of these leaves; so too are our friends and our enemies. The sun rises on the just and unjust alike in the Great Reality. Basic awareness adheres to that reality. In selfless awareness, all things have their place, and that place is determined by where they are right now. There is no staging, no self-centered price of admission. Simplicity does not screen reality's contents. Acceptance admits truth, no questions asked. Simplicity punctuates each passing moment with a triumphant "Amen!"

The Practice of Meditation

"If my eye is to discern color, it must itself be free from all color," says Meister Eckhart. Similarly, if the mind is to

---

[22] Chuck Chamberlain, Sacramento, CA, Nov. 13, 1982, www.youtube.com/watch?v=eC5KkEfzvLA

[23] Luke 17:21, NKJV

discern truth, it must be free of influences that distort the truth. The Great Reality eclipses all constructs, including theology and philosophy. It is ineffable. Words, ideas, and concepts do not do it justice. They are, at best, fingers pointing at the moon. Only silence can absorb this transcendent Reality. Meditation practices silence.

Theology and philosophy are systems of thought, and as such, keep us stuck between our ears. They build castles atop the mind but do not touch the ground of experience below. "To be attached to an experience of God is not God; it is a thought," says Fr. Thomas Keating, one of the great contemplatives of our time.[24] In meditation, we are looking to experience our Higher Power, not think about it. So while philosophy and theology have their place, that place isn't in meditation practice.

Consciousness reflects the charted depths of our experience. Meditation aims to deepen that experience, to pass through the narrow gate into the center of experience. This centermost point of contact is the body.

The body is the temple. It does not analyze or interpret. Basic awareness simply experiences. It reflects God's presence. Meditation practice uses the breath to strip consciousness of all its adornments, reducing it to its basic state. Meditation gets us out of our head, and into the body where we achieve direct contact with our Higher Power.

---

[24] Fr. Thomas Keating, *Open Mind, Open Heart,* pg 57, 2002

To begin the practice, take a seat. Find a comfortable cushion or chair. Your posture should be relaxed but upright: chest open, head straight. Roll your hips forward and pull your shoulders back, so the weight of your torso rests on the hips, rather than your lower back or stomach. This enables you to breathe freely and avoid pain.

Next, bring your awareness to the breath. Feel the coolness of the inhalation; feel the warmth of the exhalation. Don't try to control the breath. Just breathe naturally. Let the breath be a chord of silence that tethers your mind to the present moment.

When (not if) your mind drifts off, return to the breath—no more, no less. It may drift off a thousand times in a single sitting. This is not a problem. It is the point. The practice is noticing and returning. This exercise diminishes the tendency to think about thoughts, and strengthens the connection with basic awareness. Do not beat yourself up for thinking too much, that only adds to the stream of thought. Just return to the breath. The breath promotes basic awareness. It nourishes sanity and conscious contact.

We should make a daily commitment to this practice. In the beginning, ten or fifteen minutes may be all we can muster. If we stick with it, our capacity will increase. In the beginning, it might be helpful to divide the practice into two ten minutes sessions. These sessions will naturally increase in length. This a sign that we are growing in patience, one of meditation's many fruits. In short order, other fruits will begin ripening in our lives.

Meditation practice not only deepens the point of contact with our Higher Power, but it clarifies our mind and enhances our ability to abide in the present moment. These are the improvements made to conscious contact by the practice of meditation. Prayer gives conscious contact a voice. It awakens our conscience and amplifies its guidance. Together, prayer and meditation enable us to practice the presence of God in everything we do. They prepare us for Step Twelve.

16 HAVING HAD A SPIRITUAL AWAKENING

"You must live in the present, launch yourself on every wave, find your eternity in each moment. Fools stand on their island opportunities and look toward another land. There is no other land; there is no other life but this, or the like of this. Where the good husbandman is, there is the good soil. Take any other course, and life will be a succession of regrets." ~ Henry David Thoreau

In *Alcoholics Anonymous,* Wilson reduces the final rung of the Twelve Step ladder to the simple declaration, "Carry this message to other alcoholics!" In *Twelve Steps and Twelve Traditions,* written fourteen years later, he says the second act of Step Twelve, "practice these principles in all our affairs," poses "the biggest question yet." In the *Big Book,* the chapter devoted to A.A.'s final Step takes its name from the first of Step Twelve's directives, "Working with Others." The *Twelve and Twelve*, on the other hand, spends only three of the nineteen pages it dedicates to Step Twelve on working with others. The rest of the tract is about learning to "love the whole pattern of living as eagerly as we do the small segment of it we discover when we try to help other alcoholics achieve sobriety."[1]

Just as Wilson was not privy to the depths of Steps Six, Seven, or Eleven when he first penned *Alcoholics Anonymous*, the profundity of Twelve eluded him until later years when his understanding was fortified by greater experience.

This is not slight towards service work. Service is a practice unto itself. This chapter aims only to set it in its rightful place within the scheme of the Twelve Steps. Moreover, a message hyperfocused on helping the still suffering alcoholics is irrelevant to those not belonging to a recovery community.

It is important to remember there is a distinction between the Steps themselves and the way they are practiced and transmitted in recovery communities. Groups like Alcoholics Anonymous and Narcotics Anonymous have a unique relationship to service work. Obligatory service is an essential function of their fellowships, as A.A.'s *Declaration of Responsibility* makes abundantly clear: "I am Responsible. When anyone, anywhere, reaches out for help, I want the hand of A.A. always to be there. And for that: I am responsible." Service is a responsibility in Alcoholics Anonymous for two reasons.

---

[1] Bill Wilson, *Twelve Steps and Twelve Traditions,* pgs 111-112, 1953

First, A.A. is a program of "attraction rather than promotion." Thus, "carrying the message" is how they spread their message. This charge was especially urgent in A.A.'s early days, lest the movement deprive itself of later days. They had to pass their solution on to the still suffering, and they had to do it at a pace that eclipsed the high rate of relapse in order to establish a viable fellowship. In time, the *Big Book* ensured the fellowship's and the program's success, but "Twelfth-Steppers" were A.A.'s initial guarantors, none extending a larger line of credit than Dr. Bob.

Service work's preeminent role in Twelve Step culture is owed mostly to its ability to safeguard sobriety. From Wilson onto the present day, recovering alcoholics and addicts affirm and reaffirm the urgency of working with those still suffering from the affliction. In fact, the first sentence devoted to Step Twelve in the *Big Book* reads, "Practical experience shows that nothing will so much insure immunity from drinking as intensive work with other alcoholics." This insight comes to Wilson from his wife, Lois. When Bill bemoaned his failed attempts to sober others up, Lois tried to cheer him up by saying, "You're still sober." True as this anecdote may be, it is tailored to recovering alcoholics and addicts, a group to whom this book is not explicitly addressed.

The first of Step Twelve's charges must, therefore, be amended for those of us who do not identify as alcoholics and addicts. It goes without saying that we will not be carrying the message to the still suffering alcoholic. This loosens the stranglehold service work has on Step Twelve—though, the gist survives as a suggestion to be of benefit wherever possible. This approach is also in keeping with Wilson's later commentary on the twelfth Step.

When service work absorbs Step Twelve, we fail to see its broader objectives. Its richness is revealed when we step back and realize "working with others" is but one part of a larger movement. This enlarged view of Step Twelve enables us to "love the whole pattern of living," not just the segment discovered through charitable service. This is the balance Wilson strikes in his later writings.

Bill W. and Bill Wilson

On January 26, 1971, the front page of the *New York Times* read, "William Griffith Wilson died late Sunday night and, with the announcement of his death, was revealed to have been the Bill W. who was a co-founder of Alcoholics Anonymous in 1935. His age was 75." Wilson passed away on his fifty-third wedding anniversary. Hundreds of thousands gathered in memoriam at sites around the world, including the National Cathedral in D.C. and St. John the Divine in New York City.

For thirty-five years, the principle of anonymity balanced Bill Wilson's public and private lives. As the author of A.A.'s program and the architect of its fellowship he was incredibly influential, but still a member of the movement he founded. Bill W. had to be careful not to leverage his personal opinions and preferences against the fellowship's needs and norms. He struggled with this responsibility for decades, all the while longing to hand over the reins of A.A. leadership.

Bill thought stepping down best served the fellowship's long-term interests. He also hoped it would grant him a measure of personal freedom. On the first count, he was right: stepping down enabled A.A. to "come of age." However, his hopes for more freedom were dashed.

Wilson retired from leadership in 1955, but to his chagrin, he was still saddled with all the burdens and responsibilities of "Bill W., A.A. co-founder." His actions still reflected on the organization as a whole. Retirement did not permit him to pursue outside interests with his usual gusto. He had to be sensitive to the collateral impact his actions had on A.A. as a whole.

At the end of the day, Bill always saw the principle of anonymity as an enriching yoke of self-sacrifice. However, there were times when it left him and his counterparts frustrated with each other. He wanted to expand his horizons, but on more than one occasion, his extracurricular activities spooked A.A. leadership.

Gerald Heard was a prolific author, a philosopher, and a mystic, as well as a personal friend of Bill Wilson. Bill respected Heard immensely. In 1943, the Wilsons embarked on a West Coast tour, paying a visit to the emerging A.A. communities in California. Their trip included a stop at Trabuco College, an institution founded by Heard and dedicated to the study of comparative religion and contemplative spirituality. Wilson stopped by Trabuco because he wanted Heard's input on A.A.'s future. Gerald counseled him to "keep it in discrete, small units that are independent of each other and that are centered around the Twelve Steps." Wilson's Twelve Traditions echo this advice. They vest authority in autonomous groups aimed at facilitating the Twelve Step message.

Gerald Heard is also responsible for introducing Bill to the novelist and philosopher, Aldous Huxley—the grandson of Thomas Huxley[2] and the acclaimed author of *Brave New World, The Perennial Philosophy,* and *Doors of Perception.* The latter work details Huxley's spiritual experiments with mescaline and is especially pertinent to Wilson's most controversial side venture.

Heard, Huxley, and Wilson maintained a longtime friendship that centered on shared interests and mutual respect. Aldous Huxley marveled over A.A.'s "Twelve Traditions," calling Wilson, "The greatest social architect of our century." Wilson published articles by both Heard and Huxley in A.A.'s periodical, *The Grapevine.* However, this trio is best known for their collaboration with two psychiatrists conducting groundbreaking research on lysergic acid diethylamide or "LSD" for short.

The two psychiatrists were Dr. Humphrey Osmond and Dr. Abram Hoffer. Dr. Osmond coined the term "psychedelic." He first used it in a 1956 letter to Huxley, and introduced it to the world the following year in a research paper. Osmond combined the Greek words *psykhe* and *deloun*, meaning "to make spirit visible." That is what

---

[2] Thomas Huxley was a biologist and anthropologist, known as Charles Darwin's "Bulldog."

attracted Heard, Huxley, and Wilson to Osmond's and Hoffer's research. They wanted to manifest spirit. The two psychiatrists were able to use psychedelics to effect spiritual experiences in their subjects. Wilson thought this class of drugs could aid in the treatment of alcoholism and addiction. He saw a potential remedy for alcoholics struggling with the spiritual angle of the Twelve Steps. A.A. leadership thought Wilson had lost his mind.

Initially, Bill was reluctant to take LSD, so he observed the experiments from afar. But he was intrigued by the results. He went from spectator to participant on August 29, 1956. Bill W. took LSD three times with the guidance of Heard and Osmond. Of course, this troubled many of his A.A. confidantes. Although, it wasn't his participation that concerned them; it was his enthusiasm.

Huxley captures Wilson's enthusiasm in a letter to the celebrated Catholic monk, Thomas Merton: "A friend of mine, saved from alcoholism, during the last fatal phases of the disease, by a spontaneous theophany, which changed his life as completely as St. Paul's was changed on the road to Damascus, has taken lysergic acid (LSD) two or three times and affirms that his experience under the drug is identical with the spontaneous experience which changed his life."[3] Wilson himself told Sam Shoemaker that it is a "generally acknowledged fact in spiritual development that ego reduction makes the influx of God's grace possible," and LSD has "the

---

[3] Aldous Huxley to Fr. Thomas Merton, 1/10/1959, taken from: Ernest Kurtz, *The Collected Ernie Kurtz*, "Drugs and the Spiritual: Bill W. Takes LSD," pg. 39, 2008

result of sharply reducing the forces of the ego," adding that "prayer, fasting, meditation, despair and other conditions that predispose one to classical mystical experiences do have their chemical components." In short, Wilson believed that psychedelics could affect psychic changes—shifts in consciousness similar to those produced by prayer and meditation. He wasn't just impressed with LSD; he was sold.

Bill's venture didn't spark fears of relapse. The drug was still relatively new and not yet saddled with its illicit stigma. Moreover, this was clinical research supervised by reputable scientists in a controlled setting. A.A. leadership literally feared his enthusiasm. When Bill got into something, it consumed him. He possessed a one-track mind that was both persistent and persuasive. Bill quickly convinced Lois and Fr. Dowling to experiment with the spirit manifesting drug. A.A. leaders feared "Bill W." was on the verge of publicly endorsing LSD.

The prospect of a public endorsement troubled leadership because Bill's name was inseparable from A.A.'s. For all intents and purposes, A.A. would be endorsing the controversial drug. Their fears were not unfounded, either. Wilson believed "LSD to be of some value to some people, and practically no damage to anyone," but in the end, he sacrificed his convictions to the greater good of A.A.[4]

The LSD experiments are one of several examples that demonstrate the porous border separating Wilson's public and

---

[4] A.A. World Services, *Pass It On,* pg 370, 1984 (personal letter from Wilson to a friend)

private lives. When these two personages collided, his responsibility to Alcoholics Anonymous invariably prevailed, which was frustrating for the private man. This frustration was usually short-lived and never turned to bitterness.

Wilson's posthumous fame conceals the fact that no member in A.A. history sacrificed more for the fellowship than did he. The sacrificial yoke of anonymity augmented Bill's spirituality; it didn't stunt it—and he knew that, which is why he placed such high value on anonymity. No principle more effectively facilitates deflation of the ego than self-sacrifice, and this principle is central to A.A.'s Steps and Traditions. Walking the line between self-fulfillment and self-sacrifice is a high-wire act. Step Twelve is our balancing pole.

Step Twelve is about balance. "It is easy in the world to live after the world's opinion," says Ralph Waldo Emerson. However, the Steps demand more. They insist that our lives conform to spiritual principles, rather than seek to curry favor with others. Emerson continues, "It is easy in solitude to live after our own." Responsibilities are effortlessly met when we are responsible only to ourselves, but Step Twelve will have none of this. It stresses service to and relationship with our fellow man, who, in isolation, is nowhere to be found. "The great man," Emerson concludes, "is he who in the midst of the crowd keeps with perfect sweetness the independence of solitude."[5] This balance captures the spirit of Step Twelve.

The greatness of which Emerson speaks is the greatness to which Wilson aspired. Whether or not he achieved it, is

---

[5] Ralph Waldo Emerson, "Self Reliance"

uncertain. He certainly wasn't a saint, but he did endeavor to a higher order. He trudged along the path he paved. Bill's personal successes and failures are increasingly present in his writings, adding more and more weight to his words. In *Grapevine* articles, he speaks candidly about his battles with depression and his penchant for prestige. In the *Twelve and Twelve*, he conveys a greater appreciation for the latter half of Step Twelve, undoubtedly a result of struggling to live by spiritual principles for two decades. These struggles took him from the *Big Book*'s refrain, "This is our twelfth suggestion: Carry this message to other alcoholics!" to the *Twelve and Twelve's* more exalted perspective, "The joy of living is the theme of A.A.'s Twelfth Step."[6] The question is, 'How do we strike that chord in our lives?'

The Joy of Living

Joy shouldn't be confused with fleeting comfort. Joy is not a fleeting pleasure panhandled off passing circumstances. It is a state of contentment that pours forth from a place of abundance. Joy adds to the stream of life. An awareness of God's indwelling presence is the source of abundance that permits us to live with meaning and purpose.

Step Twelve reads, "Having had a spiritual awakening as the result of these steps, we tried to carry this message to alcoholics, and to practice these principles in all our affairs." It begins with "Having had a spiritual awakening" because

---

[6] Bill Wilson, *Alcoholics Anonymous*, pg 89, 1939; *Twelve Steps and Twelve Traditions,* pg 106, 1953

this awakening is the foundation of Step Twelve. As the old saying goes, "You can't give away what you do not have." Virtuous conduct and acts of altruism stem from selfless awareness. Thus, conscious contact is the perch wherefrom the twelfth Step launches its campaign of service and principled living.

In the *Twelve and Twelve,* Bill says the spiritual awakening reveals "a new state of consciousness and being," in which the awakened discovers a new appreciation for "honesty, tolerance, unselfishness, peace of mind, and love."[7] These principles give us meaning and purpose, but this new state of consciousness and being is not only fulfilling. It is also unifying. Conscious contact enables us to live with integrity because it is an integrated point of view.

Without a non-compartmentalized vantage point, it is impossible to adhere to a consistent set of principles, especially amidst the varied concerns of daily life. The prevailing winds of fear and expectation overtake us unless we stand on higher ground. Conscious contact is that higher ground. It is the one eye that sees our every thought, word, and deed; the singular will that binds our conduct to the primary principle of our spirituality, a Power greater than ourselves.

---

[7] Bill Wilson, *Twelve Steps and Twelve Traditions,* pg 107, 1953

God's Will

The twelfth Step calls us to a life that is accountable to principles, not opinions; a life that is reflective and flexible, active and in relationship, all the while rooted in a peace and joy nourished by conscious contact. Step Twelve insists on living life to the fullest—giving of ourselves so wholly and completely that only our ultimate concern remains.

"Our ultimate concern represents what we essentially are and—therefore—ought to be," says Paul Tillich.[8] In other words, our highest Self is our Higher Power's incarnational mode. God wants to be made incarnate; God wants to be realized, but for something to be realized, it must be made real. God is brought forth by acts that are consistent with the highest order of our being.

We must exercise our highest Power in the field of action and responsibility. More precisely, in the opportunities afforded by the present day. "The spiritual life is not a theory. We have to live it," says Wilson, and this moment is the only available theatre. There is no alternative. We cannot bide our time, holding out for more favorable conditions. *These* conditions await our response. We have to meet the present circumstances with principled action—however messy or complicated they may be—or our spirituality is merely a theory. This is why Step Twelve poses "the biggest question yet." It asks, 'What does it mean to bring God into our careers and intimate relationships, into our rivalries and friendships,

---

[8] Paul Tillich, *Dynamics of Faith,* pg 64, 2001

successes and failures, and even into our private ruminations?'

Human beings are not blank slates. Whatever the spiritual awakening is on the farther side, it is a connection to the infrastructure of our being on the nearer. Embedded in this structure are higher order principles, which guide us in the production of a meaningful life. The spiritual awakening makes us aware of and sensitive to this guidance. While our conception of God is negotiable, the principles that animate it are not. Love, compassion, patience, generosity, peace, humility, open-mindedness, courage, and honesty are indispensable. They are spiritual laws written on our hearts. When we conscientiously abide by these laws, we embody our true life.

Whether we believe these laws are authored by a divine intelligence or by nature itself is beside the point. The point is that we are not the author; that these decrees invade the mind from outside our conscious orbit.[9] Therefore, our nature and its constituents are revealed.

Emerson says, "Truth is the summit of being." It is *what we ought to be*. "Justice is the application of it to affairs."[10] In Twelve Step vernacular, Truth is the will of God and justice is the execution God's will in all our affairs.

God's will is the law of our being enforced against ego on behalf of our True Self. It is the force that binds us to

---

[9] In A.A. lingo: "Not God"; there is a God, and I am not him.
[10] Ralph Waldo Emerson, "Character"

principles that when lived refine our character and add value to the stream of life. This force is the interplay between conscience and conscious contact. Conscience advocates for conduct that accords with our highest nature, while conscious contact reveals that nature. This tandem keeps us true to our Self in all that we do.

God's will is not some cookie-cutter checklist; nor is it a scavenger hunt. God's will does not send us out in search of our other half: a husband, wife, kids, motorcycle, more money, or a ski boat. We can lead a spiritual life with or without a partner, on foot or in a new sports car. God's will has nothing to do with becoming something we are not; it has everything to do with becoming what we truly are. From this point of view, God does not have a will for us; we are the will of God. And the import of Step Twelve is to "carry the vision of God's will into all of our activities."

Relationships and Principles

Spiritual principles are catchphrases unless professed in daily life. The moral pronouncements of the person who fails to enter the arena are untrue. They are not false, but not yet made real. They are high ideals unsubstantiated by action. Our ideals are tested, tempered, and proven through trial and tribulation. Relationship is the arena. It is where our soul becomes flesh and blood. It is where spirit is made manifest.

She who lives in quiet isolation, though her hours are spent in prayer and meditation, never submits to the challenges of patience and tolerance that relationship has in store for her. She knows much of spiritual latitude, but nothing of longitude. He who passes his days cloistered may emerge from his hermitage to distribute insights and wisdom gleaned from reflection and countless pages read, but he never dares to test that insight and wisdom against the demands of relationship, so it is disembodied—brilliant, no doubt, but lacking the common sense and mettle forged in the fire of mutual responsibility.

The German poet, Novalis, says, "The seat of the soul is where the inner world and the outer world meet." This meeting is relationship. The realm of the spirit is a complex web of interdependency, not an isolated path of self-determinacy. We must print the principles that round out our spirituality on the pages of our daily life, which is to say, in relation to others.

The general phrase "all our affairs" points to the particular events that populate our day—everything from business dealings to conversations with our husband or wife to interactions with a nameless convenience store clerk. In fact, spiritual principles make sense only in the context of these particulars. For instance, the Fourteenth Dalai Lama said, "We can hardly call a beggar an obstacle to generosity." The beggar is, in reality, an opportunity to practice generosity because generosity requires someone or something that needs help. What we call obstacles are actually opportunities to practice spirituality, and our spirituality is as dry as dust if we fail to consent in those moments.

If our Highest Self is "a construct that serves to express an unknowable essence," as Jung says, then that unknowable essence becomes known only in the actualization of its particulars. Those particulars consist of principles like patience, honesty, peace, humility, courage, perseverance, discipline, self-sacrifice, and love. Since each principle must be actualized, yet none make sense apart from their counterpoint, all must be realized amidst adversity.

The beggar is not only *a chance* to practice generosity but *the only opportunity* this moment affords us *to be generous*. We are authentic in that moment only if we give what we can *at the moment*, be that a smile or a five-dollar bill. If we withhold recognition or resources, then we withhold our True Self. We are a false-self in that moment.

Similarly, an asshole is not an obstacle to patience. It is the only thing that makes sense of patience. Since patience is an attribute of our highest Self, we shouldn't shoo agitators away. We should welcome them onto our path. Adversaries are patience's good fortune. They are the path! This is the web of interdependence that binds our soul to friend and enemy alike.

Telling the truth is easy when there is no incentive to deceive. It is dishonesty's allure that makes honesty a character building exercise. When lying appears easier and more profitable than telling the truth, it is harder to be honest. The struggle against dishonesty carves honesty into our character.

Humility is a piece of cake in isolation. It takes effort and intention when the desire to impress tempts us to masquerade as something we are not. Likewise, courage is pertinent only in circumstances that arouse fear, and integrity is relevant only when events threaten to fracture the underlying unity of our character. We cannot talk of perseverance without trying circumstances, or discipline without chaos and the allurement of sloth.

When the Prayer of St. Francis says, "In dying, we find eternal life," it means that we cannot realize our higher Self without sacrificing our ego. There is no rebirth without self-sacrifice. Spiritual principles cannot be actualized without sacrificing base impulses, and such sacrifices are made in the name of interpersonal commitments and moral responsibility.

Relationship forces us to move beyond what we want and don't want onto a higher plane. Love is that higher plane. It easy to love those closest to us, but love goes beyond instinct and becomes a virtue when it embraces both friend and enemy.

Character building is the underlying theme of Step Twelve—although, the word "building" is misleading. We are not arbitrarily constructing a value system. We are consenting to revealed principles embedded in the structure of our being. Whether these values are the endowment of a benevolent creator or the product of natural selection is for the individual to decide. The Steps are disinterested in our personal beliefs. They are concerned with our conduct, namely that it adheres to the principles intuited by conscious contact and championed by our conscience.

Relationships and Traditions

A.A. meetings are a collective effort to "carry the message." In this sense, the fellowship is a product of the twelfth Step. Sober alcoholics can more effectively carry the message of recovery to suffering alcoholics if there is a rendezvous point where struggling alcoholics go in search of help. For this reason, A.A. meetings replaced expeditions to bars and shelters in search of those needing help.

Obviously, meetings do not facilitate themselves. They require a committed body of like-minded individuals willing to acquire a space, establish a format, conduct a meeting, and mentor the next generation of members. In brief, meetings are events put on by groups. A.A.'s Traditions provide the fellowship with principles that guard against in-fighting and cultivate group cohesion. In short, they are guides to healthy interpersonal relationships.

The Twelve Steps are traditional practices that were originally intended for a general audience; Wilson tweaked them to meet the needs of recovering alcoholics. The Twelve Traditions, on the other hand, were designed with Alcoholics Anonymous in mind. Several of the Traditions are so specifically tailored to A.A.'s needs that they merit no mention here. For example, A.A.'s ninth Tradition states, "Alcoholics Anonymous should remain forever non-professional, but our service centers may employ special workers." This Tradition bears little significance to the work before us. However, there are others that apply to common affairs. These are the Traditions that concern us.

The Traditions are group principles. A "group" is a collection of individuals with common objectives. Simply put, "group" means "relationship," but with the understanding that our destiny involves those that populate our lives; that without them, there is no journey—and vice versa.

Our paths intersect, and this intersection is the basis of relationship. So let us turn our attention to the Traditions and examine them in light of Step Twelve, as relational principles that guide us in all our affairs.

Our Primary Purpose is to Love

The fifth Tradition is Step Twelve's firstborn. It reads, "Each group has but one primary purpose—to carry the message to the alcoholic who still suffers." In other words, the A.A. group is a collective effort to fulfill Step Twelve's mandate to "carry this message to alcoholics." If we look past the particulars to the spirit of the Tradition, it becomes applicable to all of us.

Step Twelve brings our inner world into relation with others. The first half of Step Twelve identifies our role in these relationships. The gist of "carry the message" is "serve." Step Twelve is about being of benefit to others, which requires self-sacrifice. Anonymity is the essence of all A.A.'s Traditions because there can be no group without self-sacrifice.

The fifth Tradition subdues self-interest by prioritizing the common good. The A.A. group's shared objective is obvious, but what about the rest of us? What fixes us in the orbit of our co-worker? What unites us with our neighbor, a store clerk, or the talkative shopper holding up the checkout line? The answer is love, which is born out of an awareness of interdependence.

"By this everyone will know that you are my disciples, if you have *love* for one another."[11] Jesus places love at the center of his movement, and most spiritual traditions echo this sentiment. Love is our common purpose. However, the love of which he speaks is not limited to the warm, affectionate feelings we have for close friends and family. "You have heard that it was said, 'You shall love your neighbor and hate your enemy.' But I say to you, love your enemies."[12] Love is the tide that lifts all boats, friend and enemy alike. It is selflessness.

From the ego's vantage point, everyone and everything is defined by our fears and expectations; that is what it means to be self-centered. Conscious contact affords another vantage point—a broader, selfless perspective. This perspective dispels egocentricity. God-consciousness sees the whole. No one is at the center; everyone, including ourselves, is a satellite. We are called to love friend and enemy alike because from a God's eye view we are all alike. But love goes one step further. "The beginning of love is the will to let those we love be perfectly themselves, the resolution not to twist them to fit our own image," writes Thomas Merton. Love is the *act* of accepting them as-they-are.

---

[11] John 13:35

[12] Matthew 5:43-44

Love sees that others want to be happy and to avoid suffering just as we do. The conversation at checkout is not intended to disrupt our plans or cause us grief. It is not personal. They are looking for comfort in conversation and we are looking to avoid discomfort in convenience. Our motives are the same. We are not two, but one. This realization deepens our pursuit of happiness. It moves past the surface, where happiness is a zero-sum contest, and enters a space where our happiness ties into the happiness of others.

Love does not try to arrange the external world to our liking. "It does not insist on its own way; it is not irritable or resentful; it does not rejoice in wrongdoing, but rejoices in the truth" or things as-they-are. Ego tries to organize the world around self-interest. This is not love, but selfishness, which breeds irritability, resentment, and stubbornness. "Love is patient; love is kind," as Paul famously said. "It bears all things."[13] Love endures. It takes on the burden of the present moment, crucifying the false-self. In short, love is self-sacrificing.

There is no relationship without sacrifice, which is the import of Tradition Twelve. The twelfth Tradition reads, "Anonymity is the spiritual foundation of all our traditions, ever reminding us to place principles before personalities." It is easy to see the need for anonymity in Alcoholics Anonymous, but to outsiders, this tradition seems irrelevant.

Anonymity was one of the main points of contention between the Oxford Group and what was to become

---

[13] 1 Corinthians 13:4-13

Alcoholics Anonymous. A mutual aid fellowship that addresses stigmatized conditions like alcoholism and drug addiction cannot succeed in their objectives without some guarantee of "anonymousness." That said, the essence of anonymity is not confidentiality. It is egolessness. Anonymity is a willingness to sacrifice personal acclaim and recognition to the well-being of the group. Thus, anonymity is the substance of all spiritual practice.

Love uses self-sacrifice to transmute two "I's" into a "We," which is the basic unit of a group and a relationship. Love demands that we "give up personal desires for the common good," as Bill says, and in this common good, both parties find greater meaning. In A.A.'s Twelve Traditions this "sacrificial spirit" is "symbolized by anonymity," which points past namelessness to egolessness, "the spiritual substance of anonymity."[14] It fixes our gaze on principles, rather than personalities. In this way, anonymity enables us to love friend and foe.

The Common Good

The first half of Tradition One states that "our common welfare should come first." The "common welfare" is the altar upon which ego is sacrificed. The second clause of this Tradition is a statement of interdependence: "Personal recovery depends upon A.A. unity." In A.A., personal recovery is the shared objective and group unity is indispensable to personal recovery. The first Tradition

---

[14] Bill Wilson, *Twelve Steps and Twelve Traditions,* pg 184, 1953

reminds A.A. members that they need each other. The suffering newcomer is dependent upon the fellowship for support, just as the old-timer needs the fellowship's platform to fulfill one of sobriety's obligations, carrying the message to newcomers.

The first Tradition is suitable for every kind of relationship; we need only identify the point of common interest. If business partners serve the partnership, then all parties reap the rewards; if they pursue their interests at the expense of the partnership, then all involved suffer. Similarly, couples who serve the relationship first, enjoy the comforts of a happy marriage. Those who pursue self-interest without regard for the marriage languish in an unhappy affair or dissolve the union. Parents who work together for the benefit of the child, and understand that their partnership supports these efforts, forge a stronger family, which favors the child. Teams that emphasize a culture of teamwork and mutual responsibility, rather than individual talents, cease to be mere teams and become dynasties—think Bill Belichick's Patriots, Gregg Popovich's Spurs, or Alabama under Nick Saban.

The examples above pertain to defined groups, but the principle of the common good stretches beyond organizations. We all want to be happy and avoid suffering; this is humanity's common interest. Meeting a homeless person on the way to work affords each the opportunity to brighten the other's day. Just making eye contact with the other and exchanging pleasantries benefits both parties. Similarly, the convenience store clerk is not an automaton there to conduct our business, but a person who, like you, wants to fulfill their responsibilities and lead a reasonably happy life. Taking the time to make eye contact with them and wish them a good day not only makes their job easier, but is esteemable, and therefore contributes to our morale. It serves the common welfare, the pursuit of happiness.

Autonomy

There are aspects of the human condition that can be realized only in association with others, and relationship enables us to actualize those potentialities. In other words, relationship individuates individuals; it does not suck them up into an impersonal leviathan. Each relationship must acknowledge that the individual is more than the relationship; that the individual is more than a husband, more than a wife, mother, father, friend, or employee.

It is true that relationship unites us with others in a common life, but the notion that relationship erases individuality is a misconception. The shared life has its own structure; that structure is meaningful only when it accounts for the rhythms of individual life. Thus, healthy relationships are inherently democratic.

A relationship is a transpersonal reference point, a "We" with which a host of individuals identify. For that "We" to be dynamic and enriching, it must meet the needs of its constituents. No single relationship meets all the individual's needs, so there has to be balance. Space balances the rhythms of individual life with our responsibilities to the whole. Therefore, space or autonomy is integral to a healthy relationship.

The fourth Tradition reads, "Each group should be autonomous except in matters affecting other groups or A.A. as a whole." This means that each A.A. group *should* (not can) reflect the individuality of its members, barring activities that directly impact other A.A. groups or the organization as a whole. This sort of independence fosters diversity, enabling Alcoholics Anonymous to service a larger population. Groups that cater exclusively to men, women, professionals, or LGBT people owe their existence to Tradition Four.

The melody of life is composed of various relationships, each vibrating at a different frequency, and periods of silence accentuate each note. It is a symphonic movement that consists of intimacy, friendship, duty, and solitude. Individuation is found in the whole movement, not any one piece, so there must be a balance between anonymity and autonomy. It is this harmony that allows the piece to flow.

When a particular relationship monopolizes our time and energy, it jeopardizes the entire movement because it threatens to consume us. When the group consumes the individual, it ceases to be a group of individuals and becomes a totalitarian organization. When relationship smothers individuality, it is co-dependent, not interdependent.

A healthy relationship facilitates the individuation of its members. Since no one relationship can accomplish this task, no single relationship has exclusive rights to the individual. When fear usurps love, relationship becomes sick and suffocating. To love is to want what is best for the other; to find happiness in their happiness. When this ceases to be the primary aim, relationship becomes a mechanism of control. It is no longer about participation and contribution. It's about defending our territory, satisfying our demands, and clinging to our possessions, which includes our partner. This is a hostage situation.

Each party has potentialities that are fulfilled by other commitments, so healthy relationships guarantee their right to pursue those interests. These transitions must, however, be skillful because when individuals make decisions that negatively impact their partner, the common good is jeopardized. This is the wisdom of Tradition Four's stipulation, "except in matters affecting other groups or A.A. as a whole." Autonomy is vital up to the point that it encroaches upon the common good or the freedom of others.

The pursuit of our needs and interests cannot come at the expense of other's needs and interests. Balancing freedom and sacrifice is the key to healthy relations. This balance rests upon the recognition that autonomy and anonymity are not competing forces. They are complementary principles, like *yin* and *yang*. Relationships do not wash individuality away, and individuality does not seek happiness at the expense of others. Healthy relationships augment our individuality by enabling us to realize that which is hidden in solitude.

Open and honest channels of communication foster synergy. These pathways of communication are the infrastructure of relationship, which is sure to disintegrate unless we routinely service these channels. The relationship is a living organism that must be nourished and maintained. It has shortcomings, like the individuals that form it. We must identify these defects—uncommunicated expectations, conflicting agendas, resentment, and unreasonable demands—and work together to resolve them.

Without clear communication, there is no relationship. When people open themselves up, exposing not only their hopes and aspirations but their fears and tribulations, there is a meeting of the minds. Whether it be an A.A. group, a marriage, a friendship, or a business partnership this meeting produces a shared mind. Bill Wilson calls this shared mind a "group conscience."

The second Tradition reads, "For our group purpose there is but one ultimate authority—a loving God as He may express Himself in our group conscience. Our leaders are but trusted servants; they do not govern." Notice, it says, "as He *may* express Himself." There is no guarantee the group conscience will be inspired. When fear, resentment, and selfishness clog the channels of communication, the group conscience becomes a proxy for ego. This is despotism, not relationship.

Healthy relationships are democratic, not autocratic. They require free speech and informed constituents. The first step toward an informed relationship is investing in our spiritual lives. We cannot let others in if we are alienated from ourselves. Second, we have to share. We have to voice our thoughts, feelings, fears, and needs. Finally, we have to listen. When we discuss our plans with our partner and listen to their feedback, we know how our decisions affect them.

A shared mind does not convey any one of its affiliate's undiluted desires. There is nothing shared about a feed that transmits one person's ambitions into a consciousness that subordinates other partners. The shared mind reflects the common good. Therefore, relationship requires compromise.

The group conscience aims to strike a bargain that reflects the common interests of its partners, while meeting both individual and collective needs. It enables the mother to be not only a better mother, but a better wife, friend, and human being. It sets the employee up for success at work, as well as at home. The group conscience expresses God because it enables the individual to be their highest Self.

The ego struggles with concessions because it harps on what it lost in negotiations. It fails to see the gains "we" made because it sees everything through the lens of "I." The shared mind is selfless only if its affiliates are selfless. For this reason, spiritual practice is key to a healthy relationship.

Prayer, meditation, and self-analysis are just as crucial as communication to maintaining good relations. The rhythms of a meaningful life include seasons of silence and reflection, not just service and interaction. This demonstrates the continuity between Steps Ten, Eleven, and Twelve.

Conclusion

The Twelve Steps are a complete system of spiritual practice, addressing both our inner and outer lives. They aim for "the perfect sweetness" of solitude amidst "the crowd." They are contemplative and practical. The Steps are shot through with the pragmatics of William James, a philosophy that epitomizes American thought. In keeping with the religious pluralism of America, the Steps allow each person walking their path to conceive of God in terms that work for them. The Steps are more interested in *how* you believe than in *what* you believe. And for these reasons, the Twelve Steps are the quintessential American spirituality.

A Triumph of Principles

The Twelve Steps of Alcoholics Anonymous

1. We admitted we were powerless over alcohol—that our lives had become unmanageable.

2. Came to believe that a Power greater than ourselves could restore us to sanity.

3. Made a decision to turn our will and our lives over to the care of God as we understood Him.

4. Made a searching and fearless moral inventory of ourselves.

5. Admitted to God, to ourselves, and to another human being the exact nature of our wrongs.

6. Were entirely ready to have God remove all these defects of character.

7. Humbly asked Him to remove our shortcomings.

8. Made a list of all persons we had harmed, and became willing to make amends to them all.

9. Made direct amends to such people wherever possible, except when to do so would injure them or others.

10. Continued to take personal inventory and when we were wrong promptly admitted it.

11. Sought through prayer and meditation to improve our conscious contact with God as we understood Him, praying only for knowledge of His will for us and the power to carry that out.

12. Having had a spiritual awakening as the result of these steps, we tried to carry this message to alcoholics, and to practice these principles in all our affairs.

A Triumph of Principles

ABOUT THE AUTHOR

Benjamin Riggs is the author of *Finding God in the Body: A Spiritual Path for the Modern West*, *The Triumph of Principles: A Story of American Spirituality in Twelve Steps*, and the editor of *Benjamin Franklin's Virtue Journal: A Diary of Self-Improvement*. Ben has studied Buddhism and contemplative Christianity in both Buddhist and Christian Monasteries in India and the United States. He is the former director of the Refuge Meditation Group and spirituality columnist. He currently works as an author, communications director, and speechwriter in Louisiana where he lives with his wife and son.

A Triumph of Principles

The Story of American Spirituality

www.ingramcontent.com/pod-product-compliance
Lightning Source LLC
Chambersburg PA
CBHW022057090426
42743CB00008B/630